The Art of Making Wooden Toys

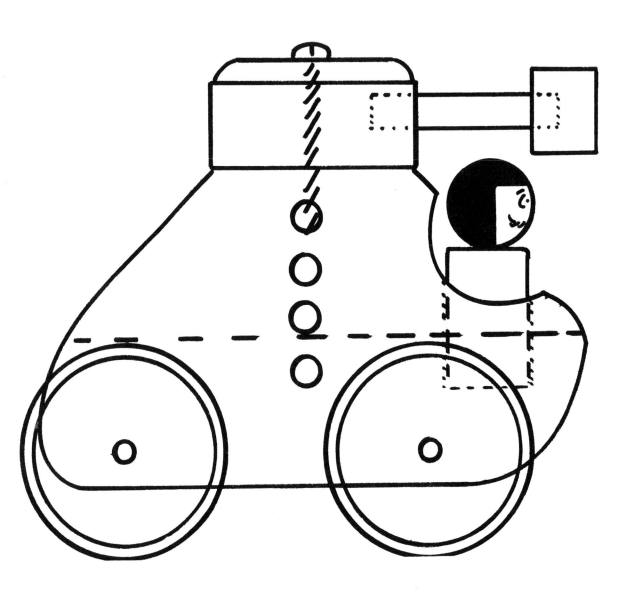

Peter Stevenson

The Art of Making Wooden Toys

Chilton Book Company

Radnor, Pennsylvania

Published in Radnor, Pennsylvania by Chilton Book Company
and simultaneously in Don Mills, Ontario, Canada,
by Nelson Canada Limited
ISBN 0-8019-5604-8 *hardbound*
ISBN 0-8019-5869-5 *paperback*
Library of Congress Catalog Card Number 77-153136
Designed by William E. Lickfield
Manufactured in the United States of America

10 11   5 4 3 2 1

Contents

For a Small Companion

Chapter 1

An Introduction to Toymaking

ON WHY TO MAKE HANDCRAFTED TOYS

At a party filled with denizens of the mainstream of Human Progress, I was once introduced to the smiling ensemble with a good deal of gratifying enthusiasm as "the fellow who makes toys."

There was a moment's hesitation while the smiles were quietly reinforced, and then one tanned, good-natured smile asked with much interest, "That's nice, but why?"

Did I make a lot of money at it? Was it for political favor? Did it attract the ladies, being the fellow who makes toys?

Why, in fact, should a grown, sane—for the sake of argument—semi-responsible adult, with no special fascination for the woodshop and no particular promise of remuneration, waste his time making toys when there are shops full of the same on nearly every street corner?

Why make toys at a time when, as never before, toymaking has become such a colossal industry—when at this very minute toys are being made that use almost every shape and theme known to man?

Well, I admit they had me for a moment. And then suddenly as I reviewed the theory of toymaking for the first time in this light, it all became crystal-clear to me. Unfortunately, everyone was talking about something else by then, so I will recount here my reasons for making toys.

As the fellow said, the solution often lies within the problem itself. Toy-making, as everyone knows, is a major industry and, as such, must obey the rules of survival for any other profit-making giant. The goal is to appeal at

1

the time of potential sale, and all else is incidental. To do this, many concerns must slavishly follow adult consumer trends, pander to short-term interests, exploit a childish fascination with the grotesque, and back it all up with a fundamental faith that man's desire to dominate will sell forever —especially to kids.

Because a toy, to the merchandiser, is not a necessity or a functional item, it must follow strict criteria to insure consumer acceptance. The commercial toy must be as gaudy and as cheaply made as possible, with a consequent loss of durability, safety, and lasting value. The toy must knock down to handy shipping size, must sell at a fixed multiple of its worth, must fill proper display requirements, and must attract a suitably significant slice of the populace. It must be so intricate to manufacture that no other concern will risk the cost of tooling to steal the idea once the first concern has the jump on the marketing promotion.

Thus the boom in twentieth-century toymaking, complete with all the technological resources of computerized research, has pushed and stretched the meaning of the word "toy" to cover everything from pliable sex-appeal dolls to fully functional miniatures of that character-building, time-honored sporting tradition of our culture—the jalopy derby.

As a result of the machinations of big business competition, only the hardiest marketing risk can survive. And so it has come to pass that in spite of the toy boom, or perhaps because of it, never has so few *true* toys been offered.

What do we call a true toy? For the purposes of this book, we'll exclude miniatures whose faithful detail completely restricts the imagination of the child. Also excluded are nonrepresentative playthings such as kites, yo-yos, tops, hoops, and the like, which are nothing more than simple expressions of mechanical phenomena.

What, then, is included? The lastingly fascinating toys throughout the ages all have had a subtle, almost intangible quality common to their design —something that prolongs the attraction of the toy long after the novelty has worn off.

These classic toys, if they can be thought of as such, tend to be abstracts, but not too abstract. They have just enough detail to capture the concept of a chariot, a soldier, or a moon-crawler—just enough defining realism to set our imaginations in gear, but not enough to confine them and stifle them with super detail. The break seems to come when we stop looking at the similarities between the toy and the real object and start looking for the differences.

The "great toys" often have subtle color combinations with softer hues than we normally associate with toys. Just because superbright colors remind us of the vividness of perception during childhood is no proof that kids necessarily go for them. As a matter of fact, when possible I let kids pick the colors for the toys I make, and the combinations invariably turn out to be quieter than I would have chosen. To test this theory, I repainted

2

a favorite truck in the traditional glaring colors that catch adult eyes so well on the shelves of toy shops. Not only did the truck suddenly look pretty shabby to the youngster, but it was banished from further play until the old browns, tans, and blacks were reinstated.

Whether kids like softer shades or not, this *does* point up one of the great advantages of making your own toys—your youthful client's individual preferences can direct every stage of the toy's fashioning with blithe disregard for the expediencies of mass production and the prejudice of merchandisers.

Another reason to make toys, be it ever so corny, is that a tailor-made, handcrafted toy is a uniquely tangible, usable piece of evidence testifying to the concern for the child on the part of someone whom the child values. And if the child can be in on all the steps of construction that somehow magically turn an inert lump of lumber into a shining, mobile, almost living entity, then so much the better every time he sees it and remembers all that it stands for.

There is still another reason for making toys; this is the one that appeals to us and is, we suspect, the real reason toymaking has cropped up in virtually every culture throughout the history of man: It's *fun*. It's an art form as well as a source of relaxing entertainment. Every subtlety of sculpture can be lavished upon it, but on the other hand, no matter how sloppy a toy may turn out, it still stands for the same affectionate concern and will probably be treasured as much as a perfect specimen.

Most of all, though, there's no pressure.

When rigging the brakes on your dune buggy, or gluing the skin on your catamaran, you can afford to squint and frown dramatically. It's serious business, and a blunder now means a good deal of embarrassment when everything comes unstuck at the wrong moment later on. But in toymaking, it's only a toy, after all. You can't really take the thing seriously. For all we talk about design approaches and concepts, a toy should above all be humble and well able to laugh at itself. The minute a toy is worshiped, it's no longer good for playing with. A toy is simply for *fun*, from the minute it's cut from the lumber stock to the day when it's finally put up on the shelf to remind someone of the good years it lasted through.

Now, assuming that the toys pictured on these pages are somewhere along the line of thought you like to pursue, we'll make a few comments about what went into the designing of them. And then we'll move from there into the more specific steps of construction for each of the toys we've included, for those of you who would like to practice on some of the recipes we know will work. Then you may want to experiment with some of your own ideas.

DESIGNING TOYS

This stage of the game, because it does the most to set the mood of the toy, tends to get a little involved in spots. Just bear in mind that anything

3

personally handmade will be better than nothing, and that it is really almost impossible to come up with an original toy that won't be appreciated by the little ones. But as long as we're trying to get as many hints and tricks on our side as possible, here goes.

It's our guess that the key to the fascination of a particular toy is its basic design—the proportions, amount of detail, weight, and texture. The themes are necessarily simple so they can be recognized.

As we said before, the great thing is to capture the concept and mood of the real object without locking in the imagination too closely. Some abstracts are so abstract they're recognizable only by a process of elimination. Remember that what may be a clever abstraction to an adult may well be completely unrepresentative to a child. It's our experience that the recurrent fad for extreme abstracts in toys is intriguing to few but the youngest set, abandoning the older kids to the mercies of the superdetailed miniatures before their imaginations may be ready for the structured rules of play demanded by miniatures.

Just how does one go about capturing the mood and the concept? Because toymaking is largely an art and not a very dependable science, there are no real constants or laws. But there are some hints we've found helpful over the years.

First, never look at another toy to get your design. Once you take a careful look at the real object that will be the theme of your toy, you'll be amazed at all the important things the other toymakers (including us, of course) forgot. Say you're going to do a dump truck; try to find one in photos or on the street that epitomizes just what you had in mind. If you can't find a single specimen that sums it all up, look at all you can find in the class that you want and note down what you like about each.

Now try to learn roughly the basic proportions. How many tire heights high is the cab roof? How many tire heights wide is the whole thing? Where is the front of the grille in relation to the front wheels? (This is probably old stuff to most of you.) It's nearly impossible to make a decent abstraction without a knowledge of the real proportions. It comes out about as intriguing as a drugstore cowboy if you don't learn what the real thing looks like.

Once you know the proportions, you can manipulate them to get the effect you want. There are some obvious hints which have been found effective for this stage, but more and more you will have to start to trust your native ability to judge what will look best and most intriguing to a child. And so the problem now becomes one of divining just what is attractive to kids. Kids are crazy about kittens, bunnies, puppies, etc.—all considered to be, if you'll excuse the expression, "cute." What features do they all have in common that make them cute? Well, they all have large component details—big eyes, big ears, big paws, and so on. And they're all short and stubby. In fact, practically anything that's short and stubby and plump with enlarged details is thought of as cute. Well, so long as you don't overdo it, why fight it? It's most likely part of our inherited predispositions and

4

probably linked to the principle of the supernormal stimuli, if you like to get philosophic.

Sketch, however crudely, the proportions you think are pretty close to those of the real object, keeping in mind the size of the toy wanted, as well as the sizes of wheels and lumber available. Include all the details you can remember and draw the object from its most defining view—usually the side. Now this is where the art comes in.

At this point, start taking out the less important details. Edit, distill, use your poetic sense, do whatever is necessary to whittle them down until only enough details remain to convey the basic idea. Try different combinations, and try to include details fairly evenly over the surface of the toy. If a certain side looks blank, you may want to put back a relatively unimportant detail to add interest to that side. Now make the proportions shorter, narrower, and generally stubbier. This moves the details together, making them relatively larger.

In two-dimensional drawings, which plan views generally are, make the object much higher than you think it should be. When it is cut into solid three dimensions, it will stand a much better chance of looking the way you wanted it to. All we know is that for some reason when you move from two to three dimensions, many strange things occur, which may explain why such abominable things are done in design processes that make no allowance for adjustment during this change.

Now finalize the lines of your sketch, cut it out, and mark it on the lumber, remembering which way the grain should go to make it as strong as possible. Then cut out the components, taking time to reason out the order in which cuts should be made to minimize the danger of breaking during the cutting. If at any point the project gets into trouble,, or otherwise ceases to be fun, then you're probably going too fast. Constantly reminding yourself to "Slow Down" is the best trick we can think of to make any project easy. Whenever a saw is running, try to slow down to about half speed. Ironically, as all the veterans will tell you, it's the surest way to get something done in a hurry and with a surprising lack of calamities. Great for the liver too.

Once you have the components cut out, tape or tack or somehow prop all the important components together so that you can get a good look at the final basic proportions. Quite a shock, eh? Well, make careful note on the pieces what the mistakes are and start retrimming. One retrimming of the components means you've done a good job of designing. Three or four retrims is more common. This may seem to be taking it all a bit seriously, but it is just this stage that does most to set the mood of a toy. Kids don't care about finish; they'll play with it as much before it's sanded and painted as after. We're the only ones who worry about that. But they really appreciate intriguing proportions and concept, and that's just what we're up to now.

Now that you have your creation in solid three dimensions, the problem becomes one of somehow being able to see it objectively, and especially through the eyes of a child. There are several design tests which can be used at this point to give you a better perspective on your work. These tests will give you much the same effect as leaving the project for a week and then coming back to look at it again, and they take, obviously, much less of a bite out of the production schedule.

One is the mirror test: By looking at the toy in a mirror you will get a surprisingly candid view of all the errors that have somehow crept into the design.

Another is the impartial-observer test: Get someone (anyone) to come take a look at the project and give you his most brutal opinion. Never pay any attention to what he says about it, but you will notice that while he's inspecting it, you will tend to look at it a little more heartlessly and may decide to change a few things.

Another alternative is the several-snorts/surprise test: If you don't mind having a little refreshment now and then, go have several snorts, and then come back thinking of something else and let the thing take you by surprise. This is invariably effective in showing up momentary design aberrations. Hemingway had it, "Good Scotch can change your mind, and there aren't many things that can do that"—or something vaguely like that. However, the snorts aren't mandatory, and any pleasant diversion will do nearly as well. No intricate trimming should be done following the snort test, of course.

Try to avoid setting a line or dimension without a reason. If you're not sure where a certain line should go—for example the front edge of a hood—move it way too far forward, then bring it back slowly until it looks right to you, and mark it. Then move it way too far back; bring the line forward slowly until it looks right and mark it. If the two marks are different, try the averaged midpoint. In this way you can be fairly sure it's the way you like it as you progress across the design. Complicated? Well, if you're interested enough in designing to try it, we think you'll find it's the best fun of the whole project. The rest is really craft, pure and simple—fun too, but of a different stripe.

Size can sometimes be a tricky point. The size of the child or the child's hands can sometimes be a clue. Let available lumber sizes set the toy size only as a last resort. Many of the toys in this book could have been made from $2'' \times 4''$ stock much easier than trimming down $4'' \times 4''$ to a little above $2'' \times 4''$ dimensions, as they were. But the result would be disappointing and remarkably reminiscent of the type of superfast projects that have given the word "homemade" such a bad meaning.

Try to look at the tape measure as little as possible when setting dimensions. If you're like us, when there's a tape too handy, you'll end up making something 5 inches long, when $5^{17}\!/_{32}$ inches would have looked better and would have been just as easy to cut if you hadn't known it was such an exotic measurement.

6

Dimensions drawn on flat sheets, as on plywood, tend to end up looking larger once the thing is together. The Gypsy Wagon-Toybox fell prey to this mistake. It wasn't until the wagon was completely finished and painted that it was discovered to be somehow unaccountably too big. The only remedy was to build a second version, two inches smaller overall with smaller wheels (as seen in the construction section). The result was somehow (still unaccountably) more satisfactory, and remains so even now that the particular gypsy for whom it was built is a good deal larger.

Of course, color can be important to the mood of the toy. One method of solving the problem is the open-can method: Open up all the cans of paint you can find and ask the child what color he wants the thing painted. As stated before, don't be surprised if it's a subtle combination of muted tones. Rich tones and contrasted wood stains seem to get a better response than the all-out, unmixed, bright colors that sell so well to parents. In some cases, of course, they can be effective if used for a specific purpose.

Don't forget that there is little to limit you in the making of handcrafted toys. They can be as unique as your imagination, or your child's imagination, allows. So consult freely the needs of your little friend. Little friends can be, and usually are, the best design consultants and sources of new ideas you can find.

Now that we have all that off our chest, perhaps a boiled-down list of the steps in the process that produced the designs in this book might be helpful:

Step 1: Look carefully at the proportions in the example of the real object that the toy is to portray. Sometimes you will need a group of examples, taking a few details from each.

Step 2: Make a rough sketch of all the details and proportions that make up your concept of the real object.

Step 3: Edit the details, keeping just enough to capture the concept well, but not so many as to stifle the imagination. Proportions can be shortened and the important components enlarged if necessary at this point.

Step 4: Mark the final outline on the wood and cut out the parts needed.

Step 5: Tack the toy together temporarily and review carefully any changes that may have crept into your original idea as it progressed from a sketch to solid three dimensions; make the needed adjustments and recuts.

Step 6: Assemble, and take one last critical look (before the glue dries, if possible), then sand and finish.

Step 7: Paint, making full use of any small design consultants that happen to be around the house at this point.

SETTING UP SHOP

Before we get into the specific steps for creating each toy, let's have a little shoptalk. You veterans who already know what you like may want to skip on to the projects. You probably know more about it than we do anyway. But for the novitiates and recent addicts, here's what we've learned.

All the toys in this book can be made with nonpower hand tools and a little extra patience. But if you get into it and find you are as hooked as the rest of us, then you might start thinking about slowly accumulating a few well-chosen power tools. Considering the low cost per year of use for good tools, it seems a little foolish to hack through life without their help. Of course, tools don't necessarily increase your standards of craftsmanship; they simply increase the scope of what can be completed in one afternoon.

It's also easy to have too many tools. Many people buy extra tools, hoping somehow to be inspired by their presence, when often just the opposite occurs. We've seen a score of fantastically well-equipped shops whose very completeness seems to intimidate the creative processes. If you have an expensive machine to do every job conceivable, somehow human ingenuity seems to dissipate. It's when you have to figure your own way around the knottier problems of the shop that you start coming up with original approaches that probably wouldn't have appeared if you had had a machine to do it the old, orthodox way in the first place. The key is to hit a stimulating compromise: enough tools to widen your scope without making things too mechanical.

At any rate, down to business: TOOLS.

Saws first, as they seem to be most important. A hand-powered coping saw will work, if slowly, for most stock up to 2 inches thick. For a curve in a 4-inch piece, it might be best to slice it in half, cut one side, use that as a guide to mark the other, then cut the second, gluing the two back together for shaping and sanding. A power saber saw can be used. A power jigsaw is better, but is usually limited to thin stock, which again means slicing, or else laminating thinner lumber.

But the best and most useful tool for toymaking in the whole shop is the band saw. With a band saw the mind runs wild. The nature of the cut is accurate, smooth, clean and almost relaxing, if a power saw can be thought of as being such. The only sore point is that a good one costs above $100, though an occasional used bargain may be found in the want ads. By hook or by crook, try to get a band saw sooner or later.

Table saws are handy for accurate straight cuts and angles. But with a little practice a power, hand-held circular saw can be almost as accurate, as well as do many other jobs at far less cost.

This next point sounds particularly obvious, but all the same we forget it much of the time: Use a saw that wants to cut straight for straight cuts, and one that cuts crooked for curves. Many's the time you seem to get going with one saw and end up trying to force it into all manner of jobs for which it isn't suited. Saws with wide blades (including circular saws) tend to cut straight, and those with narrow blades, wiggly. The only possible exception to this is the use of the hand circular saw to cut long, smooth, outside curves in plywood, but that's only for experts.

If you find you're having some trouble following a line, check the saw blade. Nothing shoots one's creative confidence like a dull blade. The blade teeth should be not only sharp to the touch, but protruding on either side alternately. A sharp blade can last for months of steady service, or it can be ruined in five seconds by being used, however innocently, to cut off nails hidden in the wood. So beware of used lumber. It's often good and straight and dry, but it can also hide a whole pocketful of nails in its bosom.

Shapers are next in importance. The old-style carpenter's plane, heavy, complex, and expensive as it is, has little use in this sort of toymaking. The new, light, simple, and inexpensive hand shapers that use a corrugated, perforated bottom surface are really a fantastic breakthrough and are absolutely essential for the toy shop. You'll probably like the short, one-handed kind better than the long one that looks a little like the old-style plane. The shorty works as well, is more versatile, and is cheaper, to boot. The new shapers can remedy a gang of cutting errors in Bristol fashion.

There's also a drum shaper, using the same surface, which can be stuck in a power drill to do the shaping almost faster than your creative eye can move. This attachment doesn't seem to hurt the drill as much as the more traditional sander, grinder, saw, etc., attachments sold to be slapped into the common, household electric drill. Few of these marvelous moneysavers do a satisfactory job without wrecking the drill in the process. A drill's cooler is typically not up to the long periods of load suffered during grinding operations. The brushes and bearings are relatively unprotected from sanding dust as well as the bits of grinding paper that eventually thicken the air. The complex gearbox at the head of the drill is poorly suited to the sheer loads placed on it by most attachments. And when the drill is being used for extended operations such as grinding, one's trigger finger tends to tire and ease off the switch, slowly burning out the drill's innards.

So perhaps building a whole shop around a small drill motor may not be the cleverest move in the final analysis. If you need a grinder, rent one. It's cheaper than getting the drill rebuilt.

Also, you might try to resist the temptation to get a quarter-inch electric drill. A three-eighths-inch drill costs only a few dollars more and is a far more satisfactory and durable machine.

Most of the mistakes we've made in sanding and finishing have been in starting with a too-fine grade of sandpaper. Start out with a real gouger to establish a reasonably lump-free surface, then smooth that out with the finer stuff. The typical mistake is to start sanding before a real surface is made, and ending up with a shiny-smooth bunch of lumps.

In painting, spray cans are made to order for toys: no cleaning, no brush marks, etc. Try to learn the peculiarities of the different brands by first experimenting on something you don't care about. However, even a single brand can be good in some colors and a washout in others. A good paint won't cover in one coat, but at least it won't bubble and have watery spots.

Getting an absolutely sparkling paint job is mostly a matter of patience and restraint. *Don't* try to do it in one day. This may sound simple, but at this stage of the game, things tend to get a little rushed, and the toy will

9

show it if they are. Get a cardboard box about two feet square and cut down across the ends diagonally and across the front about two inches from the bottom so that it forms a sort of bottom and backboard for a painting booth. This will help keep the paint from blowing away and being wasted on the garage floor. Put a piece of paper under the toy to be painted in the booth so you can turn it around without getting paw marks all over it.

Don't try to make it look nice on the first coat. Thin coats are the secret—lots of thin coats—and the first one will be mostly soaked into the wood. Don't ever rush the drying. If a coat is painted over wet somewhere along the line, it may well suddenly, before your very eyes, wrinkle up and curdle into a relief map of the moon. From about 18 inches, fog it all over evenly.

The first coat should look mottled and terrible. Sand off the fine sawdust that sticks to it. The second coat should look speckled and terrible; sand lightly this and successive layers. At about the fourth coat start watching out for drips and bubbles. Don't try to correct anything while it's wet. Spraying one last shot onto a bubbly spot will only give you more bubbles and a drip. At about the fifth coat, ease off sanding, just removing mistakes from there on. And finally, at about seven coats, depending on the paint, weather, and wood, you'll have a tough, glossy finish. Let it sit for a week and it'll be even tougher.

For two or more tones, try to brush on the other colors, dark over light, if possible. Masking and shooting on another color usually ends up in your starting over and doing it this way anyhow. If the only color you like is in spray cans, shoot some into the cap and use a brush. It'll probably take a few coats.

Of course, if you're not looking for a gloss, then it's all much easier, and two coats usually does the job.

Put your name and the date on the bottom somewhere, and try your best not to squirm every time the toy's rammed into a chair at full speed. That's what they're for, we're told.

What else do you need to get rolling? If you have a saw for straight cuts, a saw for curves, something to drill with, and a shaper, about all you need now is a hammer (for those delicate adjustments), a good screwdriver, a phillips screwdriver (optional), a pair of pliers, maybe an adjustable wrench, and a vise, or a couple of C-clamps. Oh, yes, and a hacksaw for cutting axles. Hardly a full toolbox, but it's enough to get you out of most problems you're likely to encounter.

Getting Under Way

A couple of explanations are in order that may make things a little easier throughout. It's often tempting to leave out any mention of possible pitfalls in describing a project, to make it sound easier. But, of course, this just makes the project more frustrating than it need be. So if we dwell for a little while on the pitfalls, it's just to make things easier in the long run. Just keep in mind that toymaking is one of the forgiving arts, and a few mistakes here and there won't affect the amount of fun the toys can give over the years.

Plans and instructions tend to be a little like mathematical formulas: The ones that appear simple and easy to remember are often hard as the devil to apply in actual practice; and the cumbersome-appearing ones sometimes answer all the questions as they come up. We've tried to lean toward the cumbersome side in this book, so if it's painfully elementary or repetitive in spots, please bear with us—it'll cost you less time to skip over a paragraph than it would to be left in the dark on a crucial point.

As you thumb through the toy chapters, you'll find places where entire processes have been repeated in different chapters. While this doesn't make for the most suspenseful literature, it does allow you to start with any toy in the book without missing any of the techniques needed. Each project is completely self-contained, but there are a few points that are common to almost all the toys that we might as well go into here, before we get rolling.

When you've settled on a toy that particularly fits your mood at the moment, it's best to read through the instructions once before donning the shop apron. Don't try to understand every detail of every step, because in most cases Step Three will be a complete mystery until you have actually performed Steps One and Two. The first read-through is just to get a rough idea of the method of getting the thing to go together. Even more important, it will show you how the materials are used for that particular toy, so that if anything happens to be unavailable in your neck of the woods, you'll know just what sort of substitute to look for. The list of materials is at the back of each section to remind you to get an idea of the basic methods before heading to the lumberyard or home-supply store with the list.

If you're not already a habitué of the local source of home supplies, there are a few techniques and principles involved (based on the psychology of the individual, of course). One of these is: Never assume that whoever is waiting on you knows any more about his goods than you do. You'll save extra trips to the store if you aren't too shy to peer over his shoulder and make sure for yourself that he has the right paint mix number or a piece of wood without too many gigantic cracks or bends in it. Mistakes may be the only way he has of breaking up the monotony of his days, and a little extra attention on your part may save hours spent trying to set things right later on.

Also, for the newcomers, when the recipe calls for a $2'' \times 4''$, what you actually get in standard lumber sizes is a $1\frac{5}{8}'' \times 3\frac{1}{2}''$.

Here's a handy conversion table to make things easier to remember so that when we speak of "one-inch stock," you'll know that it's actually three fourths of an inch thick.

Listed Lumber Size	Actual Size	Listed Lumber Size	Actual Size
$1'' \times 2''$	$\frac{3}{4}'' \times 1\frac{7}{8}''$	$1'' \times 8''$	$\frac{3}{4}'' \times 7\frac{1}{2}''$
$1'' \times 4''$	$\frac{3}{4}'' \times 3\frac{5}{8}''$	$1'' \times 10''$	$\frac{3}{4}'' \times 9\frac{1}{2}''$
$1'' \times 6''$	$\frac{3}{4}'' \times 5\frac{1}{2}''$	$1'' \times 12''$	$\frac{3}{4}'' \times 11\frac{1}{2}''$

The 2″ stock comes in the same widths, but is actually 1⅝″ thick. The reason for the shrinkage in the wood by the time it falls into your hands is that after all the machines have smoothed out the surfaces, the wood has lost a little weight. Some of you may wonder why they don't start with a bigger chunk of board, so that when it's finished a 2″×4″ would actually be a 2″×4″, but then it's not ours to reason why.

When we mention "hardwood" in the plans and project steps, what we really mean is that Douglas fir will do the job, but if you happen to have a piece of genuine hardwood, like oak, lying around, all the better. Fir is strong enough for our purposes if you stick with fairly straight-grained pieces, and it stains and varnishes with a good, rich color.

On parts to be shaped, a softwood is generally used, and the most common softwoods are pine, cedar, and redwood. Pine is easily shaped and is best for painted areas because it's dull as a rubber boot when stained or varnished. Cedar is also colorless and a little pulpy. The best weight and shaping ability are found in redwood, which takes on deep, rich tones when stained and varnished. However, its splinters are poisonous, they say, so I suppose we can't recommend it. We've never had any trouble from countless redwood splinters and find it hard to believe that splintery redwood furniture could be sold if it were such a threat; however, as they say on road signs in England, "You have been warned."

A few more general ruminations: Some of the toys use 2¼″ overall diameter wheels. This happens, by no coincidence at all, to be the standard size used by a number of toy-truck manufacturers. Like the trucks themselves, these wheels are all pretty much the same and they are perfectly suited to our needs. Because 2¼″ is such a popular size, used versions of the trucks may be found in nearly every secondhand, junk, and charity store, as well as at most swap meets and garage sales. If you happen onto a particularly rich lode at a good price, it might be a good idea to grab them up and salt them away until needed if you like wheeled goods.

Of course, if you lack a ready supply of these wheels, satisfactory substitutes can be cut from ⅝″ plywood with an inexpensive hole-saw attachment for the hand drill. This tool has a number of concentric circular blades attached to a ¼″ drill bit, and is handy for all sorts of projects. The cheaper, Oriental version actually has better steel than the more expensive ones, in our experience at least.

Another tool that can be had fairly cheaply is the saber saw. If you can't swing access to a band saw, most projects can be done almost as well with this versatile little tool.

While we're on the subject of handy hints, if screws don't seem to want to go in without a fight, try scraping them over an old bar of soap before sinking them. Also, beware of old paint; it tends to curdle and turn lumpy just when you need lumps least.

To transfer the lines of the plan profiles to the wood with as little distortion as possible, trace the lines through thin paper, or use carbon paper and copy over the lines. If you happen to have access to a copying machine, make a copy of the plans. Then these outlines can be cut out as the patterns and traced onto the wood.

And that's about the strength of it; just remember that toymaking is an easygoing art, and like many other things, seems like a big deal when you're talking about it, but is really very simple in practice. Now that the pitfalls have been dealt with, we can sit back and start to partake of the fun of it all.

Chapter 2

The Trailer Truck

A good trailer truck is one of the pivotal pieces in a young construction engineer's collection of heavy equipment. Fitted with any number of different trailers, the truck can be converted into a logger, tanker, stake-body, van or whatever the imagination happens to come up with.

To make this version, transfer the outlines in the plans to paper that can be cut into patterns; use carbon paper, tracing paper, or a copier to make the transfer.

Step One: Cutting

Trace around the side pattern of the cab onto the side of a clear-grained, softwood 4″×4″, with the grain running fore and aft. With a band saw or coping saw cut out this outline. The outline of the top can now be drawn on the wood and cut out. Mark the dimensions of the side profile of the hood on the 4″×4″ and cut it out with a carpenter's handsaw. Now mark on the top profile of the hood and cut that out.

Mark the outlines of the two fenders, the chassis, the trailer hitch, and the axle carriers onto a 2′ length of 1″×6″ stock. Mark the center-hole position in the middle of the hitch, and drill the hole with a ⅝″ wood bit. Now the outlines on the 1″×6″ can all be cut out with a band, jig, coping or saber saw. Mark the side profiles on the hitch and the two axle carrier pieces, and cut these out. Cut out the stacks from ⅝″ wood dowel at the angle shown in the side plan.

14

Step Two: Drilling

With a small drill bit the size of the 1¼" finishing nails to be used to attach the fenders, hitch, and stacks (or with one of the finishing nails mounted in the drill as a bit), drill the nail holes through the fenders, stacks, and hitch, as shown.

Next, position the hitch in place on the rear of the chassis platform and mark the outline of the hitch onto the top of the chassis. Mark on the chassis the position of the center of the hole in the hitch, then remove the hitch and with a ¾" wood bit, drill a hole about ¼" deep in the position marked on the chassis.

Place the cab and hood in position, centered on the chassis, and mark their outlines. Within these outlines drill two ⅛" screw holes through the chassis for both the cab and the hood.

To make the axle mounts, remove the pin from a 2½" butt hinge and cut into the edges of the looped strap pin holders in both halves of the hinge, cutting the loops in half so they no longer circle back, but now form semi-circular clamps to hold the axles in place, as shown.

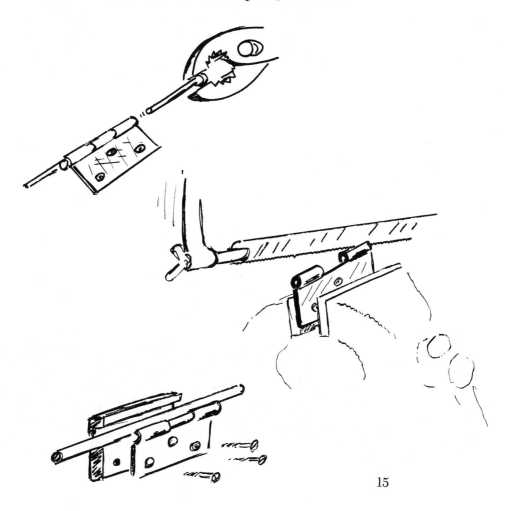

15

Place the axle clamps over the axle carriers with the semicircular clamps directly over the path of the axle grooves, and mark the screw holes to be drilled through the carriers to match the holes in the hinge halves.

Step Three: Shaping

Round off along the top of the sides of the hood, as shown in the front view, with a rasp or hand shaper. Cut a shallow groove with a hacksaw or coping saw around the sides and top of the hood about ½″ back from the front of the radiator. Smooth any rough cuts or surfaces with a shaper, and round off all corner edges (except the edge around the front of the radiator) a little. Then smooth up with the coarse sandpaper (to remove lumps), then the medium paper (to remove the scratches made by the coarse paper), then the fine (to polish to a good surface).

Step Four: Assembling

White glue should be smeared on all joining surfaces just before attaching. Place the hitch in position on the back of the chassis and drive nails

16

down through the hitch into the chassis. Nail the fenders onto the sides of the hood. Drive 1¼", Number 8, flathead wood screws up through the bottom to attach the cab, then the hood, in position, centered with the front of the cab flush with the back of the front-wheel cutouts in the chassis.

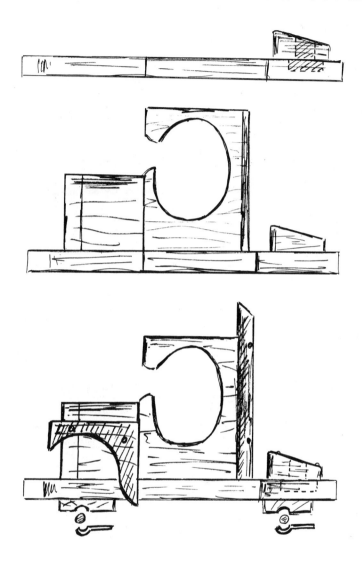

Then, with the cab firmly braced on its side, nail the stacks in place in the notches at the back corners of the cab. Place the axle carriers in position on the bottom of the chassis and drill starter holes for the screws just into the bottom of the chassis.

Step Five: Painting

As with all the toys, the color scheme is ultimately up to you and your young clients. To color it like the example pictured, spray on about five to eight coats of a rich, chocolate brown all over the cab, sanding lightly after each of the first three or four coats, as needed. Then brush-paint a couple of coats of butterscotch tan onto the sides and back of the chassis, as well as the top and sides of the hood and the wheel centers. Finally, brush on a trim of flat or semigloss black on the inside of the cab, the hitch, the top surfaces of the stacks, and the front of the grill. The bottom of the chassis and the axle carriers should also be black.

Step Six: Final Assembling

Cut the axles so that the wheels can spin freely without sticking out too much on either side. Fasten on the wheels by tapping the cut end of the axle to spread it slightly, preventing a washer placed between the outside of the wheel and the axle end from slipping off. Place the axles in the grooves in the axle carriers, then place the axle clamps over the axles, and finally insert the screws through the screw holes, and screw in place to the bottom of the chassis.

Nail two ¾″-diameter chrome chair leg bottom slide buttons in place on the front of the grill, as shown, and the cab is about ready to hit the road.

The trailer style can be another matter for personal preference. To make the earth hauler pictured, start off by cutting out the wheel carriage below the chassis at the back. Cut a 3½″ length of 2″×2″, 2″×4″, or 4″×4″, with ends square. On the end grain, draw the side profile shown in the plans. Cut this out with band saw or coping saw. Then cut out the back and top views, and sand.

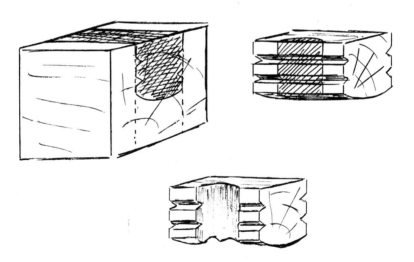

From the 1″×6″ stock, cut out a rectangular bed for the trailer, 4½″×9″. Cut out the two sides, 2¼″ by 9″ and the end 4½″×3″. Mark the top profile of the trailer front onto the edge of the front piece, and round off to this line with a saw or shaper. Drill a ¼″ hole in the center of the bottom of this front piece.

18

To make the cutouts in the sides of the trailer, a band saw is needed. Set the table on an angle of about five degrees and cut out three shallow gouges on both sides, cutting in from both ends of each gouge. With glue, nail the wheel carriage in place on the bottom of the chassis, then nail the sides to the top of the chassis, flush with the side edges; nail the front piece to the front edges of the sides and chassis. To mount the wheels, simply hammer 1½″ box nails into the centers of the wheels, leaving enough play to allow them to spin freely. The trailer hitch is a 2″-long, ¼″-diameter, roundhead bolt which is simply screwed up into the ¼″ hole in the bottom of the trailer front.

Sand the trailer smooth. To paint it like the one pictured, color the outside and wheel centers butterscotch tan, the inside brown, and the wheel carriage black.

Hook up the rig, and it's ready to hit the road for its first job.

LUMBER LIST
for the
TRUCK AND TRAILER

One foot of clear-grained softwood 4″×4″
Three feet of 1″×6″ stock (any wood)
One foot of ⅝″ dowel
One dozen 1¼″, Number 8, flathead wood screws
Two dozen 1¼″ or 1½″ finishing nails
One pair of 2½″ butt hinges
Two ¾″-diameter chrome buttons used for chair
  leg bottom slides
Two 1½″ box nails
Six 2¼″ outside diameter truck wheels
One 2″ roundhead, ¼″-diameter bolt

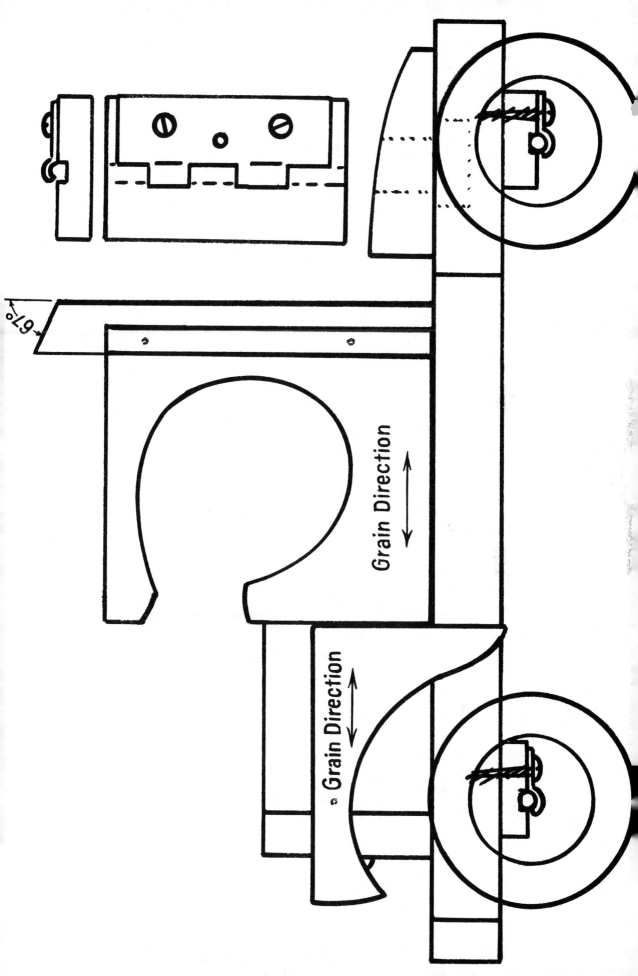

67°

Grain Direction

Grain Direction

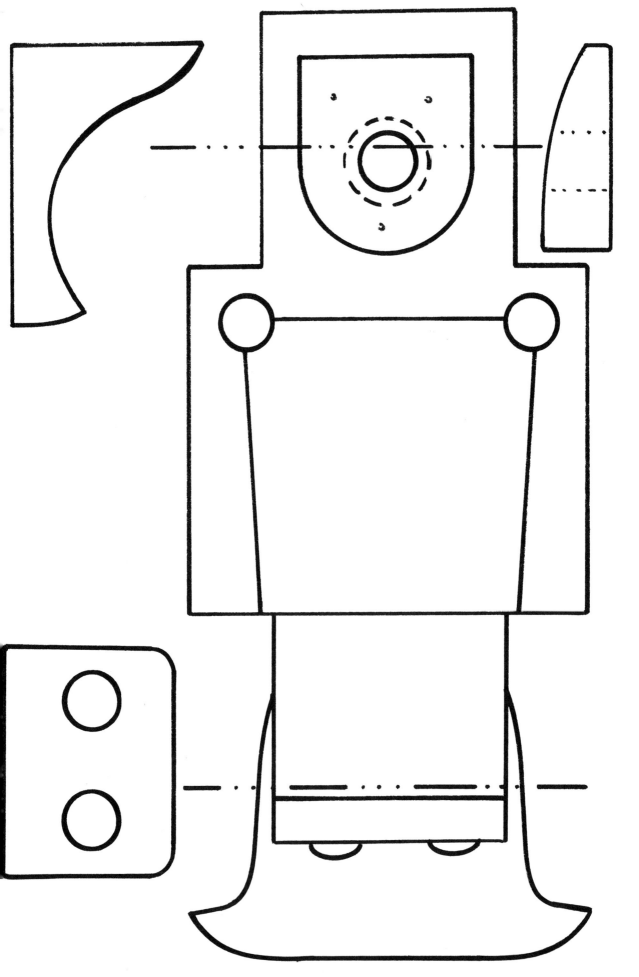

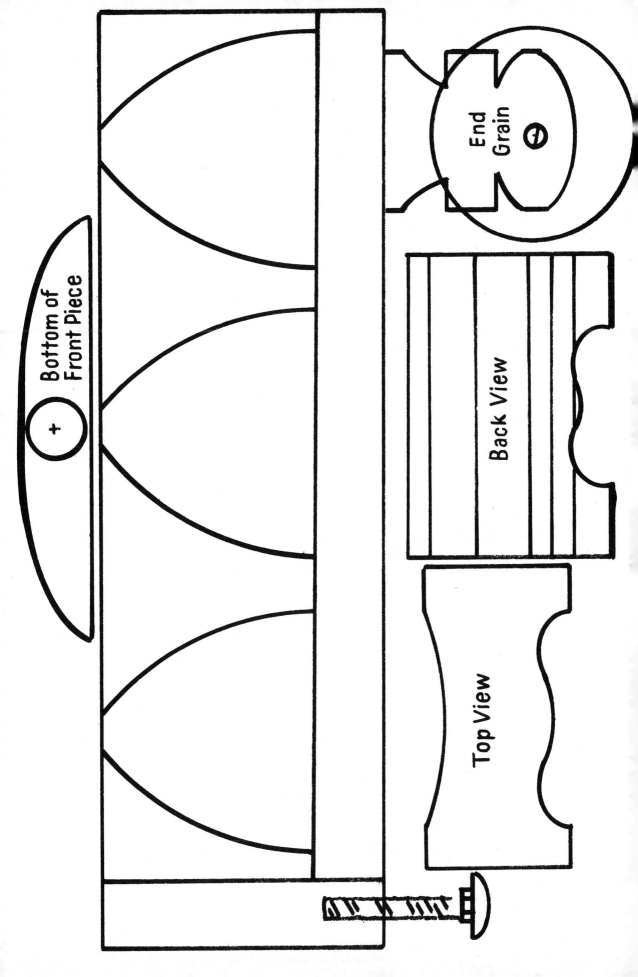

Bottom of
Front Piece

End
Grain

Back View

Top View

Chapter 3

The Steamroller

Nothing around the sandpit makes good, official-looking roads quite so fast and effectively as a sturdy, dependable steamroller. And this model happens to be beefy enough to flatten the most stubborn dirt clod without batting an eyelash.

Like the recipe that begins, "First, catch a rabbit," the first task is to hunt up a spare rolling pin. If there don't seem to be a lot of them hanging around the kitchen, the housewares department of the nearest home-supply store will spare you one for a small consideration.

Step One: Cutting

Begin by cutting off both handles of the rolling pin at the base. Then make two cuts as squarely as possible across the pin, making two sections, one 7″ long and the other 4½″ long.

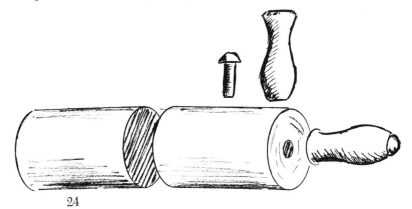

Check the basic dimensions shown in the side elevation in the plans, and then sketch these onto the longer section of the pin. It's fairly important to try to keep the cuts square to each other at this point, so make the cuts with whatever you feel most confident with.

Now, mark on the top outline and with a band saw or coping saw, cut this out, keeping the cuts square with the side cuts.

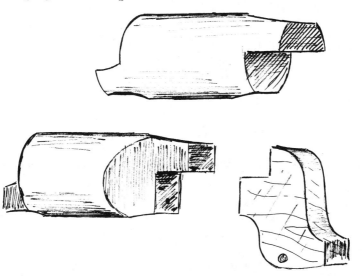

Mark two 4″ circles on a short length of 2″×6″ stock, and cut these out for the rear wheels. Transfer the top and side outlines of the rear part of the body onto a length of the 2″×6″ by making a pattern with a copier, carbon paper, or tracing paper. Now place the longer piece of the roller, which has already been trimmed, over this outline and check to see how the cuts will join up against the outline. Make adjustments in the outline, if need be, to make a good joint against the long roller piece, then cut this rear piece out with a saber, band, jig or coping saw, and trim to fit snugly against the back of the long roller piece.

Step Two: Drilling

Mark a center line straight down the top of the boiler made from the longer piece of the roller, and then mark the drilling spots for the front fork pivot, smokestack, condenser, and rear fastening hole. Drill a 1/8″ hole for the rear fastening screw, as well as one for the fastening screw in the bottom rear of the boiler. Now, with the 1/2″ wood drill bit, countersink these holes deeply enough for the 1 1/4″ long screws to get a good bite into the rear piece. The condenser, sticking out of the top of the boiler just behind the smokestack, is made from one of the spindles that the rolling-pin handles turn on. Drill a hole for this condenser that is the same diameter as the shaft of the spindle, and about 1″ deep.

Drill a 1″-diameter hole for the stack, about 1/2″ deep. Then, in the center of this hole, drill another hole that is the diameter of the spindle shaft, about 1 1/2″ deep.

On the top of the front fork mount, drill a 5/8″-diameter hole just barely down into the wood, about 1/8″ deep, to make a base for the head of the bolt that holds the fork in place. Then drill on through this spot with a 1/4″ bit, all the way through the fork mount.

Drill a 1/4″ axle hole in the center of each rear wheel, and then a rear axle hole in position in the back piece of the steam roller's body. Angling the drill up and down slightly from both ends of this axle hole, enlarge it vertically a little so that the rear wheels will be able to bounce.

To make the holes in the front fork, drill a 1/4″ hole through the center point of a 1′ length of 3/4″-wide iron strap, found close to the hinges in the hardware section of most stores. Drill two more holes in the strap 4 1/8″ away from the center hole to both sides. Cut off both ends of the strap 1/4″ to the outside of both of these holes, and round off the ends with a file.

To finish this step, drill a 1/4″ hole for the steering wheel, angled down into the back edge of the rear body piece. Then drill a 1/8″ hole in the side of one of the rolling-pin handles about 1″ from the bottom. This handle will be used as the smokestack; the wider flanged end should form the top end of the stack. Now the drill can cool off a bit.

Step Three: First Assembling

Apply a little white glue to both faces of the front and rear body pieces at the joint, and join them firmly with 1¼", Number eight, flathead wood screws.

Step Four: Shaping

With a wood rasp or, better yet, one of those serrated wood shapers, round off all the sharp edges of the body, as well as the rear wheels and front roller. Smooth up the joint between the front and rear body pieces, and sand with coarse, then medium, then fine sandpaper.

Step Five: More Assembling

Glue a roundhead ½" wood plug button (found with the wooden knobs and drawer pulls in the hardware section) in the top of the countersunk screw hole at the back of the body, and tap firmly. Cut one of the rolling-pin-handle spindles to about 2" long (including the head), add a dab of

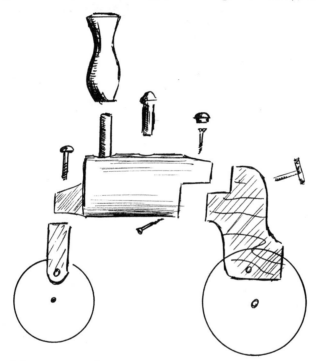

glue to it, and hammer it down into the condenser hole. Now cut off the head end of the other spindle and hammer it down into the hole for the stack after adding a little glue.

Squeeze a little glue around the spindle sticking out of the smokestack hole, then slip the handle (used as the stack) down onto this spindle, and seat it firmly in the 1" hole drilled for the stack. Now sink a ¾" roundhead wood screw through the side of the stack at the hole provided, then into the spindle shaft and tighten firmly.

The steering wheel shown was made from a standard chrome raisable

sink stopper, cut off, and then screwed into the ¼″ hole in the back of the body. This wheel can be made just as well from a short length of ¼″ dowel, to form the shaft, and a 1¼″ disc cut from ¼″-thick plywood with a hole saw, and glued onto the dowel.

To attach the wheels to the rear axle, cut off a 6″ length of ¼″-diameter threaded rod (usually found near the bolts in the hardware section). Run a nut onto this rod to about 2″ from one end. Then insert this end into the center hole of one of the wheels, and run another nut onto this end, just flush with the end of the rod. Now back the first nut onto the wheel, running the wheel up against the end nut, and tighten the nuts deeply into the grain of the wheel.

The axle can now be inserted into the axle hole in the body, and the other wheel bolted tightly to the other end of the axle.

With a vise, or heavy pliers and a hammer, bend the strap forming the front fork to the shape shown in the plans. Now sink a 1½″, ¼″-diameter roundhead bolt down through the hole in the front fork mount, through the center hole in the fork, and then fasten with a nut. Using a hacksaw, cut the bolt off flush with the bottom of the nut.

Mark a center point in the ends of the front roller, and then sink 1½″ or

2″ roundhead wood screws in through the holes in the ends of the fork, and then into the ends of the roller, leaving enough play for the roller to turn easily.

Step Six: Finishing

A coat or two of satin-finish varnish will help to bring out the patterns in the grain of the wood, and also to prevent it from drying out and cracking under heavy use. The front fork, the stack, and the plug button are all painted flat or semigloss black, or dark green if you like. And that's about it; she's ready to roll, if you'll pardon a horrible pun.

LUMBER LIST for the STEAMROLLER	One wooden rolling pin
	One-foot length of 2″×6″ hardwood
	One-foot length of ¾″-wide iron strap
	Six-inch length of ¼″-diameter threaded iron rod, and five nuts
	One 1½″-long, ¼″-diameter roundhead bolt
	Two 1¼″-long flathead wood screws
	Two 1½″-long roundhead wood screws
	One roundhead wood plug button (to fit ½″ hole)
	One raisable chrome sink stopper (or ¼″ dowel and 1¼″-diameter disc cut from ¼″-thick plywood)
	One ¾″ roundhead wood screw

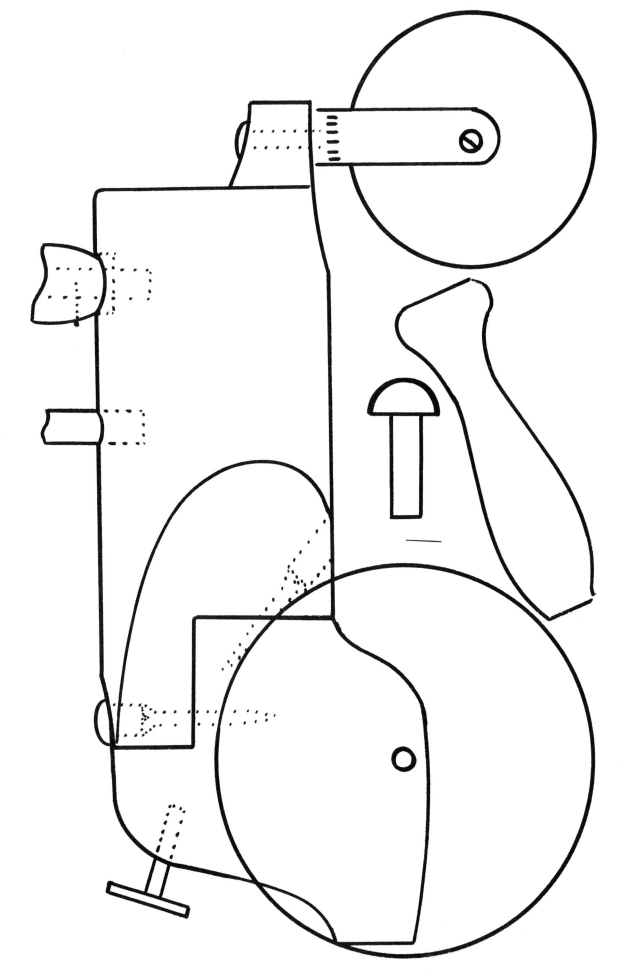

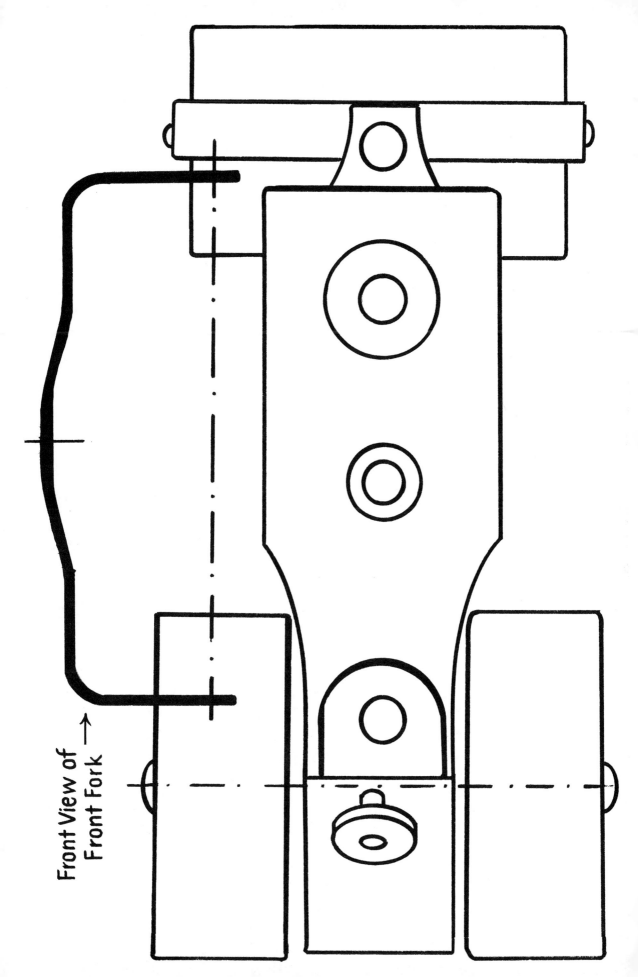

Front View of Front Fork →

Chapter 4

The Cradle

The cradle design was taken almost verbatim from a 200-year-old New England version that has made a big hit with the little ones ever since the days before George Washington and his boys got busy. For the turned legs, use ready-made room-divider posts available at most lumberyards and home-supply stores. Of course, if you have access to a wood lathe, then you're all set to make your own style posts. Or if neither ready-made posts nor lathes seem to be within your reach, the designs can be cut into the sides of 2″×2″ stock with a band saw or coping saw.

Only two of the ready-made 18″ divider posts are needed. Each post is cut near the center of the turned part, forming one of the 10″ posts for the head of the cradle, as well as the 8″ post for the foot of the cradle on one side.

Step One: Cutting

Mark the dimensions of the sides, the ends, and the bottom of the cradle onto a 6′ length of 1″×8″ stock with an interesting grain. Make the straight cuts with a carpenter's handsaw, a table saw, or a portable electric circular saw. Then cut the scrollwork at the head end of the cradle with a band, jig, saber, or coping saw. Now cut the rockers from a 2′ length of 2″×4″ stock.

Step Two: Drilling

The box of the cradle is fastened together at the corners with 1¼″, Number 8, flathead wood screws, or something close to that size. The sides and ends of the cradle box butt against the corner posts, flush with the inside edge. Starter holes for the screws are drilled through the posts in the positions shown, with a ⅛″ drill bit. Then ⅜″ countersunk holes are drilled down into these starter holes to a depth that will allow the screws to have a good bite into the sides and ends of the box. Each corner post will have a different set of adjacent joining sides, so drill the countersunk holes separately for each post. Drill starter holes and then countersunk holes where they are shown along the bottom of the sides and ends for the screws that will attach the sides to the bottom of the cradle.

Larger holes, roughly ¾″ to 1″ in diameter, can now be drilled down into the two short, flat surfaces on the top edges of both rockers to serve as seats for the turned bottom ends of the corner posts. Try to fit the diameter of the hole to the size of the turning inserted, and also to make the holes of equal depth, about ½″. Now drill ⅛″ screw holes down through the centers of these holes and out the other side. Drill ⅜″ countersunk holes in from the *bottom* side to a depth that will allow the screws to get a good bite into the ends of the posts.

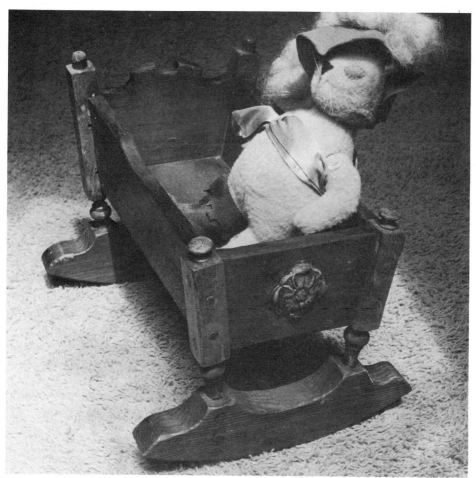

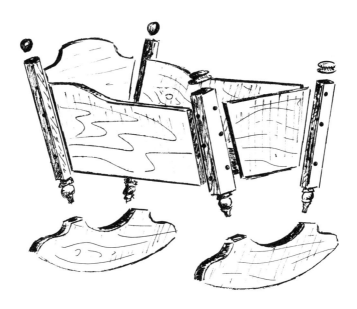

Step Three: Assembling

Place a line of white glue down one side of one of the shorter legs and attach it to the foot end of one side, flush with the inner edge. Now attach the longer post to the other end in the same way, with screws and glue.

Assemble the other side to the other legs in the same manner, making certain that the countersunk holes are always to the outside. Now attach the foot and head end pieces to the corner posts of one side and, finally, attach the other posts to the end pieces.

Slip the bottom of the cradle down between the sides, and sink screws in from the sides and ends to hold it in place.

Insert the bottom ends of the corner posts at one end down into the large holes in the top edge of one of the rockers, after placing a dab of glue in each hole, of course. Then run screws up from the bottom edge of the rocker firmly into the bottom ends of the corner posts. Repeat this performance to attach the other rocker at the other end.

A large variety of wooden drawer pull knobs can be found to decorate the tops of the posts. These can be fastened with glue and finishing nails, or double-ended screws, if you like to get fancy.

The decoration used on the head end of the example pictured was chosen from a number of nicely cast, pressed-wood "stick-ons" available at most home-supply and hobby stores.

Cut a ⅜" dowel into very short lengths, about ¼" to ⅜", with a band, hack or table saw, to make dowel plugs to cover the screwheads. Place a dab of glue in each countersunk hole on one side of the cradle, then insert the short stubs of dowel and with a mallet tap them into the hole until flush with the surface. Repeat this on the other sides until all holes are filled.

34

Round off all the upper edges of the cradle box, as well as the rockers. Then sand with coarse, medium, and fine sandpaper to remove all potential splinters.

Step Four: Finishing

The finish used can be whatever you and your young client agree upon. The cradle could be antiqued and decorated with colored embellishments, or varnished, or stained and then wiped and given a coat or two of satin finish varnish, as in this example. Now all you need is a blanket, a favorite doll, and a small girl to complete the set.

LUMBER LIST
for the
CRADLE

Six feet of 1″×6″ stock (with interesting grain)
Two 18″-long turned room-divider posts (about 1½″ thick)
Two feet of 2″×4″ stock
One foot of ⅜″-diameter wood dowel
Four decorative wood drawer-pull knobs
Three dozen 1¼″, Number 8, flathead wood screws
One or two decorative pressed-wood stick-ons

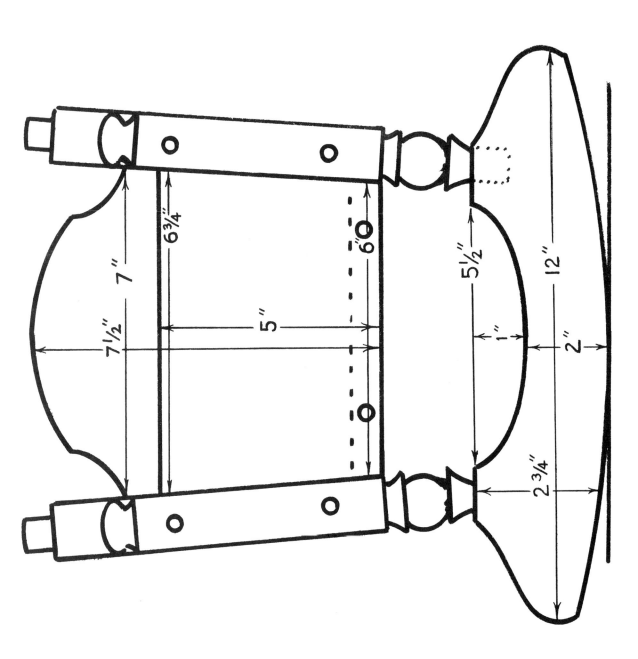

7½"

7"

6¾"

5"

6"

5½"

1"

12"

2"

2¾"

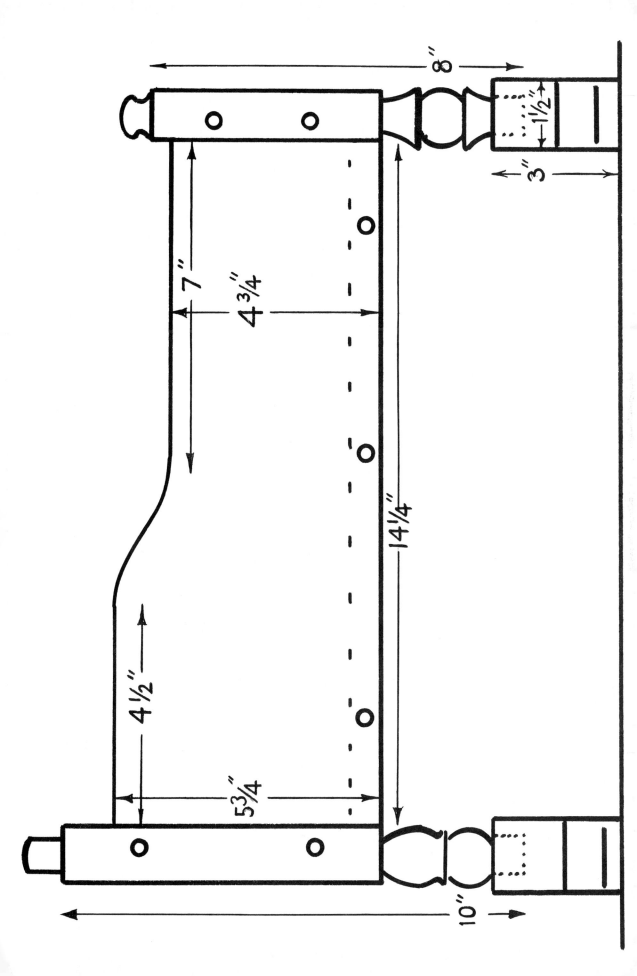

Chapter 5

The Biplane

The little French biplane, that nimble nemesis of the Kaiser's best efforts, is a composite design taken from several famous old birds, like the Nieuport, the Sopwith, and the Avro. While the rotary engines in these early beasts looked much like the radial engines of today, they were different in that instead of the crankshaft's turning the propeller, the prop was bolted to the engine and the whole engine rotated, leaving the crankshaft stationary.

Control of these engines fell somewhat short of precise, with power tending to be either Full-On or Full-Off; hence the strange *Bup, bup, barrup* sound they made when coming in for a landing.

Having two short sets of wings gave them plenty of climbing power, while still allowing great ability and strength. And in the hands of a Rickenbacker, or a Lufberry, they were quite a sight to see going through their paces.

To make this version, start with a 1′ length of clear-grained, softwood 4″×4″ stock to make the fuselage.

Step One: Cutting

Make a copy of the fuselage profile (full-scale size) in the plans, using carbon paper, tracing paper or a copier; then cut out this pattern to trace the profile onto the wood. Use a band saw or coping saw to cut out the profile of the fuselage. Then draw a center line down the top of the fuselage, and trace around a pattern; draw the top outline onto the top of the fuselage. Cut this out.

38

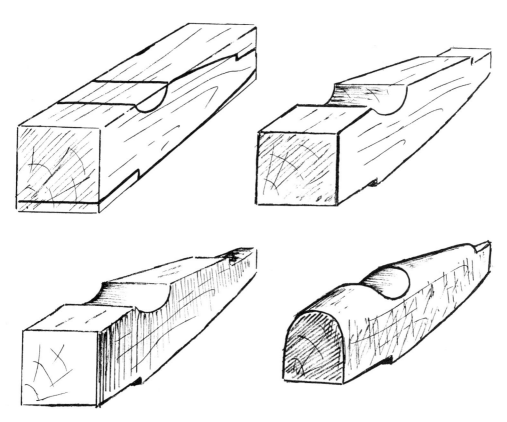

The tail surfaces and propeller are drawn onto ¼″-thick plywood or paneling, and then cut out with a band, jig, saber or coping saw.

Cut four 6″ lengths of ⅜″-diameter wood dowel and three 3″ lengths of

$\frac{3}{8}''$ dowel. Cut one last piece of $\frac{5}{16}''$-diameter dowel, $4\frac{1}{8}''$ long.

The wings are cut from tapered $\frac{3}{4}''\times6''$ or $\frac{3}{4}''\times8''$ lapped house-siding lumber. A 4' piece is as short as you can buy it in most yards, but you might be able to happen onto some cut-off ends in the scrap pile of the yard. If, for some reason, you can't find any of this standard house siding, the wings can be made from $\frac{1}{2}''$-thick stock.

When marking on the outlines of the wings, align the trailing edges of the wings with the *thin* edge of the tapered siding. Mark a center line down the piece of siding and use the wing patterns to draw the complete wings on both sides of the line.

Cut the wheels from $\frac{1}{2}''$-thick scrap plywood with the $2\frac{1}{4}''$-diameter hole-saw attachment for the power drill.

For the engine cowling, use a very short piece of hardwood $4''\times4''$ (or any wood with a color that contrasts with the fuselage wood). Slice off one end of the $4''\times4''$ as squarely as you can manage. Now mark a squared line around the $4''\times4''$, $1\frac{1}{8}''$ in from the first cut, and slice off a nicely squared $1\frac{1}{8}''$ piece of $4''\times4''$ (preferably without any cracks in it). Draw a $2\frac{3}{4}''$ diameter circle on the end grain of this slice and cut it out.

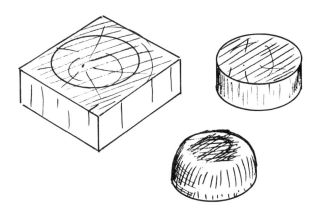

Step Two: Drilling

The two strut holes can be drilled into the top of the fuselage now with a $\frac{3}{8}''$ wood drill bit, as shown in the plans. Also drill a $\frac{3}{8}''$ hole for the tail skid in the bottom of the fuselage, angled in from the back.

Drill the $\frac{3}{8}''$ holes shown in the wing patterns into the top of the wings. With a $\frac{1}{8}''$ bit, drill a hole through the center point of the engine circle, a hole through the center of the propeller, a hole through the bottom wing near the center, as shown, and two holes in the edge of the rudder, one down through the top edge, and one in from the bottom back edge, as shown. A $\frac{1}{8}''$ hole is also needed down through the center of the pilot's head.

Now, with a $\frac{1}{16}''$ drill bit (or with one of the 1''-long finishing nails with the head nipped off mounted in the drill), space four holes around the

center hole in the propeller, as shown. Drill holes in from the edges of the wings, directly into the strut holes with this small bit, as shown in the side view.

Step Three: Shaping

To form the fuselage, use a wood rasp or, better yet, a serrated wood shaper to round over the top of the fuselage in front and in back of the cockpit. Round off the bottom of the fuselage sides slightly, and then smooth up the sides. Round off the edges of the wings, the tail surfaces, and the wheels. Place the engine cowling face-up on a firm, flat surface, and spend a little time rounding it into a smooth, bowl-shaped form.

Remove the shaper marks from all the parts with coarse sandpaper. Then use medium sandpaper to remove the scratches left by the coarse paper, and finally leave a nice, polished surface on the parts with fine sandpaper.

Step Four: Assembling

With the fuselage upside down, place the lower wing in position; drill two short starter holes through the screwholes in the wing and into the bottom of the fuselage. Attach the wing to the fuselage with white glue and 1¼″, Number 8, flathead wood screws.

Place a dab of glue in each strut hole in the top of the fuselage, insert

41

two of the 3″ lengths of ⅜″ dowel, and tap them firmly down into the holes. Insert the tops of these dowels into the holes provided in the top wing, and lower the wing to approximately the height shown in the side view.

The 6″ lengths of dowel can be inserted through the remaining holes in both wings. Adjust the position of the upper wing so that it is squared at the right height above the lower wing, as shown in the plans. With the 1/16″ bit, drill starter holes in through the holes already drilled in the edges of the wings, and into the strut dowels.

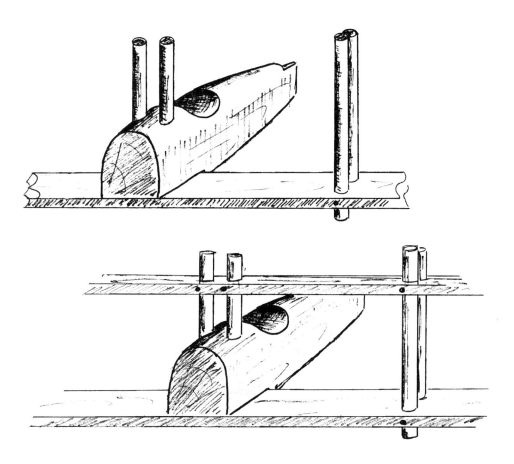

Rest the trailing edges of the wings on a firm, flat surface and drive 1″ finishing nails into the edge holes and into the dowels. Check the alignment of the wings from the top, sides, and front as this nailing progresses. The leftover struts sticking out from the top and bottom of the wings can now be trimmed off with a hacksaw or coping saw, cutting carefully and with the grain of the wings. Sand the strut ends flush with the wing surfaces. A drop of glue around each strut where it enters the wing will make the structure even sturdier.

Now the horizontal tail surface can be glued and nailed to the top of the

42

rear end of the fuselage. Insert two 2″ finishing nails in through the holes in the edges of the rudder, run a bit of glue along the edges that join with the top and end of the fuselage, and finally, holding the rudder squarely in place, drive the nails into the fuselage. Check the rudder from the front view and square it up a bit if needed.

To attach the propeller to the engine, place a dab of glue on the backside of the center of the prop and insert a 2″ finishing nail through the front of the center hole and into the hole in the engine center. Place a small finishing nail in each of the small holes around the center of the prop, and drive them in, leaving just a little of the heads sticking out of the prop. Check to see that the engine assembly can rotate freely around a 2″ finishing nail. If not, clean out the hole a little with a ⅛″ bit.

Place the engine against the front of the fuselage in the position shown in the side view, and drive in the center nail, leaving enough play for the engine to turn freely. Bend the nail slightly if the engine hangs up in one place when turning over. It will loosen up more and more as time goes on.

Step Five: The Landing Gear

The landing gear is made from aluminum counter-edge stripping. This comes in 3′ lengths with holes drilled every five or six inches. It's about

⅝" wide and beveled on both edges of one side. Lacking this, ⅝"-wide iron strap can be used.

Cut the stripping into two 4⅜" lengths and one 6¾" length. Mark a line across the long piece at the center. Now mark a ⅛" hole ⅝" away from the center line on each side, and drill these holes with the ⅛" bit. Make a mark ⅜" in from both ends of the stripping, and drill ⅜" holes at these marks. Drill ⅜" holes ⅜" in from the squared ends of the shorter pieces, and then ⅛" holes ½" in from the other ends of the short pieces. Round off the ends of the strippings with the ⅜" holes, using a file.

Bend the longer piece as shown in the plans, with the beveled side to the outside. Bend the ends of the shorter pieces over in different directions so that there is a left and a right side with the beveled side out.

Mount the long strip to the bottom wing, flush with the front of the fuselage, with screws.

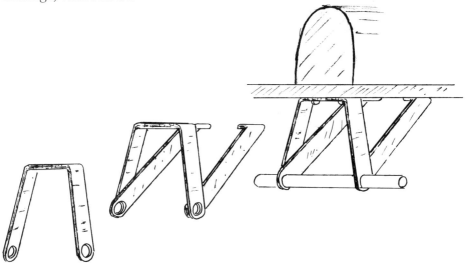

With the help of a hammer, insert one end of the 4⅛" length of 5/16" dowel through a center hole in one of the wheels, so that the dowel sticks out the other side of the wheel a little less than ⅛". Place the plane upside down on a flat surface, and insert the end of the axle through one of the end holes in the long landing-gear piece. Slip the holes in the shorter pieces over the end of the axle with the beveled sides out and the bent-over ears pointing toward the center of the plane. Now insert the axle through the hole in the other end of the mounted, long piece of the landing gear. Insert this end of the axle down into the center hole of the other wheel (lying flat on the bench) and tap the axle through so that it just barely sticks out the other side of the wheel. Now place the plane upside down again and mount the shorter lengths of stripping firmly with screws through the ⅛" holes, positioning them up against the inside of the longer piece of stripping. Tap a glued ⅜" dowel tail skid into the hole in the tail bottom and cut off on an angle about 1½" below the fuselage.

44

Step Six: Painting

After a final light sanding, a coat or two of satin finish varnish will bring out the contrasting wood tones (watch for drips along the sides of the cockpit and the struts). When dry, the rudder can be painted gloss white. When this is dry, the vertical bands of red and blue can be painted on.

With a small, round paintbrush, paint in the flat or semigloss black circle around the center of the engine cowling, as shown in the photos. While you have the black handy, paint the tires, which come about 1/4″ to 3/8″ in from the outer edge of the wheel discs.

The time has come to create a pilot for this worthy little bird. Drive a 2″ finishing nail down through the center of the top of the pilot's head (a 1½″ drawer-pull ball), leaving just the head of the nail sticking out the top. Sketch the face on the head and with the 1/16″ bit drill two holes about 1/2″ deep for the tacks that will form the eyes. Hammer in the two 3/4″-long, roundhead brass tacks, then paint on the black moustache and helmet, and place two small black dots in the center of the tack heads for eyes.

While this is drying, cut a 5/8″×6″ strip of checked cotton or other thin material, and fray the ends. Tie a double knot of the material around the nail sticking out the bottom of the head, leaving one end about an inch longer than the other.

Now the head can be hammered down into a starter hole drilled down into the center of the cockpit.

This done, it's "contact" time, heads up, tails over the dashboard, and off to the Dawn Patrol with all due haste.

LUMBER LIST for the BIPLANE	One foot of clear-grained, soft wood 4″×4″ Two feet of tapered 1″×6″ or 1″×8″ lapped house siding Three feet of 3/8″-diameter wood dowel Six inches of 5/16″-diameter wood dowel A small scrap of 1/4″-thick plywood or paneling at least 6″×6″ Half a dozen 1¼″, Number 8, flathead wood screws A small scrap of 1/2″-thick plywood at least 3″×6″ Two dozen 1″ finishing nails One short length of hardwood 4″×4″ stock Three feet of 5/8″-wide, beveled aluminum edge stripping A 1½″-diameter wood drawer-pull ball Two 3/4″-long roundhead brass tacks A 5/8″×6″-long strip of checked material

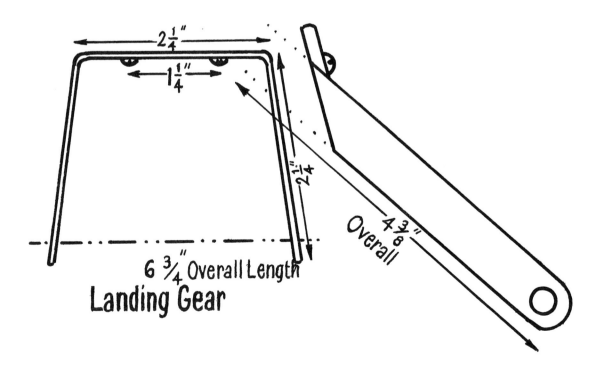

2 1/4"

1 1/4"

2 1/4"

4 3/8" Overall

6 3/4" Overall Length

Landing Gear

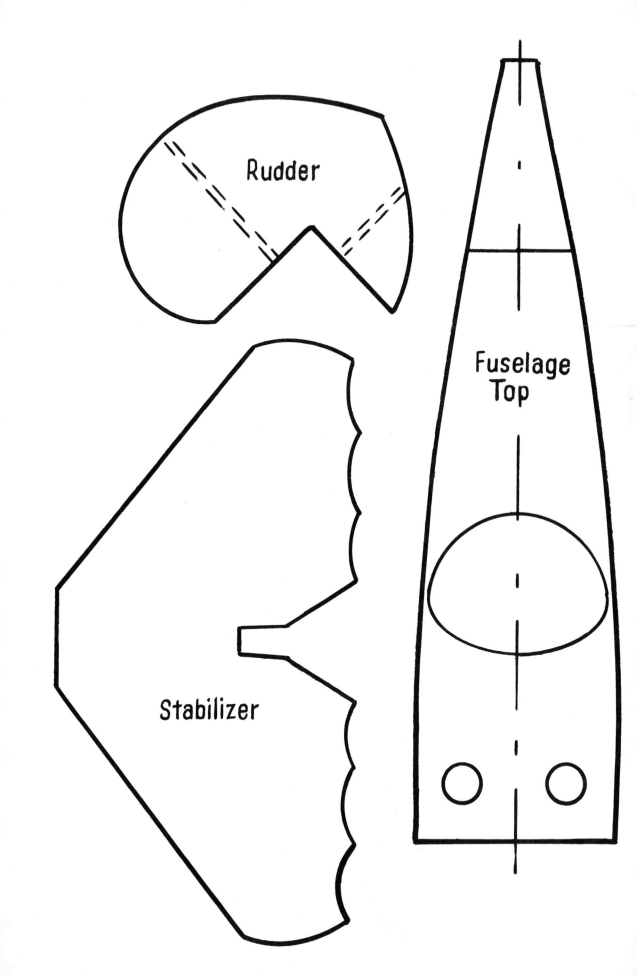

Rudder

Fuselage
Top

Stabilizer

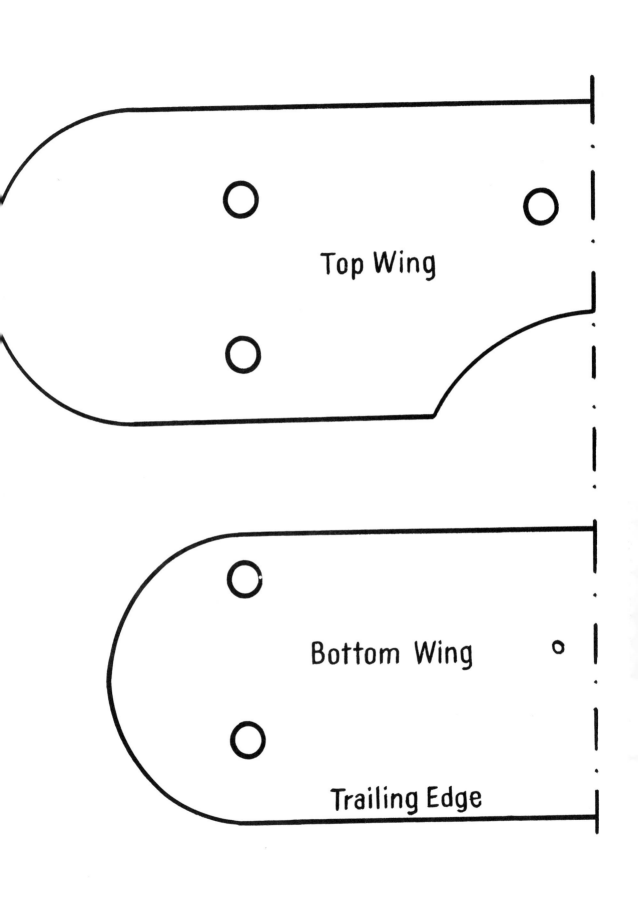

Top Wing

Bottom Wing

Trailing Edge

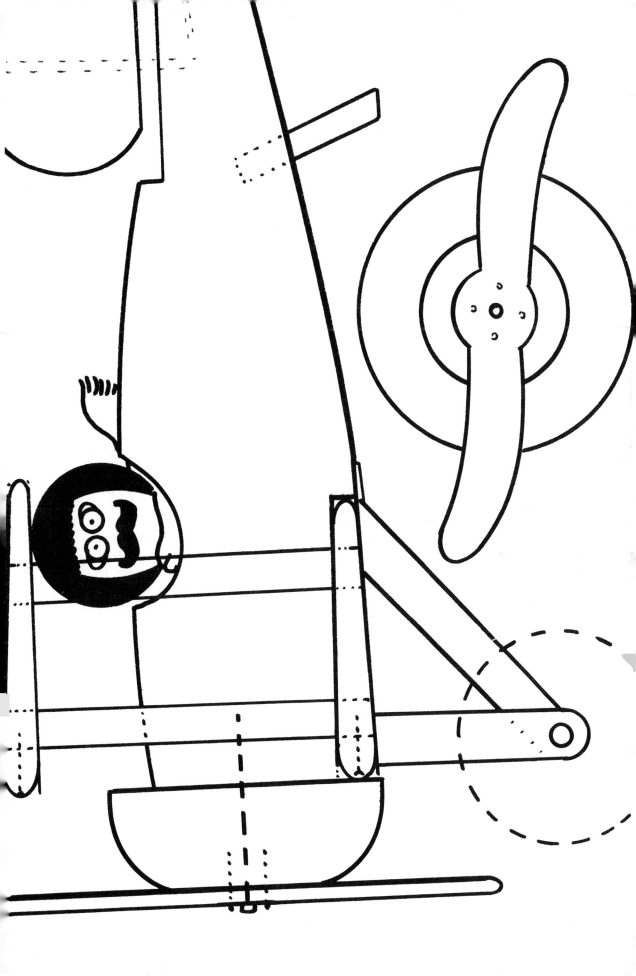

Chapter 6

The Triplane

Not to be outdone by the sturdy little French biplanes like the one in the previous project, the Germans went one better and added still another wing, resulting in the type of triplane made famous (or infamous, depending on your point of view) by the Red Baron himself.

The idea of the extra wing was to make the plane climb faster so it could get up above its opponents, which was important in those distant, sporting days. And these stubby triplanes proved to be agile fliers indeed.

Like the biplane, the toy triplane is a composite of lines taken from several planes; the manufacturers were German companies like Fokker, Pfalz, and Albatross. Typically, the engines in this type of plane were straight, in-line engines, so there's no engine cowling as on the biplane, which makes the project just a little easier. And if the V-shaped grille in the front reminds you of the toy German race car included in this book, there's a good reason—they both had the same well-known engine.

Step One: Cutting

Using carbon paper, tracing paper, or the help of a copying machine, transfer the lines of the side profile in the plans to a sheet of paper that can be cut into patterns to draw around.

Mark the lines of the side profile onto the side of a 1'-long piece of clear-grained softwood 4″×4″ or 2″×4″ stock. Because the triplane can be made from the 2″×4″ stock, and has no engine cowling, it may be easier (for those without a band saw) to build than the biplane despite the extra wing.

50

Cut out the side profile with a band, jig, saber or coping saw. Then mark a center line down the top of the fuselage, draw the outline of the top shape and cut this out. Carefully cut straight down both sides of the V-shaped grille with a hacksaw or carpenter's handsaw.

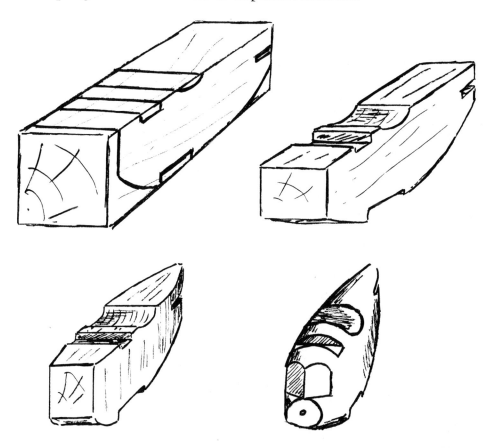

The wings are cut from a 4' length of $5/8'' \times 6''$ or $5/8'' \times 8''$ tapered house siding, the kind that is lapped around the walls of many frame houses. Mark the outline of each wing on the tapered siding, positioning the trailing edge (the longer edge in this case) along the thin edge of the tapered siding, and cut these out. Use each wing pattern on both sides of a center line to draw the complete wing shape.

Mark the outlines of the tail surfaces and the propeller onto $1/4''$-thick plywood or paneling stock and cut these out also.

Cut the wheels from $1/2''$ plywood stock with the $2 1/4''$-diameter hole-saw attachment. Finally, cut two 6'' lengths of $3/8''$-diameter dowel, two 3'' lengths and one $4 1/8''$ length of $5/16''$-diameter dowel.

Step Two: Shaping

With a wood rasp or, better yet, a serrated wood shaper, round over the top of the fuselage in front of and behind the cockpit. Round off the bottoms of the fuselage sides slightly, and smooth up the sides with

51

the shaper. Round off the edges of the three wings, the tail surfaces, and the wheels with the shaper, and then sand all the parts. Coarse sandpaper will remove the gouges of the shaper, medium paper will remove the lines left by the coarse paper, and the fine sandpaper will polish up a smooth finish.

Step Three: Drilling

Stack the three wings, with the largest on top and the smallest in the middle, so that their forward edges are parallel, as shown. Holding the wings firmly in place, drill down through the hole marks drawn on the top wing, angling down from the front, as shown, with the ⅜″ drill bit. Along the forward edges of the wings, use a ¹⁄₁₆″ drill bit (or one of the 1″ finishing nails with its head nipped off and mounted in the drill) to drill holes through the front edges of the wings and into the centers of the ⅜″ holes.

With a ⅜″ bit, drill a hole for the tail skid in the bottom of the fuselage, angling the drill in from the rear. Drill a single ⅛″ hole in through the center point of the bottom wing for a screw to attach it to the bottom of the fuselage. With white glue on the joining surfaces, sink a screw up through the bottom wing and fasten it in place firmly. With glue and 1″ finishing nails, fasten the middle wing to the top of the fuselage, squarely in place. Drill down into the ⅜″ hole in the center of the middle wing with the ⅜″ bit, deepening the hole to about 1″ into the top of the fuselage.

Drill two ⅛″ holes into the end grain of the rudder, as shown in the plans.

Step Four: Assembling

With a dab of glue on each, insert the two 3″ lengths of ⅜″ dowel, one into the hole in the top of the fuselage and middle wing, and the other into the tail-skid hole; tap them in tightly. Insert the two 6″ end dowels through the holes in the lower two wings, letting them stick out the bottom a little. Then slip the top wing down over these dowels, and adjust its positioning until it is squarely over the other wings at the angle shown. With the $\frac{1}{16}''$ bit, drill starter holes in through the holes already drilled in the forward edges of the wings, and into the dowel struts. Placing the trailing edges of the wings on a firm, flat surface, drive 1″ finishing nails down into the holes, securing the dowel struts in place. To make the plane even sturdier, put a little glue around each strut where it enters a wing.

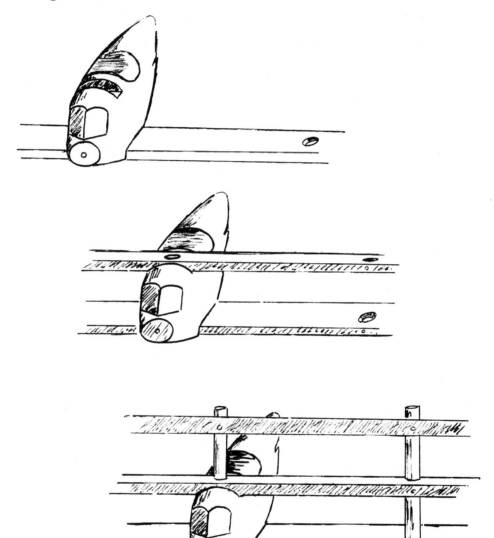

Run a little glue into the slot for the horizontal tail surface in the rear of the fuselage. Insert the tail surface into this slot with the notched trailing edge to the rear, and drive a 1″ finishing nail down through the top of the fuselage and through the tail surface, holding it squarely in place. Now,

place a line of glue along the edges of the rudder that will be joined to the top and back of the fuselage. Holding the rudder squarely in place, run 2″ finishing nails in through the holes drilled in the edges of the rudder and, with the bottom of the fuselage braced against a firm surface, drive these nails in. Then view the plane from the front, and square the tail up a little, if it is needed.

The leftover struts sticking out the top and bottom of the wings should be trimmed off flush with the wing surfaces; cut carefully along the grain of the top and bottom wings. Now the surfaces can be given a little resanding to smooth things up.

Step Five: The Landing Gear

The landing gear is made from ⅝″-wide aluminum counter-edge stripping, with edges beveled on one side. Iron strap ⅝″ wide may also be used if the aluminum stripping can't be found. With the hacksaw, cut off a 6¼" length of this stripping, then drill ⅜" holes centered about ½" in from both ends of the piece. With the ⅛" drill bit, drill two holes ⅝" out from the center point of the stripping on both sides of the center.

Now mark a line across the stripping, ⅞" out from the center line on both sides; bend on these lines with the stripping held in a vise or by a heavy pair of pliers to make the two bends that form the front piece of the landing gear, with the beveled side to the outside of the bends.

With the plane upside down, place the front landing-gear piece across the bottom of the fuselage with the front of the piece about ½" in front of the leading edge of the bottom wing. Attach this piece with screws driven up into the fuselage.

Now cut two 3" lengths of the stripping. Drill a ⅜" hole about ½" in from one end of each piece. Then bend over the ears, as shown, on the other end so that the ears on both pieces will point toward the center of the plane, with the beveled sides out. Now drill ⅛" holes for mounting screws through the ears that will fit against the bottom of the fuselage.

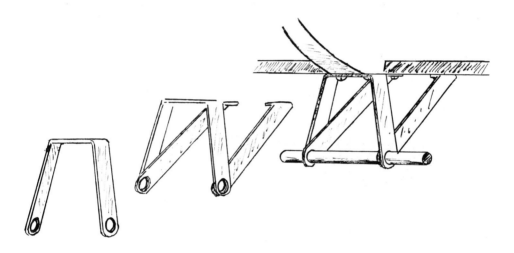

With the aid of a hammer, insert one end of the axle (a 4⅛" length of ⁵⁄₁₆"-diameter wood dowel) into the center hole of one of the wheels, driving it through until it sticks out the other side a little less than ⅛". Insert the other end of the axle through one of the ⅜" holes in the mounted landing-gear piece. Now slip the holes in the shorter landing-gear pieces over this end of the axle so that the ear mounts point toward the center of the fuselage. Insert the axle end through the hole in the other end of the mounted landing-gear piece, and then through the center hole in the other wheel in the same manner as the first wheel. Place the outside of the shorter pieces against the inside of the long piece, and then mount the bent ears to the bottom of the fuselage with screws.

Step Six: Final Assembling

Cut the tail skid off at the angle shown, about 1½" below the fuselage bottom. A ⅛"-diameter center hole should be drilled through the propeller for the 2"-long finishing nail that will hold the propeller on. Insert the nail through the front of the prop, then drive it into the front edge of the plane where shown, leaving enough play for the prop to turn easily. The prop can be attached after painting, if you're going to use spray paint.

Step Seven: Painting

Because the triplane is a fairly intricate shape to paint, it may be easier to use a brush than to spray. After a light sanding with the fine paper, spray on five to eight coats, or brush on two or three coats, of Chinese red or orange-red gloss enamel, sanding lightly after the first coats. Trim with flat or semigloss black, painting on the tires (which should come about ⅜" in from the edge of the wheels on both sides), a vertical band up the middle of the sides of the rudder, the cockpit and the sides of the V-shaped grille. Of course, if you'd like to put the Red Baron's skull and crossbones on the side or on the wings, it's a matter for your own conscience and that of your client. Varnish the propeller, and mount it if it isn't already on.

To make the Baron's head, drill a ⅛" hole on through the center of the round wood knob, and then drive a 2" finishing nail down into the hole, leaving just the head of the nail sticking out the top.

Sketch the face and helmet onto the wood knob, and drill a $\frac{1}{16}''$ hole for the tack that will form the monocle. Drive a $\frac{3}{4}''$-long, roundhead brass tack into the hole, and then paint on the face, placing a dot of black paint on the center of the monocle. The helmet should be painted a warm yellow (or "implement yellow" as it is known).

The last step is to cut out a $\frac{5}{8}'' \times 6''$ strip of red checked material, fray the ends, and then tie it around the Baron's neck with a double knot. Finally, drive the head nail down into a $\frac{1}{8}''$ starter hole drilled into the center of the cockpit about $\frac{1}{2}''$. Of course, the propeller and the axle will take a little running-in time before they will spin completely freely, but aside from that, the Baron's ready to go face those blighters in the Dawn Patrol.

LUMBER LIST for the TRIPLANE	One foot of clear-grained, softwood $2'' \times 4''$ or $4'' \times 4''$ stock Two feet of $\frac{3}{8}''$-diameter dowel One foot of $\frac{5}{16}''$-diameter dowel Four feet of tapered house siding, $\frac{3}{4}'' \times 6''$ or $\frac{3}{4}'' \times 8''$ stock (or $\frac{1}{2}'' \times 4''$ slat will do) Two feet of $\frac{5}{8}''$ wide aluminum edge stripping A $6'' \times 6''$ piece of $\frac{1}{4}''$-thick plywood or paneling A $3'' \times 6''$ piece of $\frac{1}{2}''$-thick plywood A $1\frac{1}{2}''$-diameter wood drawer-pull ball Half a dozen $2''$ finishing nails Four $1\frac{1}{4}''$, Number 8, flathead wood screws One dozen $1''$ finishing nails One piece of red checked material, $\frac{5}{8}'' \times 6''$

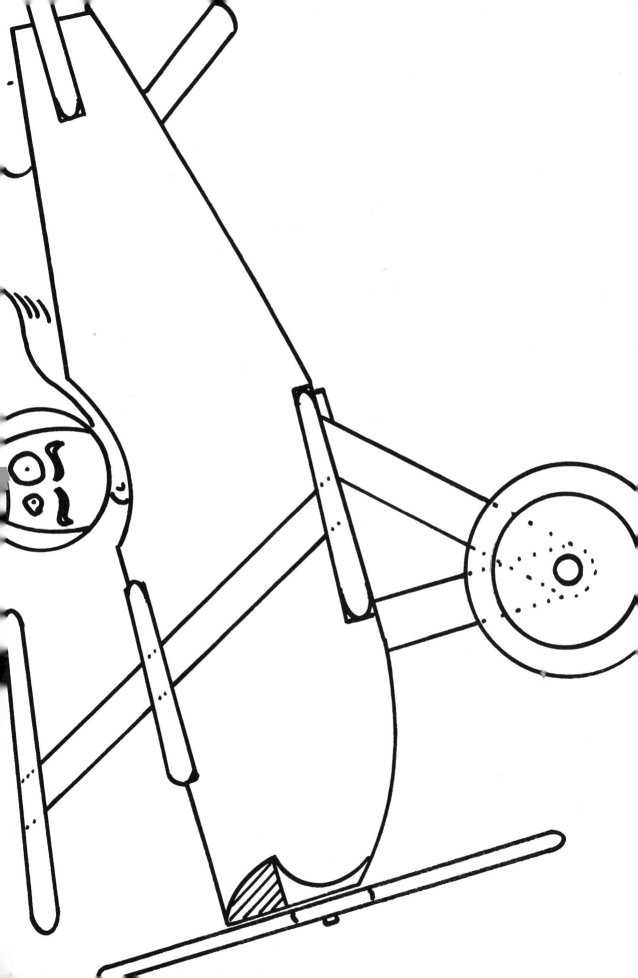

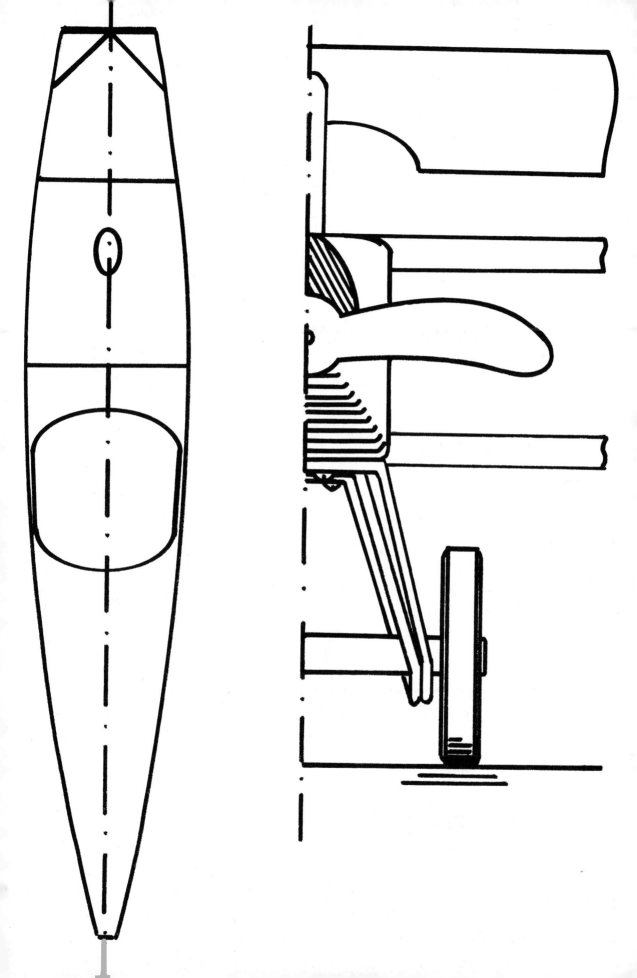

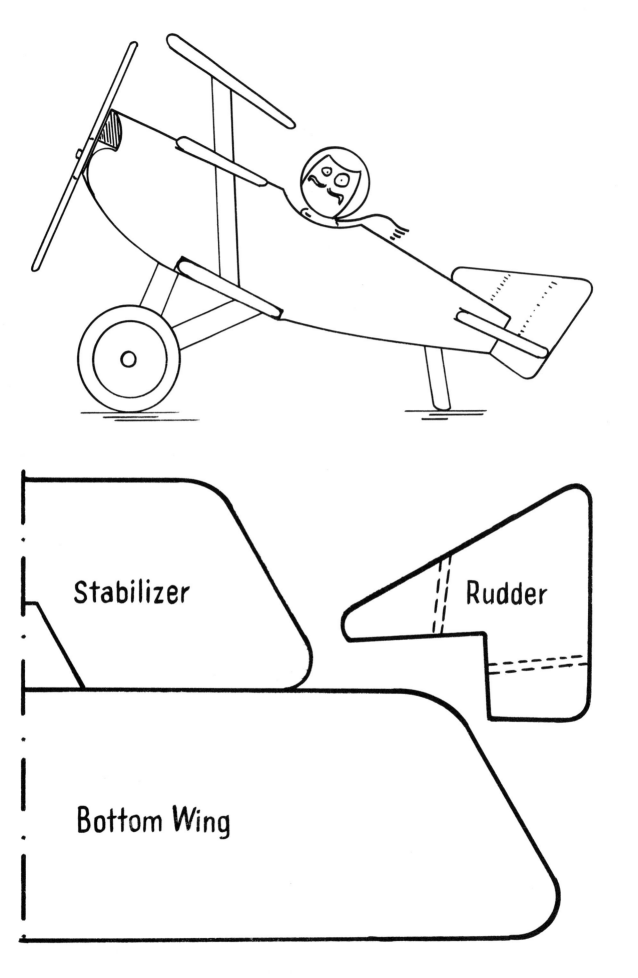

Stabilizer

Rudder

Bottom Wing

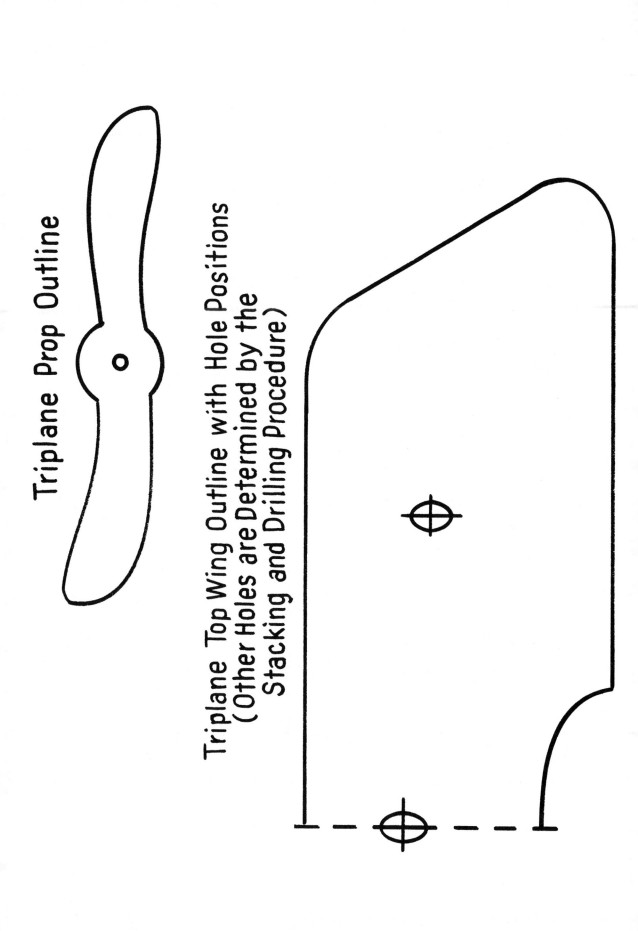

Triplane Prop Outline

Triplane Top Wing Outline with Hole Positions
(Other Holes are Determined by the
Stacking and Drilling Procedure)

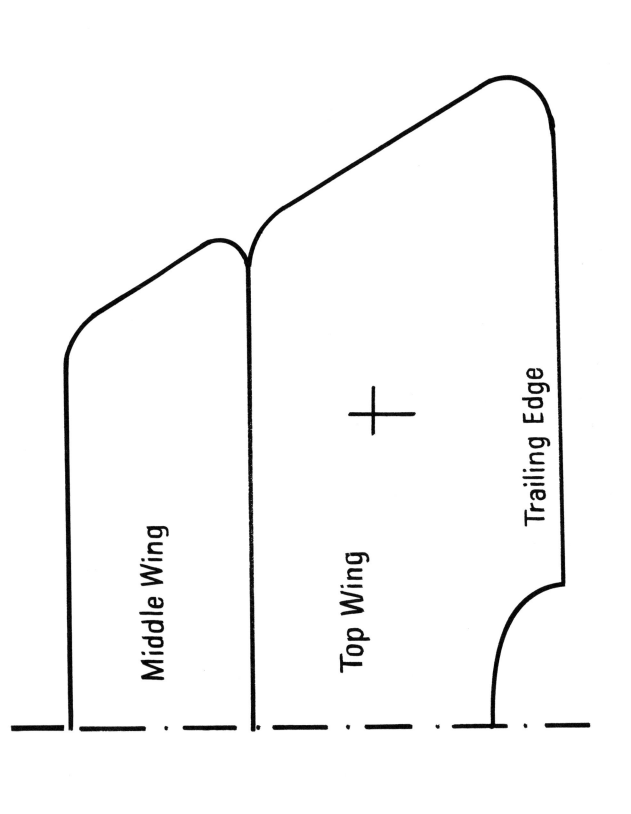

Middle Wing

Top Wing

Trailing Edge

Chapter 7

The Sword and Shield

Odsbud! what's your life worth these days without a sword and shield at your side? Of course, some may ask, what's it worth *with* a sword and shield at your side? Nevertheless, here's a set that might just fill the bill for some young rescuer of fair maidens and defender of the royal refrigerator. As far as the design goes, the coat of arms is of a composite, Middle-European origin. The reason for the coat of arms, as everybody knows, is so that you can tell friend from foe when everybody is covered with several layers of protective armament. So, if you're making more than one set, you may have to improvise a little to make up a different coat of arms for each knight.

This is an extremely easy project, the only time-consuming step being the painting, which may obviously be modified to suit your taste and patience.

Step One: Cutting

The shield shape is cut from ½″, or possibly even ⅜″, thick plywood. Draw the 18¼″ center line down the middle of a large sheet of paper (newspaper will do). Then mark a line squared perpendicularly across this center line, 1¾″ down from the top. Mark the outside top edges of the sides of the shield on this horizontal line, 6¼″ out from the center line on both sides.

Checking with the plans, sketch the outline of the shield and fold the paper down the center line. Cut out the side of the outline that you like best, cutting the other side at the same time so that a symmetrical shape will be formed when the paper is unfolded.

Using the pattern as a template, draw the shape onto the plywood, and then cut it out with the saber, band, jig or coping saw.

Cut the sword handle from a piece of hardwood 1″×4″ with a good, straight grain. Draw the lines marking the place where the crossbar overlaps the blade and handle. Cut a notch in the blade along these lines, halfway through the blade. Cut the crossbar from ¾″-thick plywood, and cut a notch halfway through the crossbar along the lines where it overlaps the blade. If you don't happen to have a scrap of ¾″ plywood, nose around the pile of discarded pieces at the lumberyard where there are often lots of nice pieces for the asking, if you have a friendly face and a little small talk handy.

Step Two: Shaping

Round off the edges of the shield with a wood plane, rasp or hand shaper.

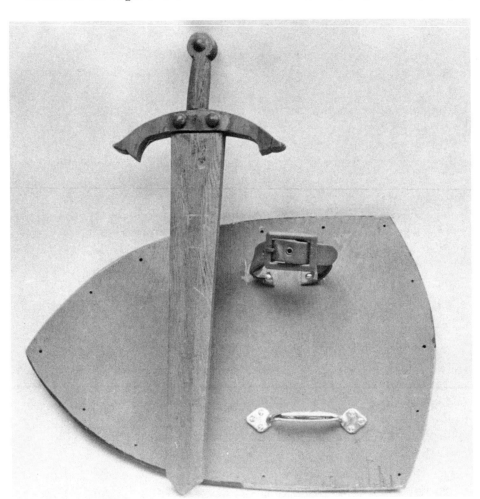

The blade of the sword should be beveled slightly, without leaving a sharp edge, of course. Round off the handle into a comfortable grip, but leave the round end of the handle as a flat disc. Sand all pieces thoroughly to remove any possible splinters.

Step Three: Detailing

With the ½″ wood bit, drill a series of holes around the edges of the shield spaced about 3″ apart and about ½″ in from the edge. These holes should be drilled to a depth of about ¼″. Drill a ½″ hole in the blade at the center of the place where the crossbar overlaps it, but on the side opposite the notch. Drill a ½″ hole into the center of the end disc of the handle, on both sides. Then drill two more ½″ holes, ¼″ into the outside of the middle of the crossbar, about ⅝″ from the center line on both sides.

Step Four: Assembling

Place a little white glue on the joining surfaces of the blade and the crossbar, then place the crossbar notch over the notch in the blade, and run two ½″ wood screws through the holes in the crossbar, and into the blade.

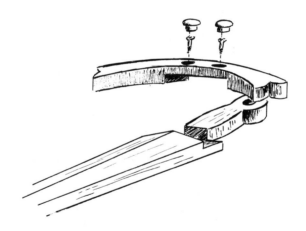

Now place a dab of glue in each ½″ hole in the sword and the shield. Tap ½″-diameter wood plug buttons firmly into these holes with a mallet or hammer. These buttons can usually be found in the hinge and drawer-pull section of the hardware department, and have a ⅝″ overall diameter of the button tops.

Attach a drawer-pull handle vertically on the back of the shield, as shown in the photo, and then a loop of belt, or strapping, mounted vertically toward the other edge of the back of the shield. If you'd like to make the strap in two halves, from both ends of a belt, then the strap can be adjusted for arms that tend to get bigger as time goes on.

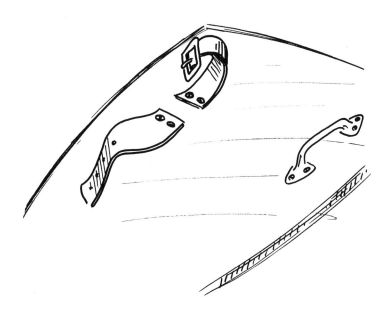

Step Five: Finishing

The sword shown was given a coat or two of semigloss varnish. It could be painted, of course; but varnished, it looks like a real toy rather than a fake sword, if that makes any sense.

The shield was painted orange-red on both sides. Then the pattern of the coat of arms was sketched on and finally outlined with the contrasting blocks of semigloss black and "implement yellow."

Sir Knight can stop avoiding the dragons in the neighborhood as soon as the paint dries.

LUMBER LIST
for the
SWORD AND SHIELD

One piece of ½″ or ⅜″ plywood, at least 18½″ × 12½″
A 2′ length of hardwood, 1″×4″
A 3″×8″ piece of ¾″ plywood
One dozen ½″ flathead wood screws
Six inches of belting about 2″ wide
One metal drawer pull
Two dozen ½″ roundhead, wood plug buttons

66

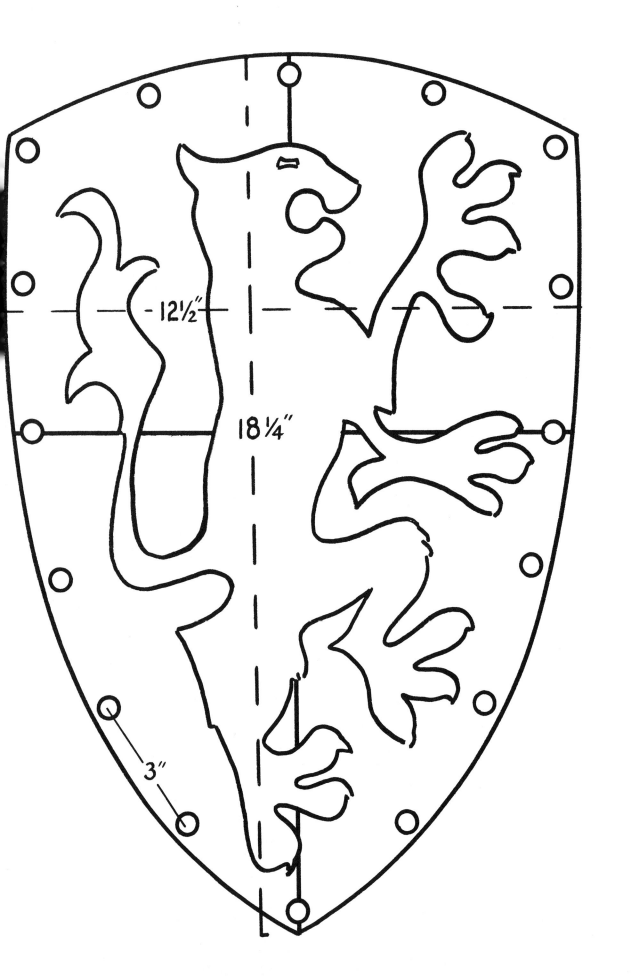

12½"

18¼"

3"

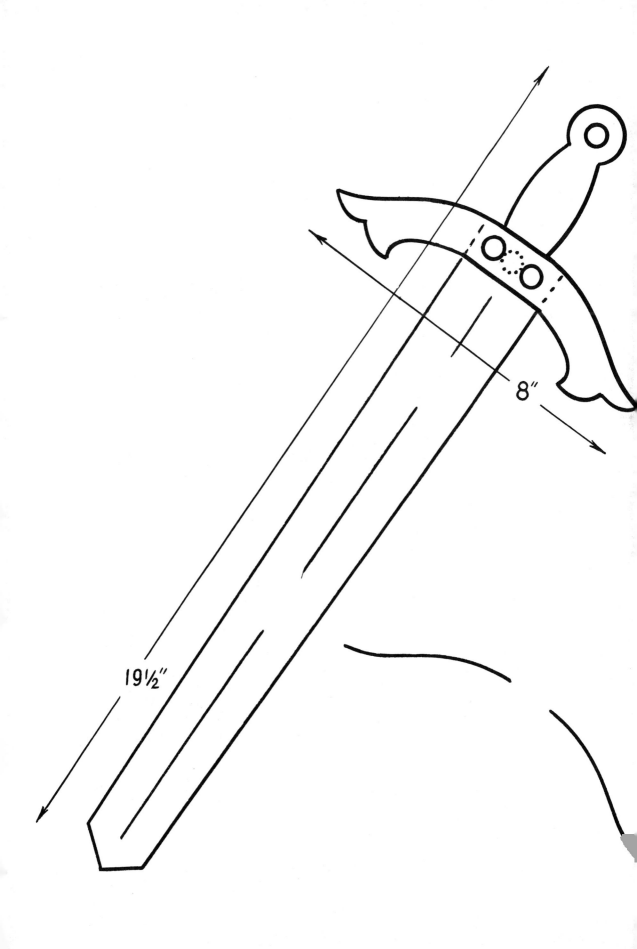

19½"

8"

Chapter 8

The Puppet / Marionette Theater

This offering is a combination puppet/marionette theater than can sit in a corner and double as a toy bin between shows.

For a performance of hand puppets, the theater is placed on a table or box with the storage bin forward, and for a marionette show, the theater is turned around and placed down low, with the storage bin behind the curtain, forming the stage floor. Of course, the bin can also serve as a storage place for the sets and props, as well as the cast.

Step One: Cutting

Mark the dimensions of the bin top lid, bin bottom and the bin front and back sides onto a 6' length of 1″×12″ stock, and 5' of 1″×10″ stock (inexpensive shelving will work for this project). Cut these pieces out with a table saw, portable electric circular saw or carpenter's handsaw. Next mark the dimensions of the stage front and wings onto ¼″ plywood or paneling stock and cut out. To cut the stage opening, drill a ½″ starter hole, and then cut out the opening with a saber or keyhole saw.

Sketch the scrollwork for the bottom and one side of the stage border onto the ¼″ stock. After cutting this out with a band, saber, jig or coping saw, flip the side border over, trace around it, and cut out the other side of the stage border. Draw the outline of the top of the theater onto the ¼″ stock and cut this out, leaving the scallop cuts along the bottom until later.

70

Step Two: Drilling

To make the round notches along the bottom of the theater front and the tops of the sides, use a 1″-diameter hole-saw attachment for the power drill. Space these holes as shown, with the centers about ⅜″ in from the edges, then drill out these holes.

Also mark in place and drill out the 1″-diameter holes that will be joined to form the handles on both sidewalls.

Now with a ½″-diameter wood bit, drill holes into the theater top, near the bottom edge, spaced 4″ apart, as shown, and centered about an inch up from the bottom edge. Cut up into these holes, curving in from either side to meet the outline of the hole on both sides, using a jig, band, saber or coping saw. Also, join the two 1″ holes in both sides with a saber or key-hole saw, to form the lifting grips. With a 2″ hole saw, cut out a disc from the ¼″ stock. Drill a ⅛″ hole into the edge of this disc, about an inch deep. Then drill another such hole down into the edge of the topmost point of the theater. You may have to make a starter hole with a sharp punch.

Step Three: First Assembling

Place the bin bottom with the long edge forward on a flat surface, run

71

a line of white glue along the short edge, and nail through the side of the stage-front wall at the bottom and into the edge of the bin bottom.

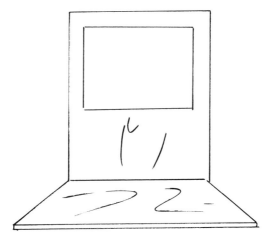

Now run a line of glue along the edges of the bin bottom and nail through the sides of the theater at the bottom and into the ends of the bin bottom (if using paneling, the finished sides should be to the outside of the theater on all three sides).

Place a line of glue on the two end edges of the bin front and on the front edge of the bin bottom, and then nail through the sides of the theater into the ends of the bin front, and through the bin front into the bin bottom.

Run a line of glue along the backside of the back brace (that supports the bin top along the stage-front wall), and place it in position against the back wall of the bin so that its top edge is parallel and at the same level with the top edge of the bin front. Nail in through both sides of the theater, and into the end grain of this brace at both ends.

72

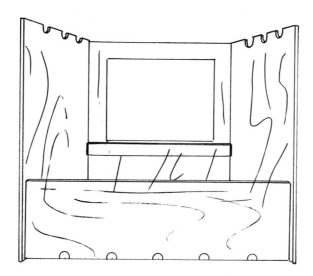

To attach the disc at the top point of the theater, nip off the head of a 2″ nail, insert one end into the hole in the edge of the disc, the other end into the hole in the edge of the top, and tap the disc down onto the point of the theater top. To fasten the tops of the theater sides to the theater stage front, screw on two sets of small, ornamental hinges, with one wing on the side and one wing on the stage front, and then nip off the screws sticking out the other side.

Step Four: Finishing

Sand off all edges and surfaces to remove possible splinters. Paint the

73

theater a warm yellow, or anything else that strikes your, or your client's, fancy. The theater can be painted either the same on both sides, or with a contrasting shade or stain on one side. Paint the theater top to match. The disc at the very top, as well as the stage border scrolls, should be given a couple of coats of gloss white enamel. Decorate the painted sides of the theater with 2"- or 2½"-wide vertical stripes of deep red or light green enamel (or any other color you like, of course).

Paint matching stripes on the top piece, tapering them in and up toward the point of the top. The bin top/stage floor is left the base color, remaining unstriped. If masking and painting stripes seems to be a bit of a bore, as they say, then use wide, colored tape instead.

Step Five: Final Assembling

Place the theater on its back, bin up, on a firm, flat surface. Cut out two

74

pieces of colored material to match the color of the stripes, both of them 1' square, and hem them, if you want to get fancy, on three sides. Run a line of glue along the top of the stage-front side above the stage. Then tack the unhemmed sides of the curtains along the top of the stage front, doubling the material back on itself about ½", every 4" or so, to get a pleated effect, and tack at these points.

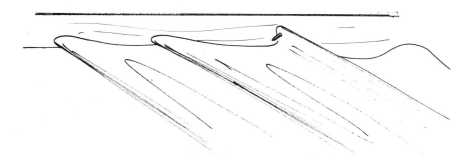

When the glue is dry enough to hold the material in place, remove the tacks, run another line of glue along above the stage, onto the material, and then nail the top of the theater to the stage front with ½" brads.

Run another line of glue around the stage border about an inch in from the edge, and nail on the stage-border scroll work with the brads.

The curtains can be tied back with a tack on either side, depending on what sort of show is to be given that day. It's just about curtain time now—time for the builder to sit back and enjoy the show.

LUMBER LIST   One 6' length of 1"×12" stock (shelving will do)
for the   One 5' length of 1"×10" stock
Puppet/Marionette   One sheet of ¼" plywood or paneling, 3'×4'
Theater   Two small, decorative butterfly hinges
A 12"×24" piece of curtain material
Two dozen ½" brads
Three dozen 1½" finishing nails

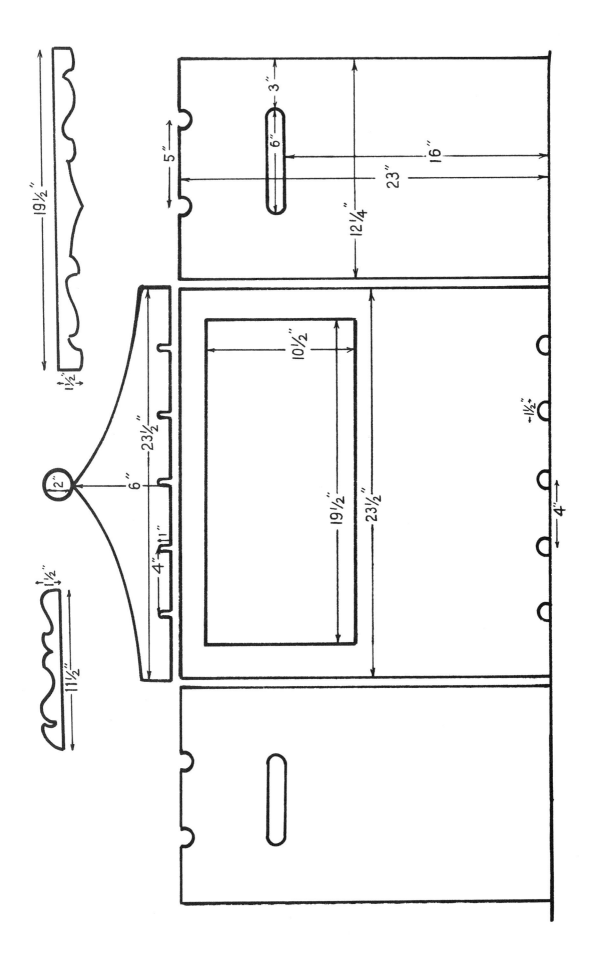

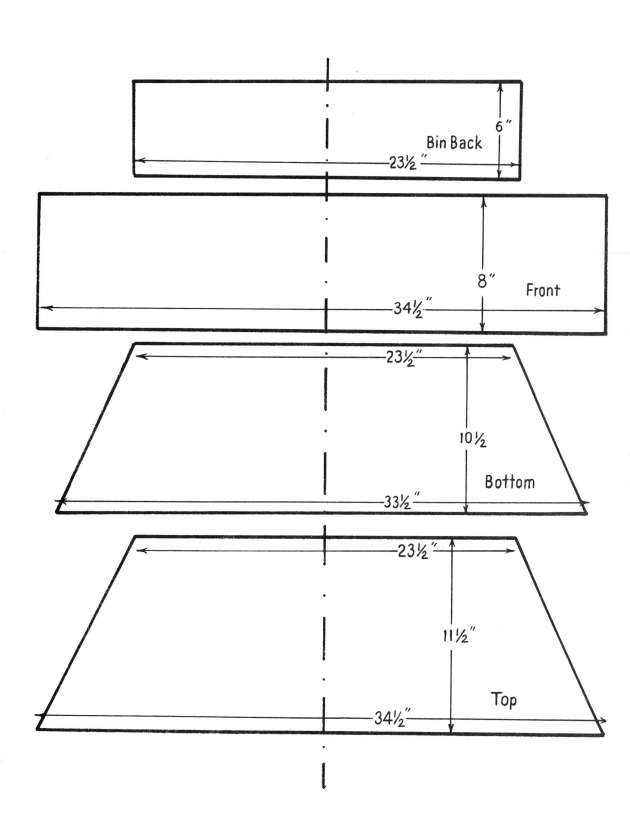

6"

Bin Back

23½"

8"

Front

34½"

23½"

10½

Bottom

33½"

23½"

11½"

Top

34½"

Chapter 9

The Dollhouse

The dollhouse was inspired by the sort of country house you might find somewhere in the quieter rural areas of the British Isles, or possibly northern France. The idea was to make a dollhouse that really was a four-sided house, but could open out to display a large number of rooms. The side pieces can open back to surround the dollhousekeeper on three sides, or they can be opened out into a straight line, forming a whole streetful of row houses. And as a special added attraction, the pins can be removed from the hinges, forming three separate, standard-style dollhouses.

Step One: Cutting

The first step is to mark the dimensions of the floors and walls onto the 1″×8″ and 1″×10″ stock (shelving will work fine). Label each part as it's cut, and try to keep all the floors in one pile, all the walls in another, and so on. When cutting out the walls, use a table saw, portable circular saw, or carpenter's handsaw for the straight cuts, and a saber, jig, band or coping saw to cut out the doors. Leave all the window cuts until the house is assembled, as explained farther on.

Cut out the walls and floors as shown, ignoring the cut along the dotted line for the walls and floors on the long side. To make the walls and floors for the two shorter pieces of the house, cut out the three pieces with the dotted line once more, this time slicing each of the pieces in two along the dotted line.

Once these walls and floors are cut out (including the two short floors

drawn next to the roof plans), the three units of the house can be built separately, starting with the largest unit first. Almost all the joints between the walls and the floors are butt joints, using white glue and 2″ finishing nails, usually driven through the side of one wall and into the edge grain of the other wall or floor. When cutting the roofs, cut out the biggest piece, ignoring the dotted line; then cut it out again, and slice across this second long roof along the dotted line. Cut out the end walls with the band, saber, jig or coping saw.

Step Two: Assembling

Place the floor of the large unit on a solid surface with the notched edge forward, and with the short end notch to your left. Place the front wall with the two doors on top of this edge so that parts of the floor stick out through the doors at the bottom to form doorsteps. Make certain the door on the left is closer to the left-hand end of the wall. Glue and nail through the front wall into the edge of the floor in this position. It would be a good idea to drill 1/8″ starter holes for the nails through the front wall to keep from cracking off the end pieces.

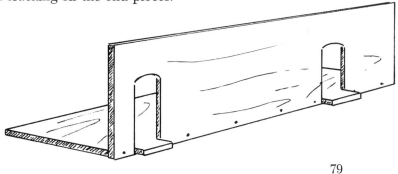

79

Now attach the end walls to the front wall and floor by nailing through the end walls and into the end grains of the floor and wall. The shorter end wall should be attached to the left end of the front wall.

Slip the notches in the upper floor and the inner divider wall over each other so that when this assembly is inserted in the back of the large house unit, the smaller rooms are on the right when viewed from the front. Check to see that the top of the inner divider wall slants up toward the center of the house.

Square up the second floor so that it's parallel to the bottom floor. Then nail through the end walls and front walls into the edges of the upper floor (using glue, of course). Square up the inner divider wall vertically, and then nail it in place through the front wall and the lower floor. Next comes the upper story front wall, which is glued and nailed in place through the end walls, and into the divider wall as well.

The long, front part of the roof can be nailed into place now, nailing in from the larger end wall, and down through the roof into the top of the divider wall.

Cut off a 24″ piece of $\frac{1}{2}″ \times \frac{5}{8}″$ inside corner molding (any wood), and nail it in place along the overhang of the bottom edge of the upper, front wall, with the rounded edge on the bottom outside corner.

Cut a 24″ length of 1″, half-round molding trim and nail it over the gap between the edge of the roof and the top of the upper wall. The end roof can now be nailed in place; run nails through the lower edge of the roof and into the top of the shorter end wall, and one through the point of the

roof and into the peak of the divider wall. Now cut a 10″ piece of the half-round molding and nail it over the gap between the end roof and the top of the end wall, overlapping the end of the other molding, but not over-lapping the base of the chimney. Round off the corner where the moldings meet. Fill in any cracks at the joints or knotholes with plastic wood, and then sand the house to remove any splinters.

Drill a ½″ hole down into the center of each chimney, about 1″ deep, then insert a 3″ length of ½″ wood dowel into each hole and tap them firmly into the holes with a hammer (add a dab of glue, of course).

Although the other two units of the house are made in much the same way, we'll go through the assembly step by step again.

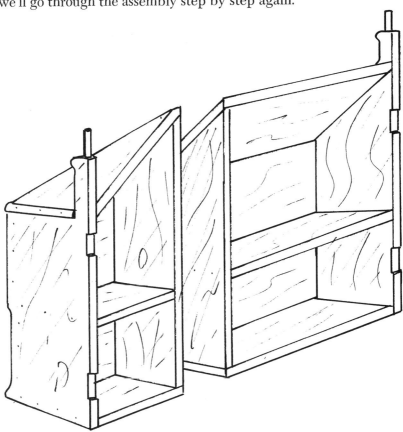

Place the completed part of the house on a flat surface with the open backside facing you. Now arrange the floors of the smaller units so that they match the size of the rooms of the completed part, when the floors are placed back to back, with the doorsteps of the smaller floors toward you. The doorsteps of both small floors should be toward the left ends of the floors. With a bit of glue, attach the lower front walls to the front of these floors, with the doorsteps sticking out through the doors at the bottom.

Attach the smaller end piece to the end of the shorter rooms with glue and nails through the end piece. Then attach the larger end piece to the end of the longer rooms in the same manner. Cut two inner divider walls (without door cuts) to form the adjacent walls of the smaller units of the house. Attach these divider walls to the inner ends of the floors and front walls of the smaller units. Then nail in the upper front walls of both smaller units.

Attach the longer roof to the top edges of the longer room, then attach the two triangular roof pieces to the top of the shorter room. Then cut more lengths of the 1″ half-round molding to be nailed around the tops of the outer walls of the smaller units in the same manner that it was attached to the completed part of the house. Also cut the two shorter pieces of the $\frac{1}{2}″ \times \frac{5}{8}″$ inside corner molding to fit under the overhangs of both units. Round off the corners where the pieces of the half-round molding meet, and then fill all gaps and cracks with plastic wood, and sand thoroughly, especially around the door cuts. Drill $\frac{1}{2}″$ holes down into the tops of the chimneys, and tap in the 3″-long, $\frac{1}{2}″$-diameter dowels used as chimneys.

Next, arrange all three units of the house in position to check the fit. If the joining is a little out of square in places, some adjustments may ensue. Once all three pieces fit together tolerably well, the window cuts can be marked on and made. Make a cardboard pattern for the two window sizes, then sketch all the windows squarely in place. With the $\frac{1}{2}″$ wood bit, drill a hole through each window near the edge of the window shape. The windows can now be cut out with a saber saw or keyhole saw. Sand off the edges of the windows to smooth things up.

To cut out the shutters, slice two strips of $\frac{1}{8}″$ masonite or plywood, one slice $1\frac{1}{2}″$ wide × 36″ long, and the other slice 1″ wide × 24″ long. With a band, jig, saber or coping saw, cut both strips into 3″ lengths. Stack the 1″- and $1\frac{1}{2}″$-wide pieces in two straight piles, and make the curved top cut of the shutters. If you're using masonite that is textured on one side, cut half of each stack with the textured side up, and half with the textured side down, to get an equal number of right- and left-hand shutters. Sand off the edges lightly.

If the notches for the $1\frac{1}{2}″$ butt hinges have not been cut in the inner edge of all the end pieces, cut these with a wood chisel. Then attach the hinges, pin edge out, between the halves of both ends, with screws.

Step Three: Texturing

The roof of the house can be painted with a semigloss paint, of course. But to get the kind of roof texture pictured on the sample, get a pound or so of crushed walnut shells (used to give boat decks a nonskid surface) at the nearest boating-supply store. Sand could be used for texturizing, but crushed walnut shells are cheap and provide a good, deep texture not easily recognizable, so the secrets of your art will be safe.

Paint the roofs a deep, rich red. Then, with the house parts on newspapers, sprinkle the crushed shells over the roof surfaces, covering every side with an even coat. Let dry thoroughly.

For the next coat, thin the paint a little, and paint the red on over the shells stuck to the roof. If you feel the color is a little too bright, use thinned-down dark stain or brown paint to antique the roof. Paint the brown over the red in small sections, and then wipe it off as you go along, to provide a deeper color and a more interesting roof texture.

Once the roof is finished to your satisfaction, give the walls a coat of warm, off-white semigloss enamel. When this coat is dry, paint on another and let it sit for a while to get a bit tacky. Then, with the end of the brush, stipple the paint to get a wall texture by repeatedly jamming the end of the brush into the tacky surface evenly all over. Make certain all window-sills and doorsteps are painted.

To paint the shutters, lay all of them out on a sheet of newspaper, with the top curves of half of each size of the shutters pointing to the left, and half pointing to the right. Then give all the shutters *one* single, thorough coat of green spray enamel (the single coat will give the shutters color without gloss). Once the walls and shutters are dry, place a dab of glue on the backside of each shutter, and nail it in place next to a window with ½" brads. With a brush, paint the chimney tops brick-red, with flat black top surfaces.

Step Four: Interior Decorating

It's usually a good idea to consult with your client along about this stage of the game to get an idea of what room goes where, what wallpaper goes with which carpeting, etc.

The wallpaper is made from contact paper, which has a great variety of colors and patterns; and with adhesive already on one side, it is a snap to install. The carpets are small scraps which are readily available at most carpet stores, if you don't have a pile of them stored away somewhere.

To put up the paper, cut it squarely to the width of the wall, or walls, to be covered, and place it in position without removing the backing. Then mark along the cut-off lines at the top and bottom, making a crease along the cutting line with a dull knife or your thumbnail. Remove the paper, cut along the lines marked, and then remove the backing. Stick the paper in place, burnishing with your fingernails to remove the air pockets caught behind the paper. The door and window outlines can then be sliced out with a razor blade.

All the patterns for the floor carpeting are rectangles and are easy to mark and cut out. Then the carpets can be held in place with contact cement, white glue, or brads.

From here on, the amount of detailing is up to your tastes and the wants of your client or clients. If, like some, you go in for electric wiring and lights, and whatnot, it might be best to install your support systems before putting on the decorative coverings.

And finally, the time has come to sit back and watch the others go at it, arguing out the ticklish points of whether it should be Danish Modern or French Provincial.

LUMBER LIST
for the
DOLLHOUSE

One 4' length of 1"×12" shelving stock (knotty, finished pine is suitable)

Two 10' or four 5' lengths of 1"×10" shelving stock

One 10' or two 5' lengths of 1"×8" shelving stock

One foot of ½"-diameter wood dowel

Six feet of 1", half-round molding

Four feet of ½"×⅝" inside corner molding

One 7"×18" or 3½"×36" scrap of ⅛" masonite or plywood

One or two pounds of crushed walnut shells, medium size

Four 1½" butt hinges with screws

Scraps of short pile carpeting

Contact paper

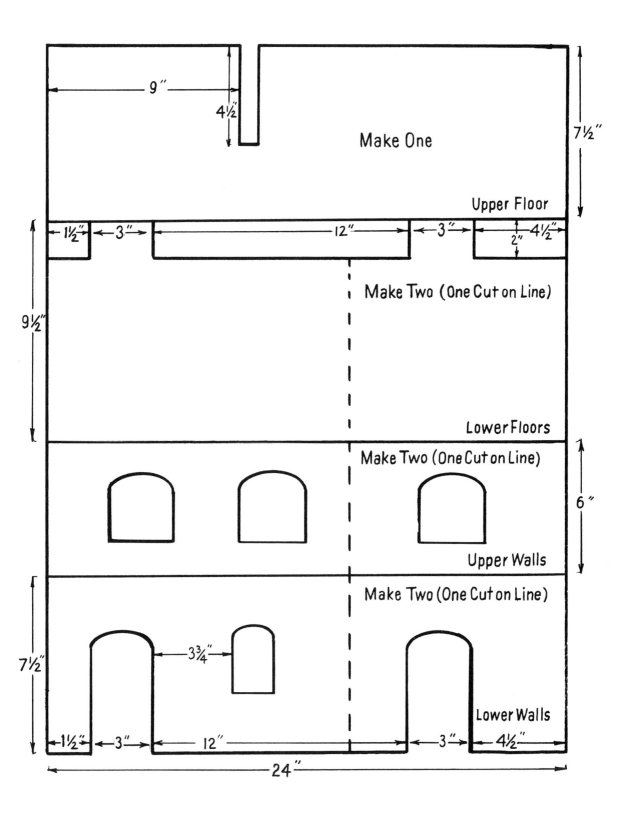

9″

4½″

Make One

7½″

Upper Floor

1½″   3″   12″   3″   4½″

2″

9½″

Make Two (One Cut on Line)

Lower Floors

Make Two (One Cut on Line)

6″

Upper Walls

Make Two (One Cut on Line)

7½″

3¾″

Lower Walls

1½″   3″   12″   3″   4½″

24″

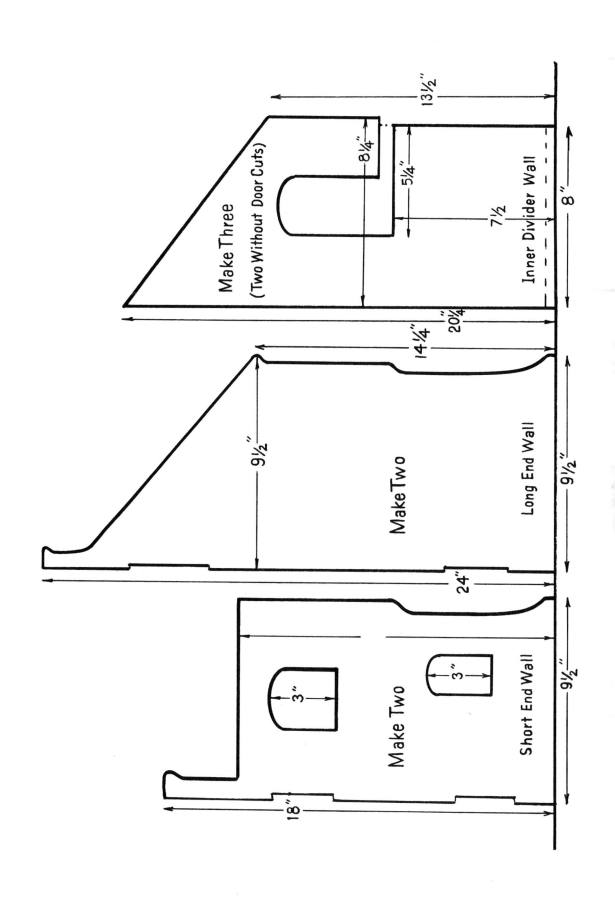

Make Three
(Two Without Door Cuts)

13½"

8¼"

5¼"

7½

8"

Inner Divider Wall

20¼"

14¼"

9½"

Make Two

Long End Wall

9½"

24"

9½"

3"

3"

Make Two

Short End Wall

9½"

18"

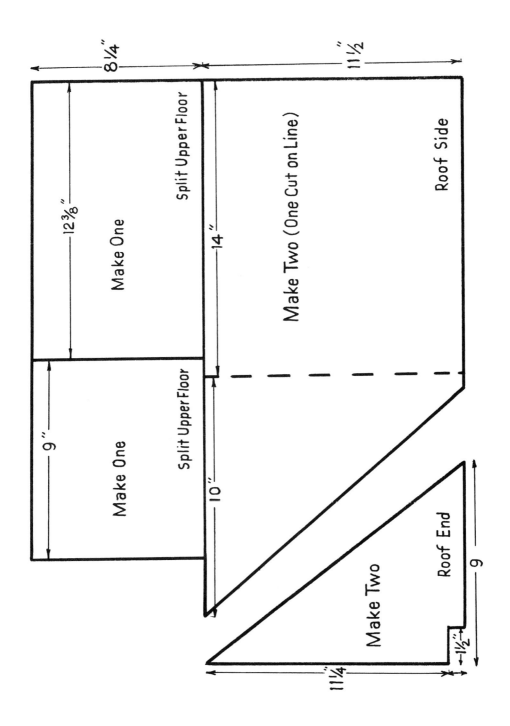

8 1/4"

11 1/2"

Split Upper Floor

Make One

12 3/8"

Make Two (One Cut on Line)

14"

Roof Side

9"

Make One

Split Upper Floor

10"

Make Two

Roof End

9

11 1/4"

1 1/2"

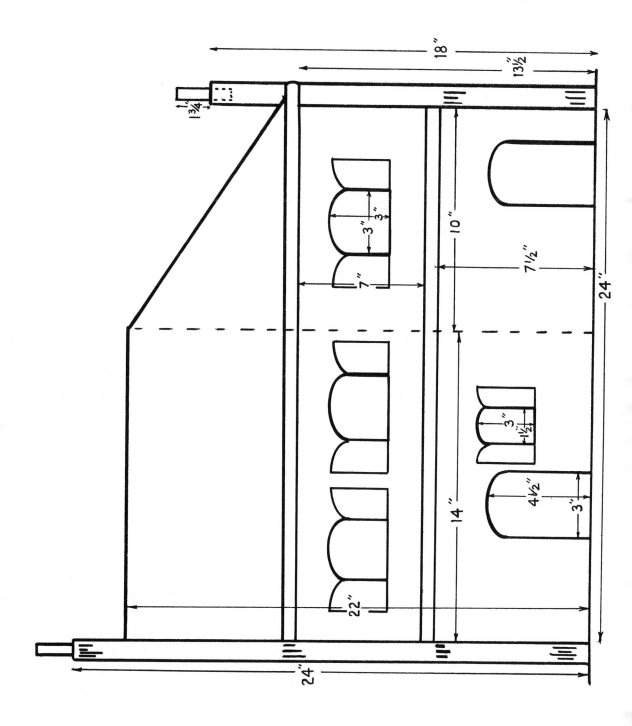

Chapter 10

The Tank

The tank is a simple, popular part of the collection and has proved itself to be rugged as a brick. The design, while admittedly pretty abstract, is a composite which takes most of its flavor from the early efforts that headed off across the hedgerows in World War II. The whole project was inspired by the tale of a certain sporting tank driver from Kent who, when finding himself surrounded by Rommel's tanks in North Africa, exercised a little quick-thinking marksmanship and bagged five of the opposition's machines in five minutes, thereby earning himself a very large medal and the unofficial title of "the tank-a-minute man" for his efforts.

Not much in the way of tools or materials is needed to fashion this version of Tank-a-Minute's trusty machine. A short length of clear-grained 4″×4″ of any wood will serve as the tank's body, and the wheels are cut from a scrap of 1″×4″ or wider stock.

Step One: Cutting

Transfer the outline of the side profile of the body onto the 4″×4″ by drawing around a pattern cut from a carbon, tracing, or copying-machine reproduction of the plans. Actually, the outline is really simple enough to draw freehand on the wood, for there aren't any joints that require much exactitude. Cut out the side outline with a band or coping saw. Now draw on the end of the body the angle cuts that form the front outline, and make the cuts with a carpenter's handsaw, table saw, band saw or even shape the wood down to these lines with a wood plane. With a 2¼″ hole-saw attachment for the power drill, cut out four discs for the wheels from 1″ stock.

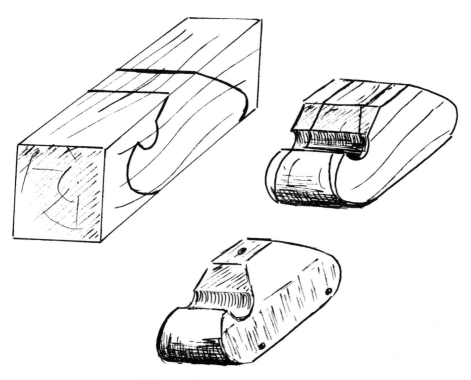

91

With the same blade in the hole saw, cut the turret from either the 1″ stock or a thicker 2″ stock, cut down to the size shown. Cut the muzzle from 1″ stock with a ¾″-diameter hole-saw blade. Cut a 1½″ length of ⅞″-diameter dowel (try a broomstick) and a 2″ length of ⅜″ dowel.

Step Two: Drilling

With the pattern, mark the position of the axle holes on the body sides. Drill these holes in from both sides, and then enlarge the holes vertically a little to allow the wheels to bounce. Next, drill a ¼″ hole about 1″ deep into the center of the top of the body for the turret pivot bolt.

Drill a 1″-diameter hole down into the center of the cockpit to a depth of about 1″. Now with the ⅛″ bit, drill a hole about ½″ into the side of the turret disc, and then with the same bit, enlarge the center hole in the muzzle about halfway through.

Drill a ⅜″ hole into the bottom of the 1″ round wood drawer-pull ball (if there isn't one already drilled), and then drill a matching starter hole just down into the center of one end of the ⅞″ dowel.

Step Three: Assembling

Drive four roundhead tacks in a vertical line down both sides, as shown, for the body rivets. Then run a horizontal line of four tacks across the rear side about halfway up to the turret base.

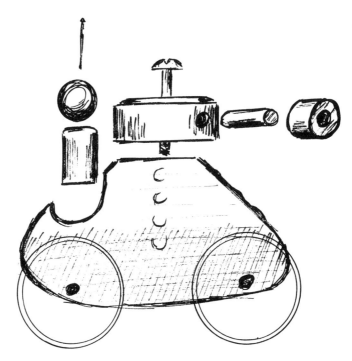

Place a dab of glue in the hole in the side of the turret, and in the enlarged hole in the muzzle. Then insert one end of the ⅜″ dowel into the

92

turret, the other into the muzzle, and then tap the end of the muzzle, setting the parts tightly together. Screw the drawer pull to the dowel body with the double-ended screw supplied with such knobs, or secure with a nail through the top. Now round off all sharp corners and sand away all possible splinters with coarse, medium, then fine sandpaper. The turret top can be rounded over with a shaper, then sanded.

To attach the turret, run a 2″, ¼″-diameter roundhead bolt with a screwdriver notch in the head down through the hole in the center of the turret, then on into the hole in the center of the top of the body, leaving enough play to allow the turret to turn.

Fix the wheels on by inserting a 5″ hexagonal head bolt through the center hole of one of the wheels. Then insert the axle through an axle hole and finally through the other wheel. Run a nut onto the end of the bolt, leaving enough play for the wheels to turn. Now cut off the bolt just outside the nut, and tap the cut end of the bolt until it flattens a little to prevent the nut from coming off. Repeat this performance to attach the other set of wheels.

93

Step Four: Painting

Since a smooth, shiny gloss isn't the most important feature of a camouflage paint job, painting can be done most easily with a brush. A base coat of khaki or a yellow-ocher sort of brown should be covered with random blobs of deep green and brown.

Tank-a-Minute's uniform can be any of the colors, with flat or semigloss black features and helmet. Paint black around the edges of the wheels, coming about ⅛″ in from the edge.

LUMBER LIST
for the
TANK

One 6″ length of clear-grained 4″×4″ stock
One 12″ length of 1″×4″, or wider, stock
1½″ of ⅞″-diameter wood dowel
2″ of ⅜″ wood dowel
One 1″-diameter wood drawer-pull ball, with screw
Two 5″, ¼″-diameter hexagonal head bolts, with nuts
One 2″, ¼″-diameter roundhead bolt
Twelve roundhead tacks

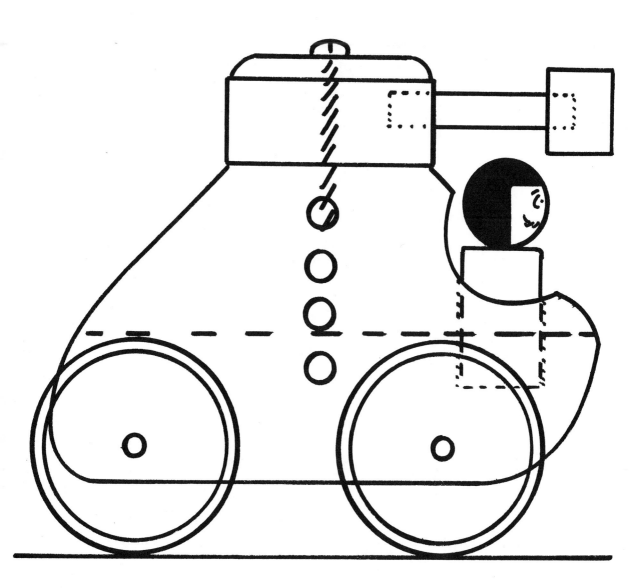

Chapter 11

The Four Racers

The four race cars in the collection are all built in pretty much the same fashion. We'll start with the red one, which happens to be the easiest to make.

Painted traditional Italian racing red, the design for this toy is taken fairly closely from the lines of a three-liter Maserati that was seen on the European tracks in the mid-thirties, and was campaigned successfully in England over ten years later by Prince Birabongse of Siam.

There isn't a lot of cutting and fitting involved in these cars, but there is a bit of shaping, so a good, clear-grained softwood 4″×4″ is used to form the bodies.

Step One: Cutting

Transfer the lines of the side profile onto the side of the 4″×4″, a foot or more long. Carbon paper, tracing paper, or a copying machine can be used to make a good copy of the lines, which can then be cut out to make a template for drawing on the wood.

A band saw or large jigsaw would be best for cutting out the shape, but a coping saw can be used; be careful to keep the cuts square with the top of the 4″×4″.

Once the side profile is cut, mark a center line down the middle of the top side, and then draw on the top profile. While you're at it, mark on the

97

lines showing the sides of the hood at the front, from the top view. Now the outline of the top view can be cut out.

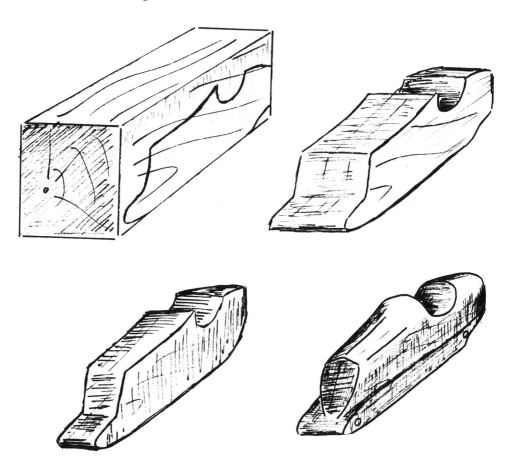

The next step is to mark the line that extends forward from about ¼″ above the rear axle hole to just above the front axle hole on both sides. Cut a groove along this line with a hacksaw, coping saw or carpenter's handsaw. Deepen these grooves at the front to meet, approximately, the line marking the sides of the hood that come in to a rounded point at the front. Being careful to keep the cuts vertical, slice straight down the sides of the hood from the top to meet the grooves.

Step Two: Shaping

Before starting the actual shaping, use your template pattern to mark the position of the axle holes on both sides. With a ¼″-diameter bit, drill in from both sides to make the axle holes as parallel as possible to each other, and to the bottom of the car as well.

Using a hand shaper, smooth off the bottom and the bottom edge of the sides, rounding slightly. Now the boattail of the car behind the cockpit can be rounded off at the corners, making a smooth, symmetrical curve over the

98

top. Don't round off the edge of the cockpit, however. Keep at this shaping until the boattail is fairly well rounded. Now mark a center line down the top of the hood, and start to round off the cowl in front of the cockpit over the top. As the hood progresses forward toward the top of the grille, it gradually loses this rounding over the top, and begins to slant down on both sides. As it reaches the top of the grille it slopes down toward the top of the sides like a low, gabled roof, as illustrated in the photos.

When you've managed to scrape away everything that doesn't look like a Maserati, as the joke goes, leave the smaller imperfections to be dealt with by the coarse sandpaper. One of the greatest skills in shaping is knowing when to quit.

Step Three: Finishing

With the ¼″ bit, drill a hole into the side at the point where the exhaust pipe enters the body at the front. Once the hole sinks in to about ¾″ deep, angle the drill back toward the rear to slant the hole along the path of the pipe.

Now you can start sanding with coarse sandpaper to remove any gouges left by the shaper. Then sand with medium paper to remove the lines made by the coarse paper, then sand with fine paper to polish up a smooth surface to paint. If small hairs persist in sticking out of the grain, leave them to be

sanded off after the first few coats of paint. Too much sanding with the finer paper may result in getting a raised-grain effect, which is not exactly what we're looking for here.

Step Four: Painting

Choose a nice deep but bright red gloss spray. A spray booth made from a cardboard box, cut away on one side, will save paint and messes. Place the car on a paper so that it can be turned without touching the car, and let it dry in the sun, if possible. Don't paint the car in the sun, however, because spray paint tends to bubble when covering a hot surface.

The first coats will look terrible, so don't try to get a nice, glossy finish in one operation, or it'll end up a mass of drips. Many light coats is the answer, with light sanding in between with fine paper. Try to find something else to do at this stage; just give the car a light sanding and spraying every few hours or so. Watched paint never dries, you know, and if you try to spray over a coat before it's thoroughly dry, it will simply curdle up like paint remover, for your trouble.

Once the Italian racing red is on to your satisfaction, paint the cockpit and grille shapes with a brush-on flat or semigloss black.

Step Five: Assembling

The exhaust pipe is made from soft copper or brass tubing, $\frac{1}{4}''$ outside diameter. Short lengths, just suitable for our purposes, can be found in the plumbing section of the hardware department. What they really are is toilet tank filler tubes. Insert one end of the tube into the hole in the side of the hood, and gently bend the pipe to shape. The pipe is held on with screw eyes, the size that just loops around a $\frac{1}{4}''$ tube. With pliers, open up the loops so that the pipe can be slipped in from the side, then screw the eyes into the side of the car along the path of the pipe. Cut the pipe to the right length, insert it in the hole, and then with the pliers close the eye loops over the pipe in position.

The wheels are the $2\frac{1}{4}''$-diameter truck wheels found in many of the secondhand stores. Most brands of this size wheel roll on an axle that will just fit inside the ¼″ outside diameter copper tubing. Cut the 3½″ axle tubes to space out the wheels as shown in the plans.

These axles generally have a head at one end, and a washer which is held on the other by an enlarged end that has been spread with a hammer. Cut off the enlarged end, and save the washer. Then insert the axle (with a wheel on it) through the tube, insert the tube through the axle hole in the car, then slip on the other wheel and the washer. Cut the axle off about ⅛″ outside the washer, then place the head end of the axle on a firm surface and tap the cut end lightly with a hammer until the end spreads enough to keep the washer from falling off the end. Before the wheels are attached permanently, check to see that all four touch when the car is placed on a flat surface. Redrill the angle of the axle holes if necessary.

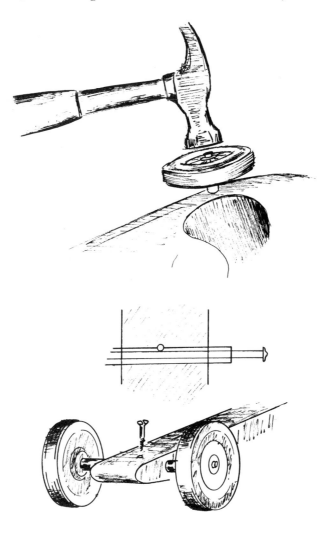

The next step is to fix the axle spacer tubes so that they're held in the center. To do this, drill a ⅛″ hole into the bottom of the car at the point where each axle crosses the center line. Don't try to drill through the steel axle, but let the bit drill to one side, grazing the axle and cutting through the tube on one side. Drill the hole about ½" deep, and then sink a ¾" or 1" screw to hold the spacer tube in place.

The car should be just about ready for the track now. At the end of the four chapters on the set of racers can be found an explanation of how to rig all four cars for use as sling racers, if you're not already a veteran at this sport.

LUMBER LIST   One-foot length of clear-grained soft-wood 4"×4"
for the   stock
FIRST RACER   Four 2¼" outside diameter wheels with axles
                       Two 1' lengths of soft copper tubing, ¼" outside
                           diameter (toilet tank filler tubes)
                       Two small screw eyes
                       Two ¾" or 1" wood screws

RACER THE SECOND

To provide a little healthy competition for the flashy red Italian racer, we've come up with an equally historic car of French racing blue. The toy design is based on the lines of the Type 59 Bugatti, one of the last great racers to leave the shops of the master—Ettore Bugatti's estate-factory in France. Resurrected during the postwar race-car shortage in England, a Type 59 Bugatti, as modified by Rodney Clarke, was said to be the fastest road car in the world, with a top speed of over 170 mph.

To make this version, a short length of clear-grained 4"×4" is needed. Construction is almost the same as in the Italian racer project, with a couple of added embellishments.

Step One: Cutting

Transfer the side profile in the plans with carbon paper, tracing paper, or a copier to make patterns to trace around and onto the wood. Cut out the side outline with a band saw or coping saw, keeping the cuts square with the sides of the 4"×4".

Now draw a center line down the middle of the top, and mark on the outline of the top shape. At this stage, mark the lines showing the sides of the hood in the top view too. Cut out the top shape. With the side pattern, mark the positions of the axle holes on both sides, the positions of the gas filler caps on the top behind the cockpit, and the positions of the lightening holes on both sides near the bottom. With a carpenter's handsaw, hacksaw, or coping saw, cut a groove along the line which extends forward from just above the rear axle hole to just above the front axle hole on both sides.

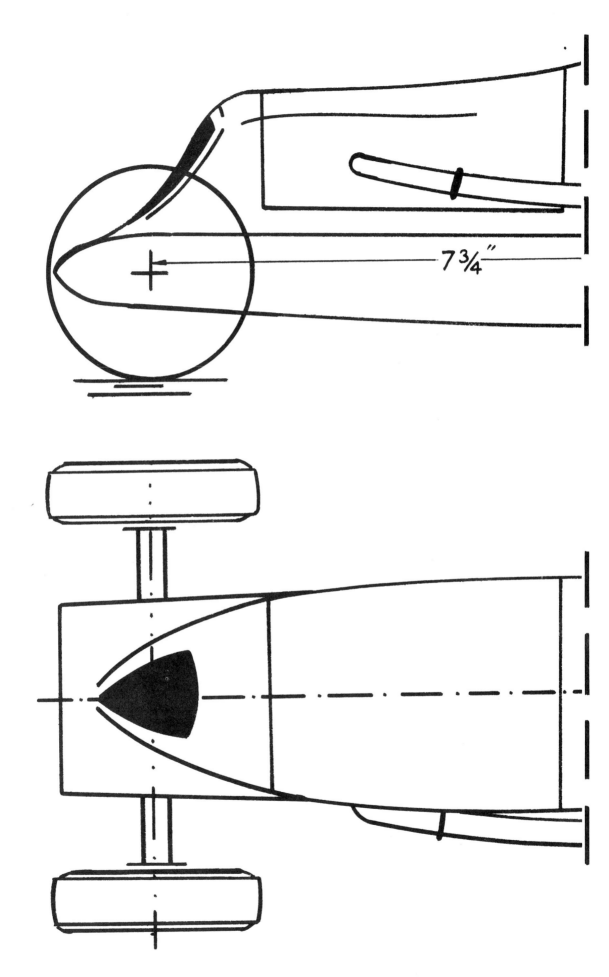

7 3/4"

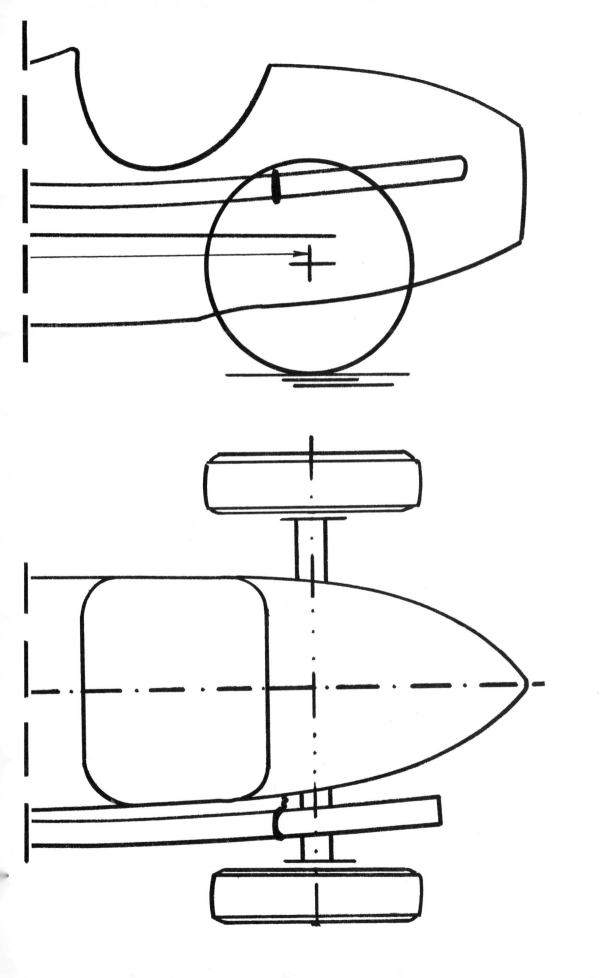

Toward the front of the hood, cut this groove to run into the bottom of the side of the hood cuts. Now, with a carpenter's handsaw or hacksaw, make straight, vertical cuts down from the top, cutting straight down the sides of the hood, and meeting the groove in the side.

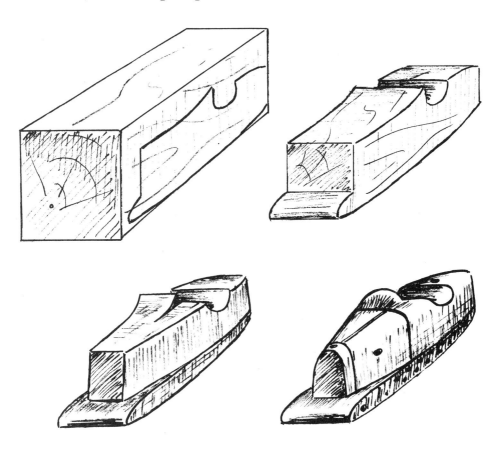

Step Two: Drilling

With a ½" wood bit, drill the two holes marked for the gas caps on the rear deck to a depth of about ½". Then with the ¼" bit, drill the axle holes in from both sides; then drill the lightening holes in the sides of the frame near the bottom to about ¼" deep. Drill a ¼" hole down through the center line on the top of the hood, about ⅜" back from the front point of the hood, for the radiator filler cap. Finally, with the ¼" bit, drill a hole in position in the side of the hood for the exhaust, about ½" deep; then slant the hole back along the path of the pipe.

Step Three: Shaping

With a hand-held wood shaper, smooth up the bottom of the car, then the bottom edges of the sides, rounding only slightly. Round off the top, outside edges of the rear boattail of the car, and shape the tail to match the plans and photos, leaving it boxier and more slab-sided than the boattail of

106

the Italian car. Sketch the outline of the grille on the front of the grille surface. Now shave off the top side edges of the hood, shaping a curve over the top of the hood that tapers in and matches the outline of the grille in front.

Mark another center line on the hood if the first line has been scraped away, and then, with the shaper, remove the left-hand half of the cowl in front of the cockpit, down to the level of the top of the hood, as shown in the photos.

Use a convex shaper or rasp, or a round drum power shaper, to shape the cowl on the right side of the front of the cockpit. The cowl should arch over the top when viewed from the front or rear, and it should slope down to the top of the hood in a concave curve when viewed from the side.

When the shape of the body is close to what you see in the photos, remove with coarse sandpaper the scrapes made by the shaper. Then with medium-grade sandpaper remove the lines left by the coarse paper. Finish with fine sandpaper, but if grain hairs persist, wait until after the first coat of paint to remove them. Don't sand too long with the fine paper, or a raised-grain effect will ensue.

Mark the lines over the hood onto the car and with a hacksaw, or coping saw, cut shallow grooves along these lines and sand with the edge of a piece of fine sandpaper.

107

Cut off a ½"-long piece of ¼"-diameter wood dowel, place a dab of glue into the hole in the top of the radiator, and tap the dowel down into the hole until it sticks out the top of the radiator about 1⁄16". Place dabs of glue into the holes for the gas caps, and tap in wooden plug buttons (usually found near the wood drawer pulls in the hinge section of the hardware department) with a ½"-diameter insert.

Step Four: Painting

The painting process is the same for this car as it was for the red car. Place it on a piece of newspaper in a spray booth made from a cardboard box with one side removed, and paint with a good, light French racing blue (a sort of robin's-egg blue) gloss enamel. Spray lightly, sanding after each of the first few sprays, and allow each coat to dry thoroughly. It should take about five to eight coats of spray paint.

When the blue is on to your satisfaction, brush a coat or two of flat or semigloss black into the cockpit and front grille surfaces. Then paint the sides of the radiator shell in front of the hood line with aluminum paint, making a narrow border around the top of the grille front, as shown.

Step Five: Assembling

Once again, the processes in this step will be the same as they were for the previous car, but in case you're not yet intimate with the Italian car, we'll repeat the program. See the previous section for the illustration.

The exhaust pipe is made from soft copper, or brass, tubing, ¼" outside diameter (sold as toilet tank filler tubes). Short lengths, just suited to our purposes, can be found in the plumbing section of the hardware department. Insert one end of the tube into the hole in the side of the hood, and gently bend the pipe to shape. The pipe is held on with screw eyes, the size that just loops around a ¼" tube or dowel. With pliers, open up the loops so that the pipe can be slipped in from the side, then screw the eyes into the side of the car along the path of the pipe, as shown. Cut the pipe to the right length insert it into the hole in the head, and then with the pliers close the eye loops over the pipe in position.

The wheels are the 2¼"-diameter toy truck wheels found in many secondhand stores. Most brands of this size wheel roll on axles that will just fit inside the ¼" outside diameter copper tubing. Cut 3½" spacer tubes from this tubing to space out the wheels as shown in the plans.

These axles generally have a head at one end, and a washer which is held on the other by an enlarged end that has been spread with a hammer. Cut off the enlarged end, and save the washer. Then insert the axle (with a wheel on it) through the tube and insert the tube and axle through the axle hole in the car. Slip on the other wheel and the washer. Now cut the axle off about 1⁄8" outside the washer, and place the head end of the axle on a firm surface. Tap the cut end of the axle lightly with a hammer until it spreads enough to keep the washer from falling off.

108

Before attaching the wheels permanently, check to see that all four touch when the car is placed on a flat surface. Redrill the angle of the axle holes if necessary.

The next step is to fix the axle spacer tubes so that they're held in the center. To do this, drill a ⅛″ hole into the bottom of the car at the point where each axle crosses the center line. Don't try to drill through the steel axle, but let the bit drill to one side, grazing the axle and cutting through the tube on one side. Drill these holes about ½″ deep, then sink ¾″ or 1″ screws to hold the spacer tubes in place.

The car is ready for The Big Race now, and at the end of the chapters on how to build the set of racers is a section on how to enjoy the thrills and spills of sling racing with these cars, if your client isn't already a champ at it.

LUMBER LIST	One-foot length of clear-grained, soft wood 4″×4″
for the	Four 2¼″ outside diameter wheels with axles
SECOND RACER	Two 1′ lengths of soft copper tubing, ¼″ outside diameter (toilet tank filler tubes)
	Two small screw eyes
	Two ¾″ or 1″ screws
	A short stub of ¼″-diameter wod dowel (can be whittled)
	Two roundhead wood plug buttons with ½″-diameter insert

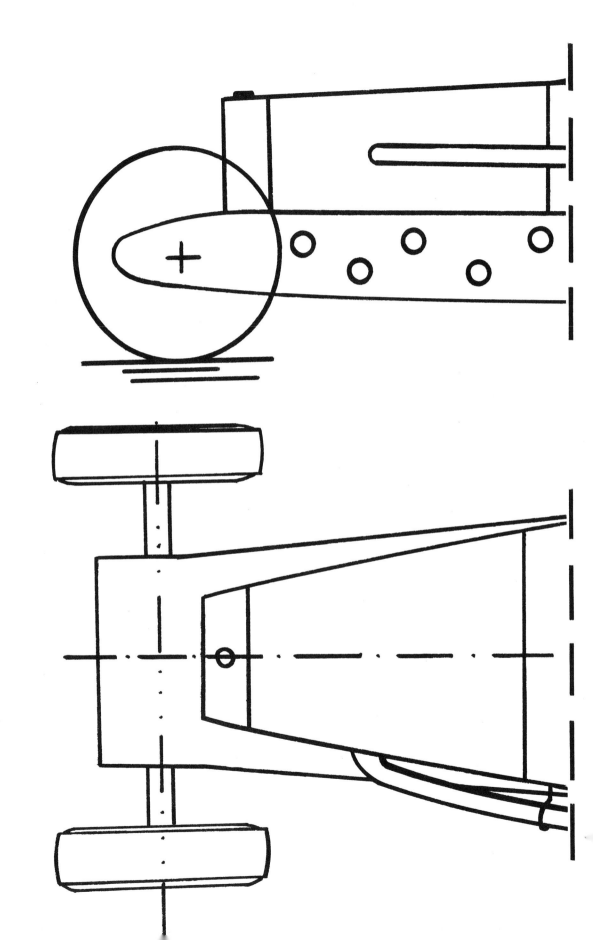

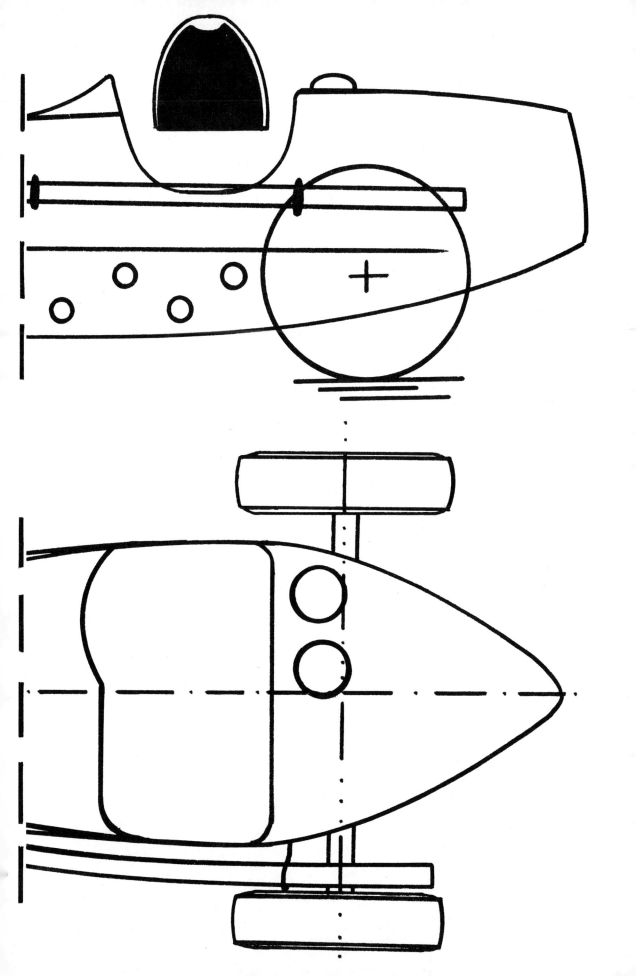

The lines for this third part of the set of racers were taken from the old blood-and-thunder Blower Bentleys. These Jolly Green Giants of British racing were raced successfully through the roaring twenties, especially at the LeMans twenty-four-hour race by Sir Henry Birkin and the rest of the "Bentley Boys," who had things well in hand there for a number of years. "W. O." Bentley was originally trained in the engineering of railroad machinery, and as a result, he was a true believer in making things sturdy, if a little on the beefy side. Race-car creators from other lands tended to refer to his machines as "thinly disguised trucks"; but trucks or not, their enormous, finely made, supercharged engines made them often impossible to catch.

To make one for your collection, start with a short length of clear-grained, soft wood 4″ × 4″ stock.

Step One: Cutting

Transfer the outline of the side profile onto the wood by using carbon paper, tracing paper, or a copier to make patterns to cut out and sketch around. With a band saw or a coping saw, cut out this profile. Draw a center line down the middle of the top side, and mark the outline of the top view, marking also the lines showing the sides of the hood from the top, and the V-shaped cut of the grille. Cut out the top shape.

Mark the positioning of the axle holes on both sides. Then mark the line that extends forward from just above the rear axle hole to just above the front axle hole, as shown in the plans. With a carpenter's handsaw or hacksaw cut a groove along this line, angling the groove in deeper toward the front so it will meet the vertical cut down the sides of the hood.

Now, with a carpenter's handsaw, cut straight down the sides of the hood to meet this groove. Cut vertically down the V-shaped sides of the grille front also, but only down as far as the top of the block that sticks out the front.

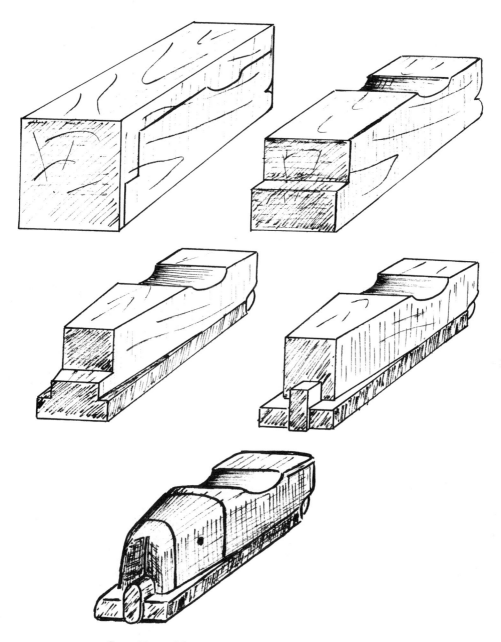

Step Two: Shaping

With a sharp wood chisel and mallet, carve out the areas on both sides of the front blower housing, which sits in front of the center of the grille at the bottom. The blower should be about $5/8''$ wide, arching over the top. The top of the areas on either side should be at the same level as the grooves cut in the sides, and should blend back into them. Vertical cuts should be made on both sides of the blower at the very front of the car so that the blower sticks out about $1/8''$ in front of the frame, as shown in the plans and photo.

The sides of the gas tank at the bottom rear are also indented about $\frac{3}{8}''$ from the sides of the car. Carve out these sides, as shown in the plans and photo, with the wood chisel.

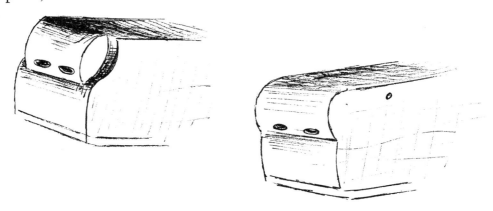

With a hand-held wood shaper, round off the corners at the back end of the body and the gas tank. Smooth off the bottom of the car and the bottom edges of the sides. Draw the outline of the radiator shape onto the front of the car, and then round off the top outside edges of the hood so that it arches over the top, starting at the cowl in front of the cockpit and becoming slightly more arched farther forward to match the outline drawn on the front of the grille. The hood should then curve down, as shown in the side plan, to blend into the vertical V-cuts of the radiator grille. The top and rear edges behind the cockpit are rounded slightly.

With coarse sandpaper remove the marks left by the shaper, then with medium-grade sandpaper remove the lines made by the coarse paper. Finally, smooth off with fine sandpaper. Any grain hairs that won't seem to go away with sanding can be removed more easily after the first coat of paint. Oversanding with fine paper on soft wood will only bring out a raised-grain effect, which is fine in its place, of course, but not wanted here. Mark the hood lines over the hood and cut grooves along these lines with a hacksaw or coping saw, and sand with fine paper. A groove should also be cut around the back three sides of the cockpit, about $\frac{1}{4}''$ down from the edge.

Step Three: Drilling

Mark and drill the axle holes in from both sides with a $\frac{1}{4}''$ drill bit, as squarely as possible. With the same bit, drill a hole in place for the exhaust pipe, about $\frac{1}{2}''$ deep, angling it down along the path of the pipe; and then drill a hole about $\frac{1}{2}''$ deep in the top center of the radiator, about $\frac{3}{8}''$ in front of the front hood line.

With a $\frac{1}{2}''$ wood bit, drill two holes for the gas caps in the top, back of the gas tank, as shown, to about $\frac{1}{2}''$ deep. Finally, drill a $\frac{1}{8}''$ hole in the side of the body opposite the exhaust pipe at the center of the spare-wheel position.

114

Step Four: Assembling

Cut off a ½″ length of ¼″-diameter wood dowel (or whittle a short stub), place a dab of glue in the hole in the top of the radiator, and then tap the dowel down into the hole so that it sticks out above the radiator about ¹⁄₁₆″. Sand the end of the dowel smooth. Place dabs of glue in the two holes in the top of the gas tank and tap firmly in place two roundhead wood plug buttons (found near the wood drawer-pull knobs in the hardware department). If there is no more light sanding to be done, it's time to start painting.

Step Five: Painting

From here on out, the painting and final assembling processes are exactly the same as the ones used on the other two cars, but if you're starting with this one, we'll repeat ourselves.

Pick out a nice, deep green gloss spray enamel for the British racing green color. Place the car on a piece of newspaper in a spray booth made from a cardboard box with one side removed. Using many light coats, and sanding after each of the first few sprays, cover the car with five to eight coats of paint, allowing each coat to dry thoroughly.

When the green is on thick, smooth, and glossy, brush a coat or two of flat or semigloss black on the cockpit and flat tonneau surface behind it, and on the front of the grill. Then paint on a couple coats of aluminum to cover the radiator, outlining the grille shape, and the blower at the bottom front.

Step Six: Final Assembling

The exhaust pipe is made from soft copper or brass tubing, ¼″ outside diameter. Short lengths of this tubing (sold as toilet tank filler tubes) can be found in the plumbing section of the hardware department. Insert one end of the tubing into the exhaust-pipe hole, and with the help of pliers bend the pipe down and back, forming it into shape; cut it off as shown.

The pipe is held on with two screw eyes, the size that just loops around a ¼″ outside diameter tube. Open up the loops of the eyes with pliers so that the pipe can be slipped in from the side, then screw the eyes into the side of the car along the path of the pipe. Insert the pipe into the hole in the hood, and with pliers close the loops of the eyes over the pipe in position. See the section on the first racer for the illustrations.

The wheels are 2¼″-diameter toy truck wheels found in many second-hand stores. Most brands of this size wheel roll on axles that will just fit inside the ¼″ outside diameter tubing. Cut 3½″ spacers from the tubing to space out the wheels, as shown in the plans.

The axles generally have a head at one end and a washer that is held on the other by an enlarged end that has been spread with a hammer. Cut off the enlarged end and save the washer. Then insert the axle (with a wheel on it) through the tube, and insert the tube and axle through the axle hole

115

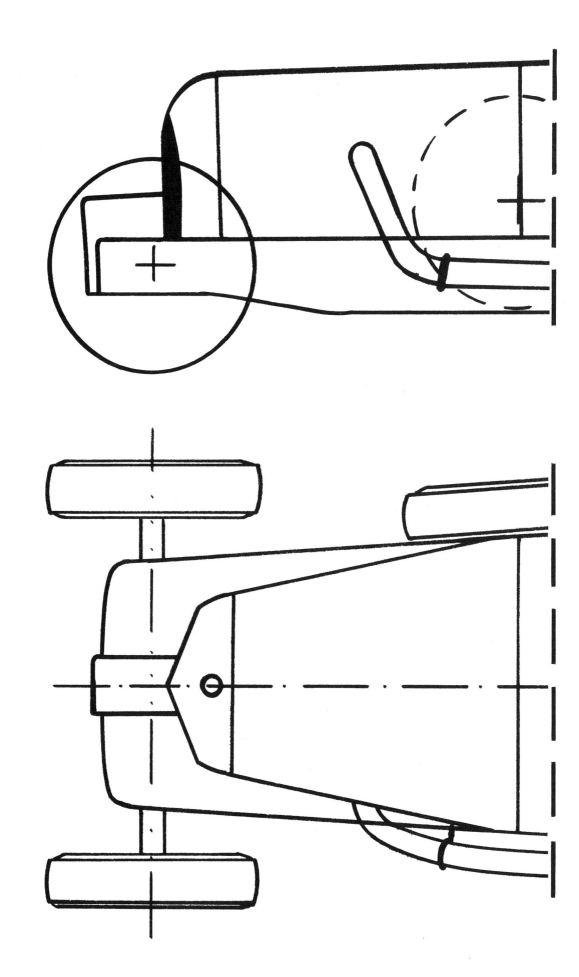

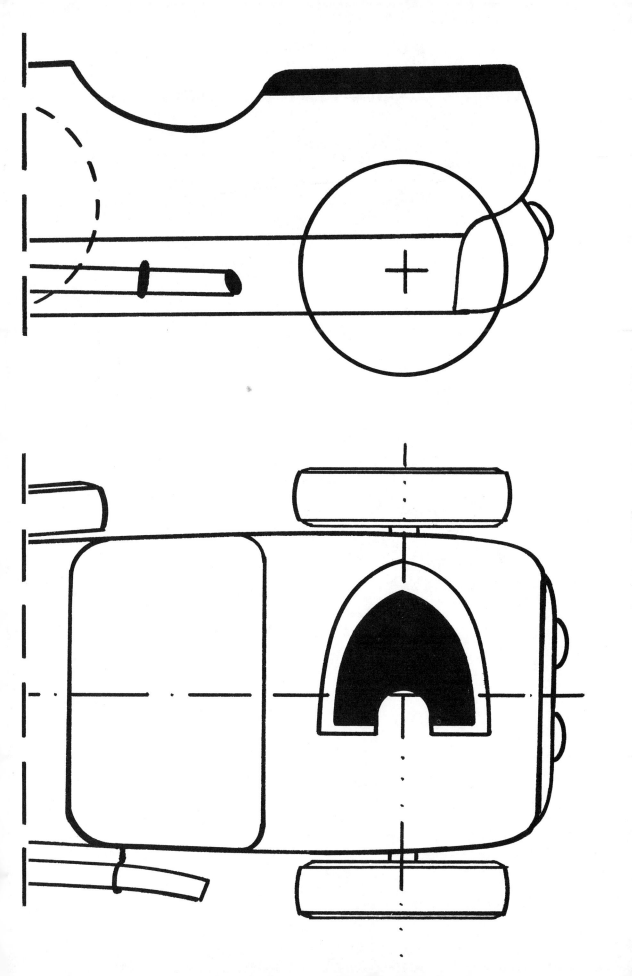

in the car. Slip on the other wheel and washer. Now cut the axle off about ⅛″ outside the washer, and place the head end of the axle on a firm surface. Tap the washer end lightly with a hammer until the end spreads enough to keep the washer from falling off.

Before attaching the wheels permanently, however, check to see that all four touch when placed on a flat surface. Redrill the angle of the axle holes, if necessary.

The next step is to fix the axle spacer tubes so that they're held in the center. To do this, drill a ⅛″ hole into the bottom of the car at the point where each axle crosses the center line. Don't try to drill through the steel axle, but let the bit drill to one side, grazing the axle, and cutting through the tube on one side. Drill these holes about ½″ deep, then sink ¾″ or 1″ screws to hold the spacer tubes in place.

Attach the spare wheel in place on the side opposite the exhaust pipe with a 1½″ screw through the center.

The car is now just about ready to do a little racing in the grand old manner, and if your client would like to try sling racing with it, there is at the end of these chapters on how to build the set of racers a section that explains the theory and principles of sling racing for any newcomers in the crowd.

LUMBER LIST	One-foot length of clear-grained, soft-wood 4″ × 4″ stock
for the	Five 2¼″-diameter toy truck wheels with two axles
THIRD RACER	Two 1′ lengths of soft copper tubing, ¼″ outside diameter (toilet tank filler tubes)
	Two small screw eyes
	Two ¾″ or 1″ screws
	One 1½″ screw
	A short stub of ¼″-diameter wood dowel
	Two roundhead wood plug buttons with ½″-diameter inserts

118

A Racer to Complete the Set

The mighty white racer from across the Alps in Germany is another fire-and-brimstone machine from the roaring twenties. The lines for this toy were taken from a particularly historic offering from Mercedes which, when in the hands of Rudolf Caracciola or Hans Stuck, managed to write a good-sized chapter in the history of auto racing.

To re-create this terror from Stuttgart, the first thing that is needed is a short length of clear-grained soft wood, 4" × 4".

Step One: Cutting

Transfer the lines of the side profile with carbon paper, tracing paper, or a copier onto a sheet of paper that can be cut to make a pattern to trace around. With a band saw or coping saw, cut out the side profile. Then draw a center line down the middle of the top side and draw on the top-view profile; cut this out. Now draw the lines marking the sides of the hood and the angle of the V-shaped grille on the top side. Mark the position of the axle holes on both sides and then draw the line that extends forward from just above the rear axle hole to just above the front axle hole. Cut a groove along this line with a carpenter's handsaw, hacksaw or coping saw, on each side. Cut the grooves in deeper toward the front to a depth that will meet the vertical side cuts. Now make these cuts by sawing with a carpenter's

handsaw straight down along the lines marking the sides of the hood from the top. While you're at it, cut the sides of the V-shaped grill, cutting as straight as possible.

Step Two: Drilling

With a ¼" diameter bit, drill the axle holes in from both sides as squarely as possible. Then drill a hole down into the top center of the hood about ⅜" back from the front of the V-grille and about ½" deep. Drill two holes in the side of the hood for the exhaust pipes, angling them down along the path of the pipes. Now, with a ½" wood bit, drill the lightening holes in the sides of the frame, near the bottom, to a depth of about ¼", as shown. Then with the same bit, drill the two holes down into the top of the car just behind the cockpit, as shown in the top view, for the gas filler caps.

The spare wheel is positioned behind the cockpit on the rear deck. To make a circular, flat base for the wheel, drill down into the center of the wheel position with a 2¼"-diameter hole-saw attachment for the power drill. Drill this circular cut about ½" deep at the front, leaving the back of the cut flush with the rear deck at the very back.

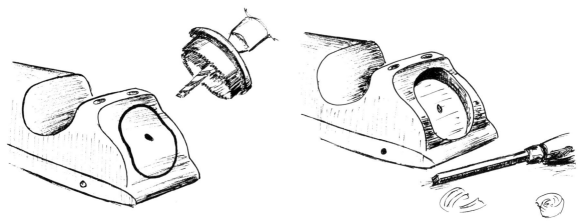

Step Three: Shaping

With a sharp chisel, gouge out the wood within this circular cut, forming a reasonably flat bottom surface for the spare wheel to rest on. With a hand-held shaper, smooth up the bottom of the car and the bottom edges of the sides. Next, draw on the shape of the grille front. Round off the top corner edges of the hood, arching the hood over slightly just in front of the cockpit; as the hood progresses forward, make it gradually more arched to match the shape of the grille front.

Smooth up the sides of the car and round off the corner edges of the rear deck slightly.

Sand off with coarse sandpaper any gouges left by the chisel and the shaper, then with medium-grade paper remove the lines left by the coarse paper; finally, polish the car with fine sandpaper. Mark the lines over the front and back of the hood squarely with a pencil, and use a hacksaw blade

120

or a coping saw to cut grooves along these lines; sand lightly with the fine paper.

Cut off a ½" stub of ¼"-diameter wood dowel, place a dab of white glue in the hole in the top of the radiator, and tap the dowel down into this hole until it sticks out the top of the radiator about ¹⁄₁₆". Sand off the end of the dowel. Place dabs of glue in the gas-cap holes, insert roundhead wood plug buttons with ½"-diameter inserts and tap them in firmly. After a final, critical check of the sanding job, the car should be ready to paint. Small grain hairs can be removed after the first coat of paint.

Step Four: Painting

Once again, the painting and the assembling steps are the same processes as those used on the other three cars. But if you haven't yet looked over those projects, we'll repeat the program here. See the section on the first racer for the illustrations.

Place the car on a sheet of newspaper in a painting booth made from a cardboard box with one side removed. Using many thin coats, and allowing each spray to dry thoroughly before repainting, cover the car wtih five to eight coats of white gloss enamel, sanding lightly after each of the first few coats. Avoid spraying over a hot surface to keep the paint from bubbling. When the white paint is on thick, smooth, and glossy, brush a

121

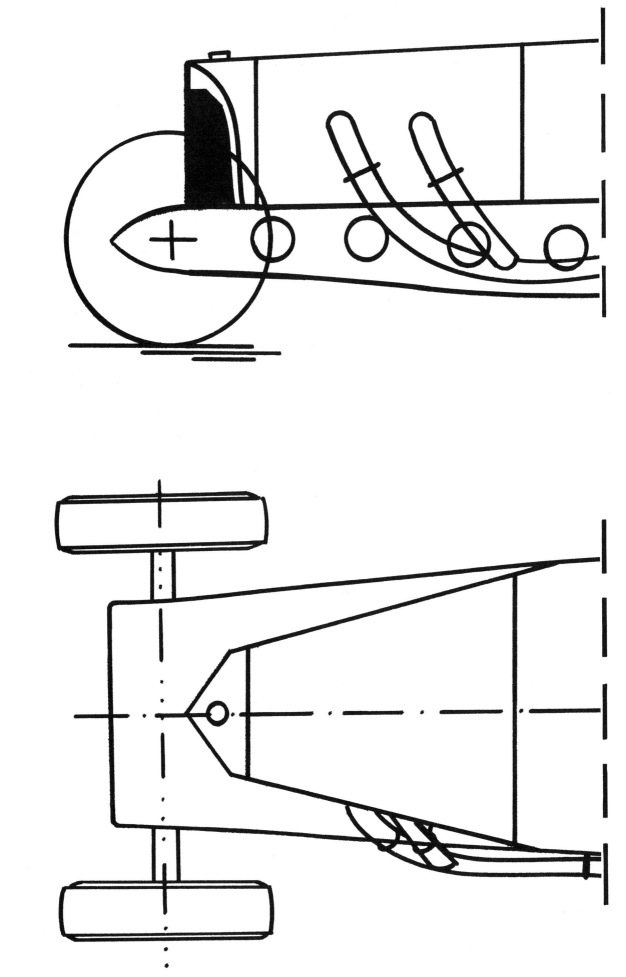

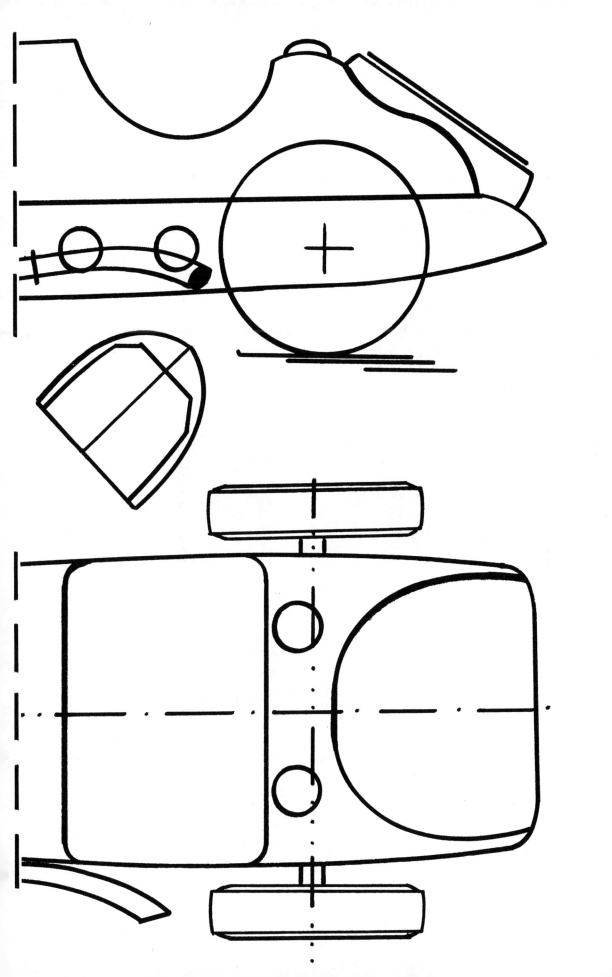

coat or two of flat or semigloss black enamel on the cockpit and on the front surface of the grille. When this is dry, paint on a couple coats of aluminum paint to cover the sides of the radiator, outlining the grille shape in front.

Step Five: Assembling

The exhaust pipes are made from soft copper or brass tubing, ¼″ outside diameter. Short lengths of this tubing (sold as toilet tank filler tubes), just suited to our purposes, can be found in the plumbing section of the hardware department. Insert one end of the tubing into the front exhaust-pipe hole, and with the help of the pliers, bend the pipe down and back, forming it into shape, as shown. Then cut it off. Stick the end of the cut-off, unbent portion of the tube into the rear exhaust hole and bend it down in the same manner, cutting it off at an angle so that it will rest on top of the longer pipe when in place.

The pipes are held on with screw eyes, the size that will just loop over the ¼″ outside diameter tubing. Attach the longer pipe first with two eyes. Open up the loops of the screw eyes with pliers so that the pipe can be slipped in from the side, then screw the eyes into the side of the car along the path of the pipe. Insert the pipe into the hole in the hood, and close the loops of the eyes over the pipe in position.

Insert the end of the shorter pipe into the rear hole in the hood; open up the loop of one screw eye to hold on the shorter pipe, then screw the eye into the side of the hood along the path of this pipe. Now insert the end of this pipe into the hole in the hood, and close the loop over the pipe in position.

The wheels are 2¼″ diameter toy truck wheels, found plentifully in secondhand stores. Most brands of this size wheel roll on axles that will

124

just fit inside the ¼″ outside diameter copper tubing. Cut 3½″ long spacers from this tubing to space out the wheels as shown in the top view.

The axles generally have a head on one end, and a washer that is held on the other by an enlarged end that has been spread with a hammer. Cut off the enlarged end and save the washer. Then insert the axle (with a wheel on it) through the tube, and insert the axle and tube through the axle hole in the car. Then slip on the other wheel and washer. Now cut the axle off about ⅛″ outside the washer, and place the head end of the washer on a firm surface. Tap the washer end lightly with a hammer until the end spreads enough to keep the washer from falling off.

Before attaching the wheels permanently, however, check to see that all four touch when placed on a flat surface. Redrill the angle of the axle holes, if necessary.

The next step is to fix the axle spacer tubes so that they're held in the center. To do this, drill a ⅛″ hole into the bottom of the car at the point where each axle crosses the center line. Don't try to drill through the steel axle, but let the bit drill to one side, grazing the axle, and cutting through the tube on one side. Drill these holes ½″ deep, then sink ¾″ or 1″ long screws to hold the spacer tubes in place.

Attach the spare wheel in place with a 1½″ screw through the center hole.

The time has now come for this racer to hit the track. If your client would like to try a little sling racing with it, there is a section at the end of this chapter explaining the theory and practice of this ancient sport for any newcomers in the crowd.

LUMBER LIST
for the
FOURTH RACER

One-foot length of clear-grained, soft-wood 4″×4″ stock

Five 2¼″-diameter toy truck wheels and two axles

Two 1′ lengths of soft copper tubing, ¼″ outside diameter (toilet tank filler tubes)

Three small screw eyes

A short stub of ¼″ wood dowel

Two ¾″ or 1″ screws

One 1½″ screw

Two roundhead wood plug buttons, with ½″-diameter inserts

SLING RACING EXPLAINED

To rig all the racers for sling racing, attach two small screw eyes (about ⅛″ diameter inside the loop) to the left side of the car about ⅜″ up from the bottom of the side. Position the front eye just behind the front wheel, and the rear eye just in front of the rear wheel. Cut off a 10″ piece of coat-hanger wire. Bend a right angle in the wire, 4½″ from one end. Now, with the shorter side held to the left, bend the ends of the wire down and back on themselves, forming a vertical U-shape bend at both ends.

Hook both ends of the wire through the screw eyes, then tie one end of a 15′–20′ length of strong string to the wire at the right-angle bend. Tie the other end of the string to a 3″ or 4″ piece of dowel to form a handle at the free end of the string.

Place the racer on a smooth paved surface wide enough to serve as a 30′–40′ diameter track. Position the racer near the edge of the track so that it will rotate in a counterclockwise direction. Let out about ten or fifteen feet of the string, standing in toward the center of the track circle.

Now, pull up the slack and begin to walk in a counterclockwise circle, pulling the racer forward and in from the side. Once a little speed has been built up, let the string out and continue to pull the racer around the circle faster and faster by walking in smaller and smaller circles and using a little arm action. Great speeds can be reached after a while, and teams of cars, as well as jumps and obstacles, can be used when your confidence is built up a little.

While the wrecks are often spectacular, usually nothing is hurt but the driver's pride and the paint job. So, if you revere the glossy paint, a little tape applied to the top of the hood and rear deck might be in order before going racing, to preserve the cars for later generations of racing fans.

126

Chapter 12

The Racing Pits

The pits pictured behind the race cars in the previous chapters are a natural companion to the set of racers and form the focal point of any good sling-racing track. The scale used was one that was thought to be a good compromise, so that the building could be used with a variety of different scales of toy racers. If you're a stickler for scale accuracy (which most kids aren't), the plans are simple enough to scale up or down to fit any special size you need. The design was taken loosely from a number of tracks the world over.

Step One: Cutting

Most cuts are straight and can best be made with a table saw or carpenter's handsaw. Mark the dimensions of the roof, roof front piece, back wall and front wall on the 1″×6″ stock and cut these pieces out. Cut five pieces of ½″-diameter wood dowel 4½″ long, and four pieces of the dowel 3½″ long.

Mark the outlines of the end walls on the 1″×6″ stock and then cut these out. Mark and cut out the beveled timing tower roof. Then sketch the clock board on the 1″ stock and cut this out with a jig, band, saber or coping saw. Mark the outline for the base of the timing tower onto a short length of 2″×6″ stock and cut this out with the same saw.

To cut the garage doors in the back wall, sketch a pattern onto a piece of paper or cardboard, and then trace around this pattern to mark the four garage doors on the back.

127

Step Two: Drilling

The ends of the pits butt up against the inside edges of the front and back walls, so $\frac{1}{8}$" nail holes should be drilled in through these walls, about $\frac{3}{8}$" in from the ends. Drill more nail holes down through the roof, about $\frac{3}{8}$" in from the back edge, spacing them between the garage door cuts in the back wall.

Still more nail holes go in through the front of the roof, spaced about 5" apart, and about $\frac{3}{8}$" down from the top edge.

Holes for the flagstaffs are drilled down into this top edge, about 3" apart, and about $\frac{1}{2}$" deep.

Now place the base of the timing tower and the clock board in position on the roof and draw a light line around these pieces on the roof. Drill two nail holes down through the roof within each of these outlines. Draw a line lightly on the top of the roof, $1\frac{1}{2}$" back from the front edge of the roof piece. With the $\frac{1}{2}$" wood bit, drill a hole down through this line at the midpoint, an equal distance from both ends of the roof. Then drill four more holes along this line to both sides, spacing them out 5" apart.

Drill five $\frac{1}{2}$" holes down into the top edge of the front wall of the pits, about $\frac{3}{4}$" deep and spaced exactly as the five holes through the roof were drilled.

Drill four $\frac{1}{2}$" holes down into the top of the timing-tower base at the corners, about $\frac{3}{4}$" deep. Then drill four more holes through the roof of the timing tower spaced apart to match the holes in the base of the tower.

Step Three: Assembling

With 2" finishing nails and white glue, nail up through the roof of the pits and into the base of the timing tower. Then nail up through the roof and into the base of the clock board.

With nails and glue, attach the roof front piece to the front edge of the roof. Then attach the front wall of the pits to the front edge of both end walls, and then attach the back wall of the pits to the front edge of both end walls, and then attach the back wall of the pits to the back edge of the end walls.

Now the roof assembly can be glued and nailed to the top edge of the back wall. Place dabs of glue in the holes in the top edge of the front wall of the pits and then slip the dowel pillars down through the holes in the roof and into the holes in the top of the front wall.

Making sure that the roof is level, sink nails in through the end edges of the roof and the front wall, and into the end dowels, securing the roof in place. It may be a good idea to drill guide holes for these nails first.

Place dabs of glue in the holes in the top of the timing-tower base and drive the dowel pillars down into these holes firmly, then slip the tower roof over the dowels, level the roof, and fix the roof in place with nails in through the edges of the roof and into the dowels.

128

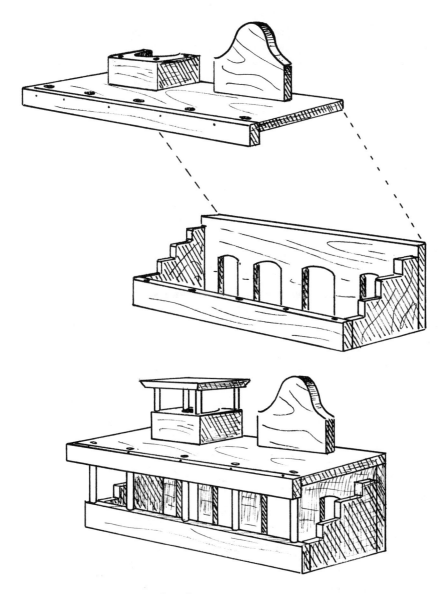

Step Four: Finishing

Sand the building and remove any rough edges or joints with a shaper. The building can then be painted with semigloss white or off-white enamel.

To decorate the pits with racing advertisements, run through a few old sports-car magazines, or whatever kind of race-car magazines you can find, and clip out any trademarks that seem to have something to do with racing. These can be glued on at random wherever they seem to fit. The flagstaffs are made from nails or cut-off matchsticks, and the flags are cut from scraps found in the ragbag and then glued around the staffs.

Add a few grease stains and oil smudges, and the pits are ready for the Big Race Day.

129

LUMBER LIST
for the
PITS

Eight feet of 1″×6″ shelving stock
Three feet of ½″ wood dowel
A scrap of 2″×6″ stock, 6″ long
Three dozen 2″ finishing nails
Seven or eight matchsticks or 3″ nails for flagstaffs
Material scraps for flags

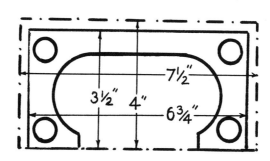

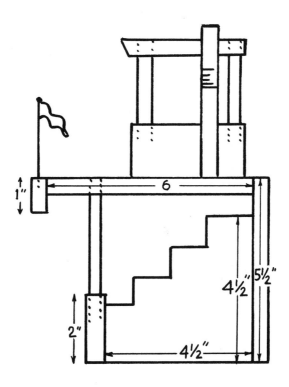

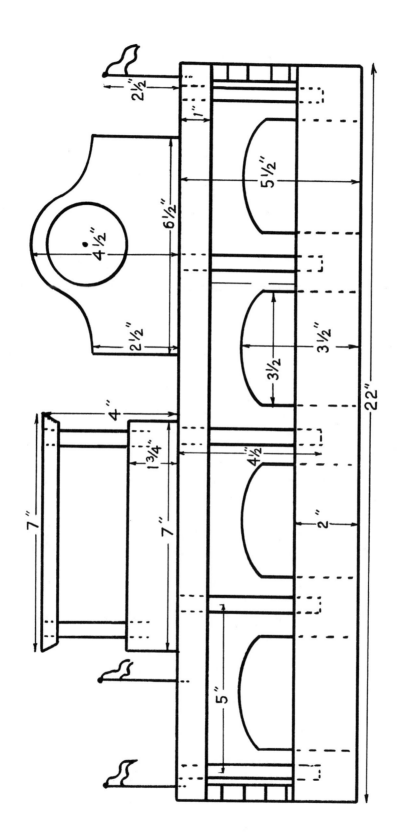

Chapter *13*

The Grandfather Clock

This grandfather clock doesn't exactly keep time with the best of them, but it does tend to teach the wee ones how to tell time pretty well, and also how to read Roman numerals.

The works are fairly simple. When the small hand on the face of the clock is turned to point to "IV," for instance, a disc is turned behind the face so that the number in the upper part of the window at the top of the face reads "4," and when the hand points to "III" the top of the window reads "3," and so on. When the large hand points to "VI," however, the number in the lower part of the window reads "30," and when the large hand points to "IX," the number in the lower part of the window reads "45," and so forth, so that wherever the hands point, the time, in Arabic numerals, can be read in the window.

If this doesn't fascinate you, the bottom of the clock serves as a book-shelf, and below that is a toy bin, as extra added attractions.

The clock is a fairly simple project, and even simpler if you want to leave out the teaching parts and let the hands just rotate.

Step One: Cutting

Mark the dimensions of the side profile onto the 1″ × 12″ shelving stock and cut this out, using a table, portable electric or carpenter's handsaw for the straight cuts, and a band, jig, saber or coping saw for the curved cuts. Once this piece is cut, use it as a pattern to draw the other side onto the shelving. Cut the other side out. Also, mark the dimensions for the shelf and bin bottom on the 1″×12″ stock and cut these pieces out.

Now mark the dimensions and sketch the outlines of the back, the bottom front, the face and the top scroll, as well as the hands and the discs, onto a 4′×4′ piece of ¼″-thick plywood or paneling. To mark the discs, drill two small holes in a yardstick or any thin stick, with the holes spaced as far apart as the length of the radius for each disc. Place a nail through one hole and onto the plywood. Then, with the tip of a pencil through the other hole, rotate the pencil around the nail to draw the right size circle.

Mark the window in position on the face of the clock and after drilling a ½″ starter hole, cut the window out with a saber or keyhole saw.

Step Two: Drilling

With a ⅜″ wood bit, drill a hole through the center of the clock face and through the centers of the two discs. Carefully drill ⅜″ holes through the pivot points of the two hands, also.

Step Three: First Assembling

Run a line of white glue along the back edge of one of the sides of the clock, and then with the side placed front edge down on a firm surface, nail the back of the clock onto the back edge of the side, flush with the outside, using 1½″ finishing nails spaced every 5″. Repeat this to attach the other side to the back.

Now run a line of glue along the side edge, back edge and other side edge of the shelf, and with the sides of the clock resting back edges down, aligned with each other, insert the shelf squarely into position, nailing through the sides and back of the clock. Run a line of glue around the edges of the bin bottom, and insert it into position about an inch up from the bottom of the clock, and then nail in from the sides and back, fixing it in place. After running a line of glue nine inches up both front edges of the sides, position the bottom front of the clock and attach it with nails through the front into the edges of the sides.

Now the face can be nailed on in the same manner, and then the top scroll nailed on over that. Before nailing on the top lid of the clock, the discs should be attached, and before they can be attached, they should be painted, so we might as well paint the whole clock at this point.

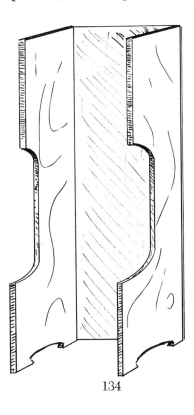 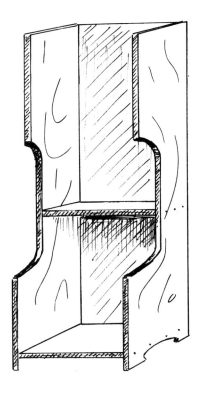

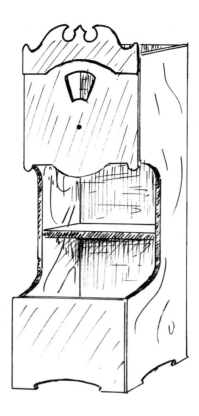

Step Four: Painting

The painting is nearly always according to your own whims. The clock can be stained, varnished, antiqued, or painted—like the one pictured. To follow the color scheme in the example, the entire clock was first painted a warm yellow, then the sides and bottom were striped with deep red (wide, colored plastic tape can be used). The face was painted gloss white, as were the two discs on one side. The top scroll was colored dark gray-brown and the hands were painted semigloss black.

When the face of the clock is thoroughly dry, the Roman numerals can be drawn on with the aid of a drafting square and a wide-tip felt marking pen.

Step Five: Assembling the Works

To hook up the hands to the discs, first run a 4″-long ⁵⁄₁₆″-diameter, roundhead bolt (with the threads all the way to the head) into the hole in the small hand. Run a nut all the way onto this bolt, and tighten the bolt securely to the hand.

The longer hand is attached to a 3″ length of ⅜″-diameter threaded brass tubing. This tubing is the sort that normally attaches light sockets to lamp bases, and can be found in all lengths in the lighting section of the hardware department. When you get the tubing, grab four of the nuts and two of the wide washers that are made for it. They are usually found in plastic packets right near the tubing.

135

Run a nut just onto this tube, then insert the tube through the hole in the large hand. Run another nut on from the other end of the tube, and tighten the nut deep into the grain on the backside of the large hand to hold the hand securely. The hand should be positioned as close to the end of the tube as possible.

Insert the tube into the center hole in the clock face. Then run a nut, and then a washer, onto the end of the tube inside the clock, and up to about ⅛″ from the back of the clock face. Now place the smaller disc over the tube from the back, and run another washer and then another nut onto the tube, tightening up against the back of the disc to hold it firmly to the tube. Check to see that the small disc turns freely as the large hand is rotated. Cut off the tube flush with the back of the last nut attached.

Now insert the bolt attached to the short hand into the tube, and run a nut onto the back of the bolt to about ⅛″ from the back of the tube. Place the hole in the larger disc over the bolt, then run on another bolt and tighten it securely, holding the disc firmly to the bolt. Check to see that the small disc turns freely when the large hand is rotated, and that the large disc turns freely when the small hand is rotated.

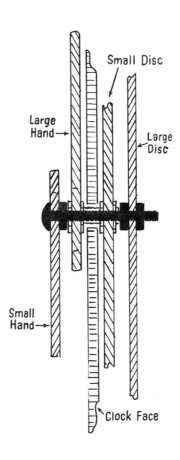

Once the top piece is nailed on, it's a simple matter to point the hands toward each numeral, one by one, and write on the discs in the window the Arabic numerals corresponding to the time that is shown on the face in Roman numerals. Put the hours on the large disc and the minutes on the small disc, of course. After long and heated discussions, it was finally decided to write the Roman numeral four as "IV" instead of the "IIII" found on most clocks, with the idea of teaching the children the right numerals first. They can learn the idiosyncrasies of clock face numbering when they're older and presumably better equipped to cope with such intricacies of life.

It may be more fun if you let them discover by themselves how the whole clock works. It's amazing what they can puzzle through when they're stalling off putting their books and toys away.

LUMBER LIST
for the
GRANDFATHER CLOCK

Two 5' lengths of 1″×12″ shelving stock
A 4'×4' piece of ¼″-thick plywood or paneling
Three dozen 1½″ finishing nails
One 4″, 5⁄16″-diameter roundhead bolt (threaded to the head), with three nuts
One 3″ length of 3⁄8″-diameter threaded brass lamp tubing, plus four nuts and two wide washers

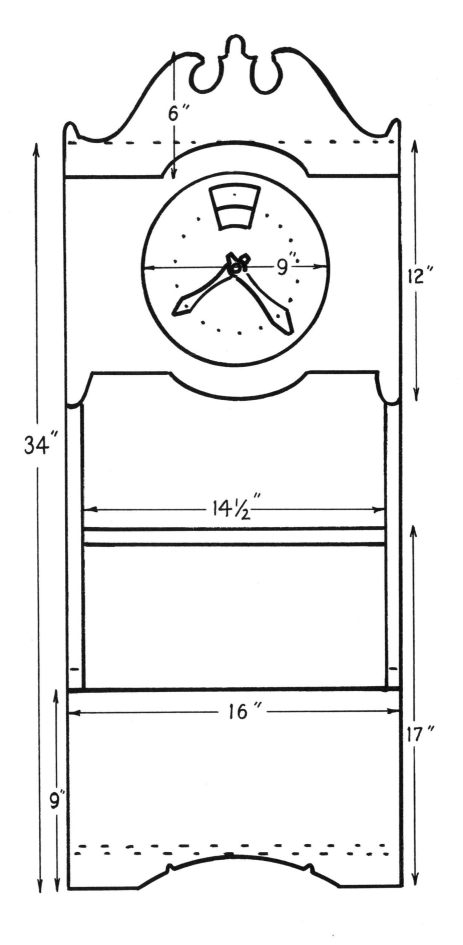

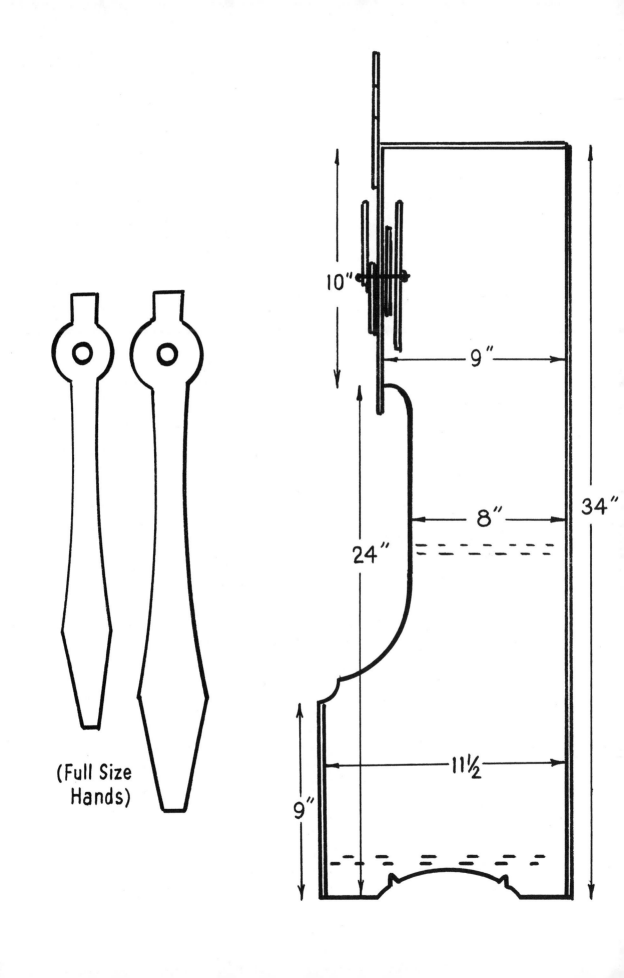

(Full Size
Hands)

10"

9"

8"

34"

24"

11½

9"

Chapter 14

The Train

This little train came from a composite of French and English narrow-gauge machines that used to puff their way over the countryside, bringing a touch of the city to the rural villages, and vice versa. Like the steam-roller, the train engine is made around one crucial component—a wooden rolling pin. If you don't happen to have a spare, the housewares department of the local home-supply store will be glad to spare you one for a small sum, or try the secondhand store.

Step One: Cutting

From 1″×4″ or 1″×6″ stock, mark and cut a rectangular piece, 2¼″× 4½″. Mark the outline of the profile of the axle carrier piece onto the 1″ stock with the grain running lengthwise, and cut this out with a band, coping, jig or saber saw.

Now, from a piece of 4″×4″ stock, cut a 3″ piece with one end cut squarely. Use carbon paper, tracing paper or a copier to make a pattern. Trace the side profile of the engine cab onto the side of the 4″×4″ with the grain running fore and aft. Cut out the side profile with a band saw or coping saw, then sketch the outline of the end view of the cab onto the squared end of the cab, and cut this out.

To cut the front piece of the engine, reverse the process. Sketch around the pattern to draw the end view on the side of 2″×4″ stock, cut out the end view, and then make the side cut, slicing the piece to a 1″ thickness.

140

141

Before cutting the curved top of this piece, which sits against the bottom of the rolling pin, check the size of your pin, and if there is a difference, use the end of the pin to draw on the top line of this piece.

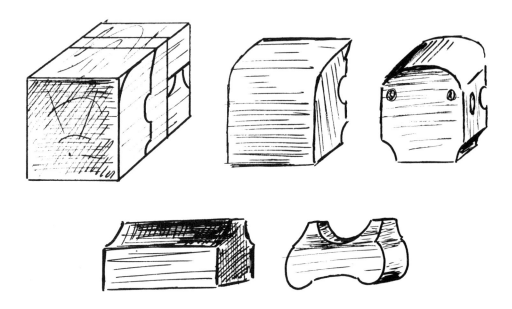

Now the handles at the end of the rolling pin can be whacked off. Cut the roller down to a 5″ length to form the boiler of the engine.

Remove the spindles that the pin handles spin around, cut one spindle to 2″ long and cut off the head of the other spindle at its base. Cut the four wheels from ½″ or ⅝″ thick plywood with the 2¼″-diameter hole-saw attachment.

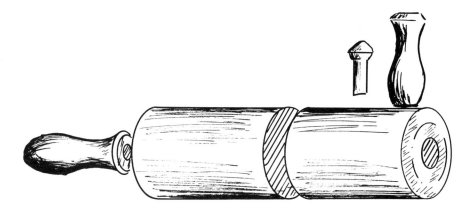

Step Two: Drilling

Mark the shape of the cab windows in place on the sides of the cab, and then drill three holes, as shown, into the windows to about ¼″ deep with

142

the ⅜″ wood bit. Mark the positions of the windows in the front of the cab, and drill these to a depth of about ¼″.

Drill a ⅛″ hole in the center of the cutout on the backside of the cab, for a screw hole to attach the cab to the back of the boiler. Countersink this hole with the ⅜″ bit to a depth that will allow the 1½″-long screw to get a good bite into the back of the boiler.

Drill two ⅛″ screw holes through the center line of the axle carrier, as shown, just in from the axle notches. Mark a center line down the top of the rectangular chassis part, and drill a screw hole through this line, 1¼″ from the back end, and 1½″ from the front end.

Mark a straight line along the length of the boiler, and then, exactly on the other side of the boiler, make another line straight along the length of the rolling pin. Use the squarely cut off end of the rolling pin as the back end of the boiler.

Place the boiler directly over the chassis so that one of the center lines on the boiler sits on the center line down the top of the chassis. The boiler should sit on the chassis with the front end of the boiler overlapping the front of the chassis 1⅛″. Holding the boiler in place, drill through the screw holes in the chassis and into the bottom of the boiler about ¼″. Attach the chassis to the bottom of the boiler with screws and glue.

143

Now the positions for the holes which will hold the smokestack, condenser, and bell can be marked along the top line of the boiler.

The condenser, behind the stack, is made from the 2″ piece of spindle. Drill a hole down into the position marked for the condenser hole with a drill bit the same size as the shaft of the spindle, to a depth of about 1″. With a 1″ bit, drill a hole down into the stack-hole mark about ½″ deep. Then with the same bit used for the condenser, drill another hole down into the center of the 1″ stack hole, to a depth of about 1″. Drill two small holes about ⅝″ apart for the bell hanger, which will be made from coat-hanger wire.

Step Three: Assembling

Attach the front piece to the bottom front of the boiler by drilling a screw hole up through the bottom of the piece, and just into the bottom of the boiler, then running a screw through the piece into the boiler (using glue, of course). The bumpers on the front are made from ½″, roundhead wood plug buttons. Drill a small hole in the center of each one, then glue and nail them in place with short finishing nails. Now, with a little glue spread on the joining surfaces, sink a screw through the back of the cab and into the back of the boiler, holding the cab in place.

Place a bit of glue in the condenser hole, and then tap the 2″ spindle piece firmly in place. Set the headless spindle shaft into the hole for the stack in the same way. Put a little glue around this shaft, and then slip the roller-pin handle down over the shaft, with the flared end up. Now a small hole can be drilled through the side of the stack and into the shaft. Fasten the handle to the spindle with a ¾″ screw.

The bell used on the engine shown came from a piece of junk jewelry lying around. If you happen to be short on such essentials, bells can be found by the dozens in dime-store decoration departments.

144

With pliers, shape the bell hanger from coat-hanger wire, slip on the bell, and then tap the hanger down into the holes provided. With screws and glue, attach the axle carrier to the bottom of the chassis.

The condenser pipe is made from a soft copper, $\frac{1}{4}''$ outside diameter tube (a toilet tank filler tube is perfect), found in the plumbing department. With the $\frac{1}{4}''$ bit, drill a hole in the front side of the condenser, a little to the left, and about $\frac{1}{4}''$ deep. Then drill a hole in the back of the left side of the front piece to about the same depth. Gently bend the tube to the shape shown, and cut it off to a length that will extend into both holes. Bend the pipe into a tighter S-curve, insert one end in one hole, then bend the pipe back to the original curve shape, and fit it into the other hole, which will hold the pipe in place.

The axles are made from $4''$ roundhead, $\frac{1}{4}''$-diameter bolts. Insert the bolt through one wheel, tap the head in so the base of the head is flush with the side of the wheel, insert the bolt through the axle carrier and through the other wheel. Run a nut on the bolt, leaving enough play for the wheels to roll, then cut off the bolt sticking out beyond the nut, and tap the end with a hammer to spread the bolt and keep the nut from coming off. Repeat this to attach the other axle.

Step Four: Finishing

With a sharp wood chisel gouge out the space between the holes forming the side windows in the cab. Smooth off all rough edges and surfaces with medium and fine sandpaper. A couple of coats of satin-finish varnish may bring out enough contrasting wood tones to give the engine interest. If it looks a little dull after varnishing, touch up the smaller components like the stack and the front piece with semigloss black or dark green. Sink a screw eye in the front of the chassis and in the back of the cab for attaching a pull string to the front and a coal car to the back.

THE COAL CAR

Transfer the side profile of the coal car onto the side of a piece of $4'' \times 4''$ stock and cut it out. Now draw the end profile onto the front, and cut this out. Sand with medium and fine sandpaper to remove rough edges. The wheels are cut with the $1\frac{1}{4}''$-diameter hole-saw attachment for the power drill, using $\frac{1}{2}''$- or $\frac{5}{8}''$-thick plywood stock. Attach the wheels with $\frac{1}{2}''$ wood screws, leaving them enough play to roll freely. The car can be varnished, or painted black, deep green, or whatever color strikes you. Attach a screw hook at the front and a screw eye at the back for couplings.

THE PASSENGER CAR

There are any number of different cars that can be designed to run with this train—flatcars, boxcars, gondola cars, tank cars, cranes, etc. And for those who have the inclination this is a good place to start their experiments in designing toys. We'll go through the basic layout of a passenger car to get the ball rolling.

This car is made from a 6″ length of 4″×4″ stock and two 6″ lengths of 2″×4″ stock.

Slice the 4″×4″ stock into a piece 2″ wide. Now mark a line along one side, 1″ in from one of the long edges. Draw the center marks for the four 1″ holes to be drilled along this line, as shown. Drill these holes, then make the vertical cuts up into these holes to form the profile of the car, as shown.

Mark the side profile of the car's top on the side edge of one of the 2″×4″ pieces, and cut this out with a band saw, a table saw, or a carpenter's handsaw.

Now mark on the end shape and cut this out with a table saw or carpenter's handsaw.

Mark the end shape of the chassis on the remaining 2″×4″, and cut out in the same manner. Then sketch on the side profile of the chassis and cut it out. The wheels are cut with the 1¼″ hole-saw attachment, just as they were for the coal car, and are attached with the 1½″ screws the same way.

Place the roof of the car squarely over the body, drill ¹⁄₁₆″ nail holes down through the roof, and then glue and nail the roof to the body. Attach the chassis to the body in the same way, attach the wheels, sand, paint, screw on the eye and hook on the ends, and you're ready to start on the next effort. To make a flatcar, simply make the chassis part alone. A tank car could be a length of 2″ dowel mounted lengthwise on a chassis, with a stub of 1″ dowel sticking out the top.

From there on, the imagination reels, and your only limits are your time and interest (or rather, the interest of your clients).

LUMBER LIST	One wooden rolling pin
for the	A 2′ length of 4″×4″ stock (preferably soft wood)
ENGINE AND	A 1′ length of 2″×4″ stock
TWO CARS	A 1′ length of 1″×4″ stock
	About one square foot of ½″ or ⅝″ plywood scrap
	Two dozen 1½″ wood screws
	Two 4″ roundhead, ¼″-diameter bolts, with nuts
	One dozen 1″ finishing nails
	Two ½″-diameter, roundhead wood plug buttons
	A 1′ length of ¼″ outside diameter soft copper tubing
	One small bell
	One coat hanger
	Two screw hooks
	Four screw eyes

Train Cab
Front Outline

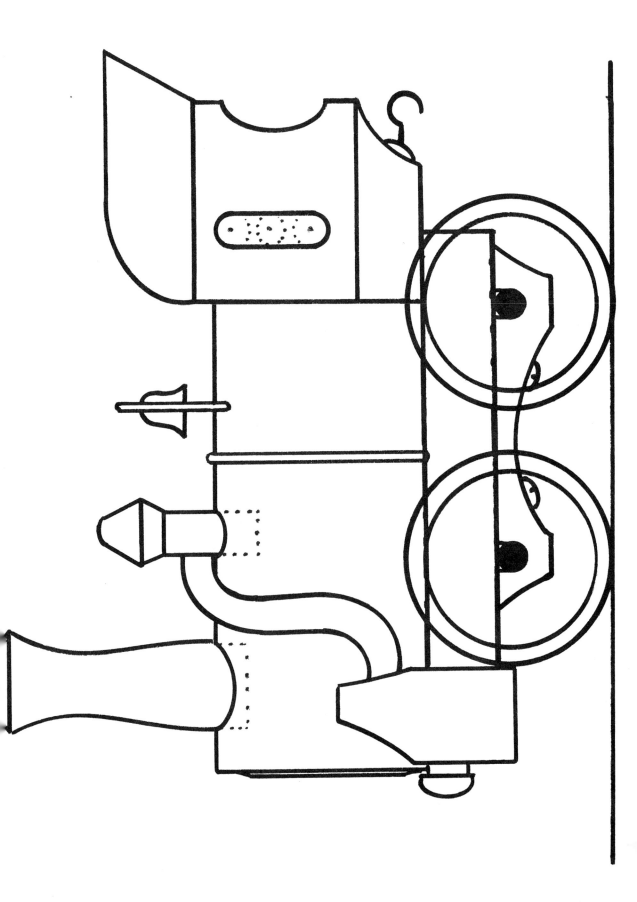

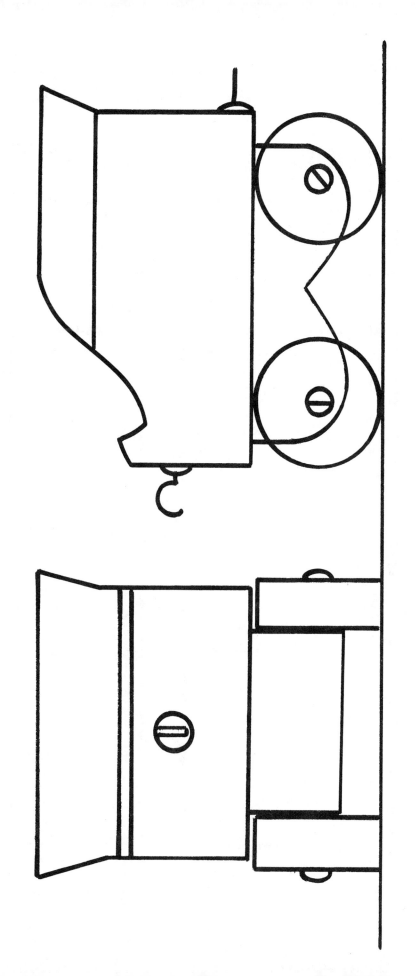

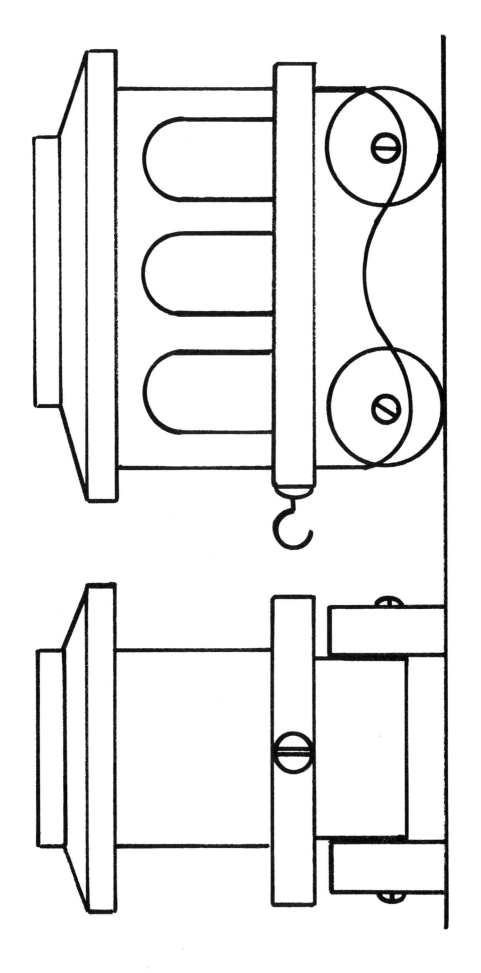

Chapter 15

The Forklift

A forklift is a tool of endless uses for the young construction engineer. Arranging misplaced blocks and building logs, loading trains, lifting bales, toting barges—its work, like that of the fabled female, is never done. Well, hardly ever.

This particular forklift works with a twist of the steering wheel, which raises or lowers the fork. It has six wheels (being a heavy-duty model), two in the back and four in the front to support the heavy loads lifted by the fork. In the real versions, the back wheels steer, making it easier to line up the forks with the pad to be lifted. And the engines are also in the back to help balance the weight on the front. Sometimes even the rear bumper is used as a counterweight, being made from iron several inches thick to help beef up the rear end.

Step One: Cutting

The body is cut from a short length of 2″×4″ stock. Transfer the outline of the side view of the body piece by making a copy with carbon paper, tracing paper, or a copier, then cutting out a pattern to trace around. Cut out the body with a saber, jig, band or coping saw.

Sketch the outline of the fender piece onto a length of 1″×2″ or 1″×4″ stock, and then cut this out. Use this fender piece as a pattern to draw the other fender piece, then cut it out.

Now cut out a strip of hardwood, ⅜″ thick and ½″ wide, 13″ long. The table saw is best for this, but the job can be carefully done with a band

151

saw or carpenter's handsaw. On one ⅜" edge of this strip, make a groove between ¹⁄₁₆" and ⅛" wide, and about ¼" deep down the middle. Now cut this strip into two 6½" lengths.

Cut a ⅜"-diameter wood dowel into one 4½" length and two ½" lengths. For a steering wheel, cut off a ½"-thick slice of 1½"- or 1¼"-diameter dowel, or cut a 1¼"-diameter disc from a scrap of ½" thick plywood with the hole-saw attachment for the power drill. Fluted wooden curtain rod makes a perfect source of doweling to be sliced, and no one will really notice if the curtains are ½" shorter. After all, it's for a noble cause.

To make a pad, which supports the load to be lifted by the fork, cut two rectangular pieces of 1" stock, 2" x 3½". Now cut out four 1⅜"×5⅛" pieces of ⅛" masonite or plywood. Cut the fork from soft, sheet aluminum, soft iron or thin plywood with the slider made from a strap, as shown.

The wheels pictured in the photos are the standard, 2¼"-diameter size toy truck wheels used in some of the other toys. If, for some reason, these are in short supply around the shop, cut the wheels from 1"×4" stock or plywood with the 2¼" hole-saw attachment. Use ¼"-diameter threaded rod for the axles, if using wood wheels, and attach the wheels with a nut on each side of each wheel, as in the steamroller project.

Step Two: Drilling

With the ¼" bit, drill the axle holes in from both sides. Enlarge these holes vertically a little so that the wheels may bounce. Now drill a ⅜" hole for the steering column down into the center of the footwell, just in front of the seat. Angle this hole down toward the front so that it comes out the bottom just behind the front axle hole. Enlarge this hole slightly by running the bit through several times while applying a little side pressure so that a ⅜" wood dowel will turn freely in the hole. Drill a ⅜" hole through the center of the steering wheel so that it will fit snugly over the steering-column dowel. Now drill two ⅛" holes through the steering column, one 2" from one end, and the other ½" from the other end.

The forklift is put together with white glue and 1½" finishing nails. To avoid splitting the fender pieces, drill guide holes for the nails, as shown, with a 1/16" bit or by using a nail with the head nipped off for a drill bit.

153

Drill nail holes in through the grooved edge of the hardwood strips, ⅜″ in from both ends. Now drill nail holes through the same strips, but this time through the ½″-wide sides of the strips. Place both strips on a firm surface, side by side, with the grooved edges facing each other. Now drill nail holes ¾″ in from the near end of the strips. Drill more holes 2¼″ in from this same end.

Before attaching the steeling wheel to the steering column, remember that the bottom end of the steering column has a hole drilled ½″ in from the end. Now place a dab of glue in the center hole of the steering wheel, and insert the end of the steering column into it. Then drill a small nail hole in through the edge of the steering wheel, into the column, and through the other side of the wheel, and attach the wheel by gently tapping a nail into the hole.

The two short, ½″-long pieces of dowel are used as pulleys for the lifting string. Hold one of the dowels, end grain up, in a vice or with pliers, and drill a ⅛″ hole through the center of the dowel end. Then with a hacksaw, coping saw or handsaw cut a shallow groove around the side of the dowel at the midpoint from both ends.

With a ¾″ wood bit, drill down into the hole for the steering column in the footwell, about ⅛″ deep, making a flat base around the top of the column hole.

154

Step Three: Shaping and Assembling

Round off the tops of the hood sides with a shaper, and then with a hacksaw or coping saw cut the grooves up both sides and across the top of the hood, as shown in the side view. Round off the top ends of the hardwood strips (the ends away from the side nail holes) with the shaper.

Run a line of glue along the inside of the fender pieces, and nail the fenders on, as shown. Then round off the rear edge of the bumper.

Now the grooved, hardwood slide strips can be glued and nailed in place to the front of the body. Position the slide strips parallel, flush with the sides of the body on the outside, with the bottoms of the strips extending down about ⅛" below an imaginary straight line running through the axle holes.

With a hacksaw, coping saw or handsaw, grind off the sharp corner at the bottom front of the body piece between the hardwood slides, so that one of the lifting strings can pass easily from the bottom of the body, around and up the front of the body.

Do this by a number of closely spaced, side-by-side cuts of the saw. Now a nail can be inserted into one of the holes in the edge of a slide strip near the bottom. Place one of the short dowel pulleys between the slides at the bottom, and insert this nail through the pulley, then through the hole in the other slide. Tap the head of the nail in firmly.

The wheels can now be attached. If using the 2¼" truck wheels, run the front axle through two wheels, through a ¼" nut (used as a spacer), through the front axle hole, and finally through the other two front wheels. Place a retaining washer, fitting snugly over the axle, on the end, and then cut the axle off, just outside the washer. Place the head end of the axle on a hard surface, and tap the cut-off end of the axle with a hammer until it spreads enough to keep the washer from falling off. Repeat this process to attach the two rear wheels.

To attach the steering column, run a short, stubby screw into the hole near the center of the column. Insert the column through a loose washer, then down into the hole in the body.

If you're using the all-metal fork, drill the hole in the top of the slide, as shown, with a $\frac{1}{8}''$ bit, bend the fork to the shape illustrated in the sketch, and then file off any rough spots on the edges of the slide. If using the wooden fork, cut the slide strap to shape, drill the holes, bend to shape, and then attach to the back of the fork with screws.

Run a little oil down into the steering-column hole, around the center hole in the pulleys, and into the grooves of both slide strips.

Place the slide of the fork down into the grooves of the slide strips. File off the fork slide if the fork doesn't fall freely in the slide. Now insert a nail through the top hole in the slide strips and the top pulley in the same way that the bottom pulley was fixed on.

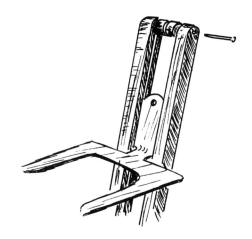

Step Four: Rigging

Turn the forklift over, and insert a 2′ length of good nylon string through the hole near the bottom of the steering column. Tie a strong knot around the base of the column with about a foot of string on either end.

Now turn the column so the string hole is parallel to the front axle, and extend one end of the string out to your left, and the other to your right. Take the right end of the string and insert the end of it between the bottom dowel pulley and the body. Bring this end of the string up between the slide strips, up behind the top pulley, over the pulley and then back

156

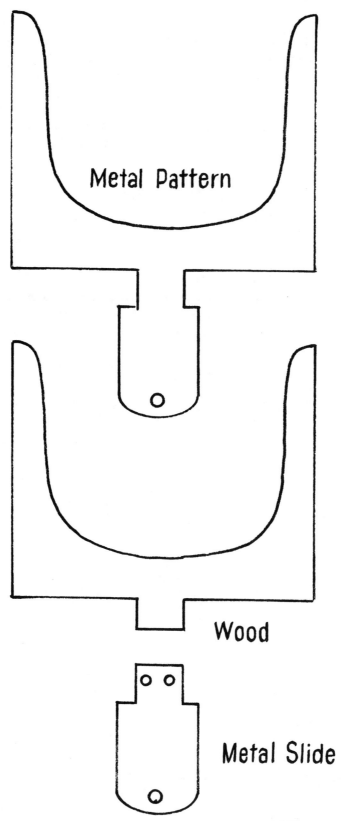

Metal Pattern

Wood

Metal Slide

157

down the front, where it is tied securely to the hole in the fork slide when the fork is in the "up" position.

Then with the forklift upside down, run the left end of the string around the column dowel (clockwise when viewed from the bottom) three times, passing between the right end of the string and the bottom of the body. Then the string should go around the outside of the bottom pulley, and up behind the fork slide, where it is tied securely to the hole in the fork slide.

Now, lo and behold, if you took the steps slowly and patiently, the fork should raise on command when the steering wheel is turned.

Every forklift worth its salt needs at least one pad to lift things on, and where pads are concerned, the more the merrier. Place the two 2″×3½″ pieces of the 1″ stock on edge, and then nail and glue both ends of the ⅛″-thick pieces to the edges, flush with the sides and the ends. Repeat this on the other side, and it's ready to work.

Give the forklift a coat or two of satin-finish varnish and then paint the steering wheel, seat, fork and rear grille flat black. Be careful to keep the paint and varnish off the slides, of course. And finally, the wheel centers are painted "implement" yellow (what else?).

LUMBER LIST	One-foot length of 2″×4″ stock
for the	Two-foot length of 1″×4″ stock
FORKLIFT	One hardwood strip, ⅜″ thick, ½″ wide, 13″ long
	One-foot length of ⅜″ wood dowel
	One 6″×6″ piece of ⅛″-thick masonite or plywood
	One short piece of 1⅛″ or 1¼″ wood dowel
	Six 2¼″-diameter wheels with two axles
	A 4″×6″ square of soft aluminum or iron sheet (or a short length of thin iron strap, and a 4″×4″ piece of ⅜″ plywood)
	A ⅜″ washer
	Two dozen 1½″ finishing nails
	A 2′ length of good nylon string

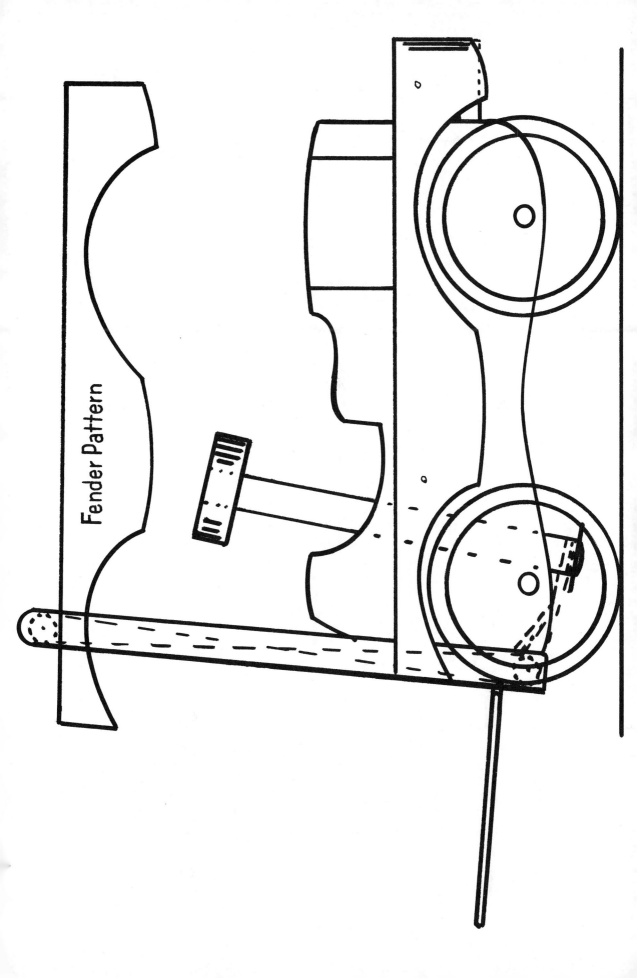

Fender Pattern

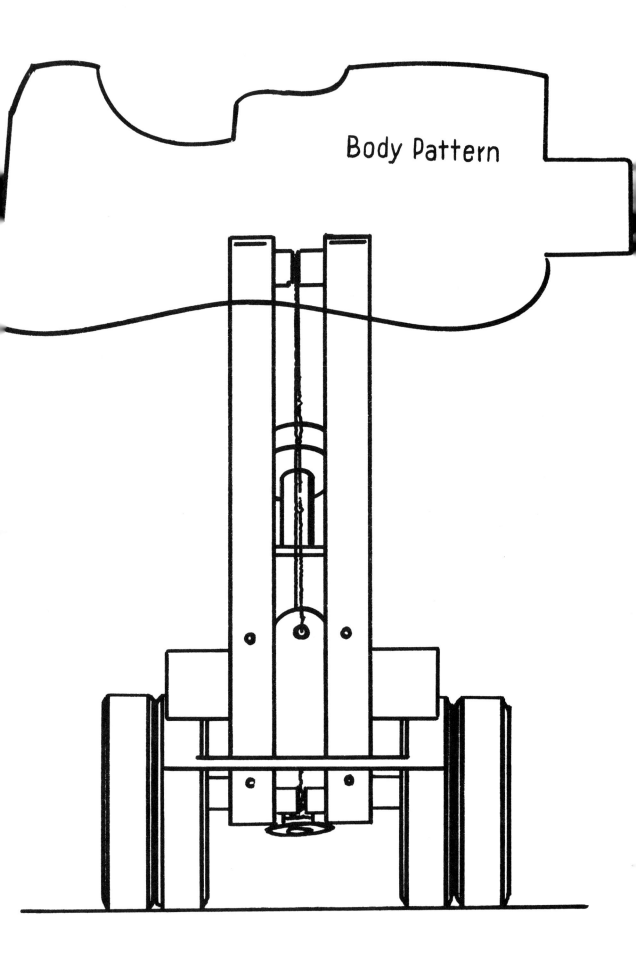

Body Pattern

Chapter 16

The Fish Boat

The fish boat is designed for cruising o'er the billowy reaches of the living-room floor. The lines of the boat were taken fairly literally from those of the purse seiners that chug along patiently up and down the fog-bound coast of California. Their enormous nets are handled in the water by the skiffs, and are drawn on board with the help of a huge power winch and the boom. When the boat is heading for home with a full hold, the skiff is usually carried flopped over on the nets to hold them down in a blow.

To make the toy fish boat, the most difficult step will be finding a short length of softwood 4″×6″, or 6″×6″ stock. Such timbers are expensive by the time you end up paying for the four- or six-foot minimum length sold. So, if you don't want to take the time for laminating a piece out of thin stock glued together, then the best bet is to nose around the cut-off scrap pile at the lumberyard where the timbers are trimmed and where short scraps can usually be had for a little friendly shooting of the breeze.

Step One: Cutting

Using carbon paper, tracing paper or a copier to make patterns to sketch around, draw the side profile of the hull onto the 4″×6″ or 6″×6″ stock. Use a band saw or a coping saw to cut this shape out. Next mark a center line down the top of the hull, and draw on the top outline of the deck. Cut this out with the band saw or the coping saw so the side of the hull leans in toward the bottom about 10° from perpendicular.

161

The side profile of the top part of the boat (the bridge) can be drawn on 2″×6″ or 4″×6″ soft-wood stock, and then cut. Now draw the top outline of the bridge, and make the straight cuts that form the sides. Then make the curved cut around the front of the bridge, angling it down and back 10° from perpendicular.

Draw the cabin profile onto 4″×4″ hardwood stock. Check to see how the bridge and hull pieces already cut will rest against this outline, and use these pieces to make any changes that may be needed in the deckhouse outline to get a good fit. Cut out the side profile, and then mark on the out-line of the top. Make the straight side cuts, and then cut around the front curve, angling it back like the bridge front cut. From the same hardwood stock, cut the side view of the skiff, then mark on the deck plan outline, and cut this out, angling the sides in about 10° toward the bottom.

Cut off a 2¼″ length of 1″-diameter wood dowel, and then another piece 1¾″ long, angling back about 60° from the end, so that the long side is 1¾″ long, and the short side is 1¼″ long. Cut a ⅜″ dowel into one 6½″ length and one 5″ length.

Step Two: Drilling

With a 1″-diameter wood bit, drill a hole in the center of the deckhouse 1¼″ in front of the backside, angling it down somewhat from the rear (or stern, of course), as shown, to a depth of about ¾″.

With a ⅜″ bit, drill a hole straight down into the center of the hull, 3¾″ forward of the back of the hull (or stern, or transom, that is to say), about ¾″ deep. Holding the short, angled length of 1″ dowel (the crow's nest) firmly in a vice or with pliers, drill a ⅜″ hole up into the bottom of the crow's nest, about ¼″ in from the short side, and about ¾″ deep.

With the same bit, drill the four front ports in the forward wall of the deckhouse, about ¼″ deep; drill the ports on the side walls and back (or aft) wall of the deckhouse, and the two anchor line holes in the sides of the hull near the bow using a ½″ bit. Drill two ⅛″ holes through the mast, one about 1″ down from the top, and the other about 2″ up from the bottom.

Drill two ⅛″ nail holes down through the top of the deckhouse about 2″ apart and about 2″ back from the forward point of the deckhouse. Drill two nail holes down through the top of the bridge, about 2″ apart, and about 2″ back from the forward point of the bridge.

And finally, drill two nail holes about 2″ apart along the center line of the bottom of the skiff.

Step Three: Shaping

Make certain the hull, deckhouse, and bridge fit reasonably well together in place. Make adjustments, if necessary, with the saw or shaper. Then with a wood rasp or shaper, smooth off all surfaces. Remove shaper marks with coarse sandpaper, remove the lines left by the coarse paper wtih medium paper, and then smooth up with fine sandpaper.

Step Four: Assembling

Place a little glue on the bottom of the deckhouse, then place it in position on the deck. Insert a 2″ finishing nail in both nail holes, and nail the deckhouse in place. Run glue onto the top front of the deckhouse, then place the bridge squarely in position, and nail the bridge in place. Put a dab of glue in the hole in the crow's nest and a dab in the mast hole; then insert the top of the mast into the crow's nest, the bottom of the mast into the hull, and tap the parts together firmly. To attach the boom, run a 2″ box nail through the hole in one end of the boom, and then bend the nail into a "U" shape. Run the pointed end of the "U" through the hole near the bottom of the mast. Finally, cut the pointed end off so that the nail sticks out through the mast about ⅜″, then bend this end back on to the head, completing a loop through the holes in the boom and the mast.

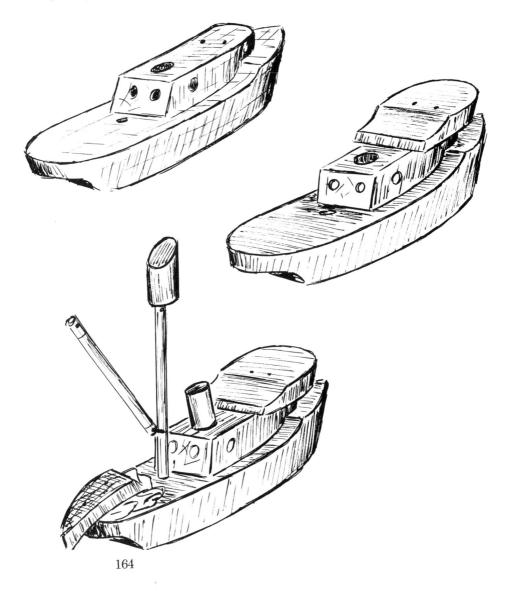

Run some glue into the smokestack hole, then insert the stack and tap home with a hammer. If you like, the stack can be painted first and then inserted, to get a neat line around the bottom.

Step Five: Finishing

The boat can be painted, stained or varnished to suit your tastes. The specimen pictured here went through all three processes.

The deck, the topside of the bridge, the mast and boom, and the crow's nest were all stained and wiped, using a dark oak stain. Then the entire boat was given a coat of satin-finish varnish. The sides of the bridge and a band around the top of the bow were given several coats of gloss white enamel. The stack was painted glossy yellow. The bottom of the skiff was painted Chinese red, with bands of red around the stack and the crow's nest. And finally, the tops of the crow's nest and the stack were painted flat black.

Step Six: Final Assembling

Wad up (or fold artfully) a 6″×6″ piece of green plastic window-screen mesh, place it on the back deck, position the skiff upside down on the net, and drive two nails through the skiff and into the deck. Cut two narrow triangles of ping-pong (or similar) netting, about 2″ across the base and 5¾″ high, and glue them in place on either side of the mast, as shown. Of course, if you're big on detail, you can rig the shrouds with individually knotted lengths of string, and so on, but then you're likely to be a little less philosophic when they spill ice cream on it later. There should be a boom line running from the hole just under the crow's nest to the end of the boom, as shown.

To make the craft fully ready for the blessing of the fleet, all that's needed now is a name on the bow. Your clients may be able to help you there.

LUMBER LIST	A 1′ length of 4″×6″ or 6″×6″ softwood stock
for the	A 1′ length of 4″×4″ hardwood stock
FISH BOAT	A 6″ length of 2″×6″ softwood stock
	A 6″ length of 1″-diameter wood dowel
	A 1′ length of ⅜″ dowel
	A 6″×6″ piece of green plastic screening
	A 2″×8″ piece of ping-pong (or similar) netting
	A dozen 2″ finishing nails
	A 1′ piece of string

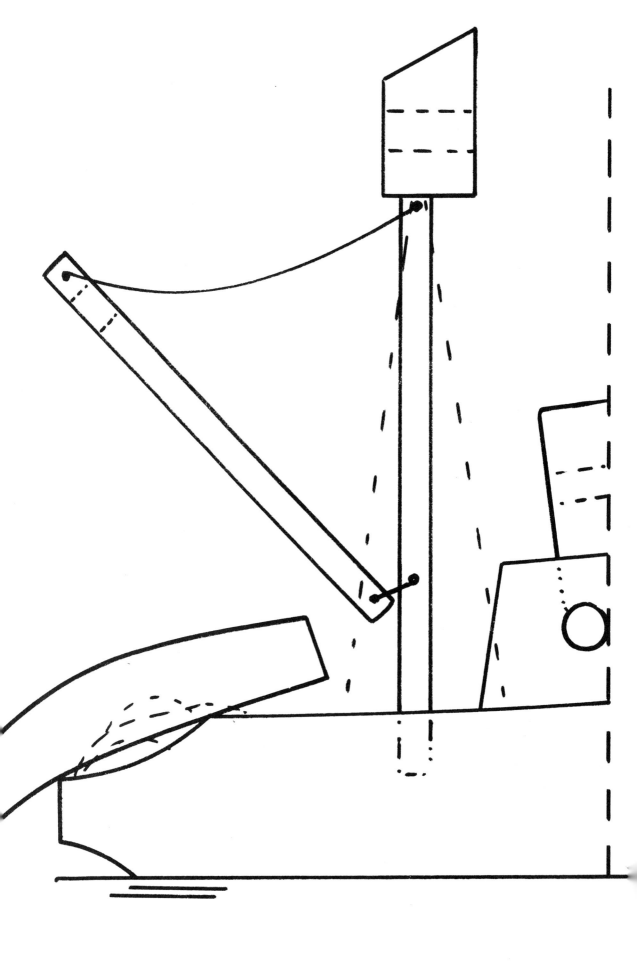

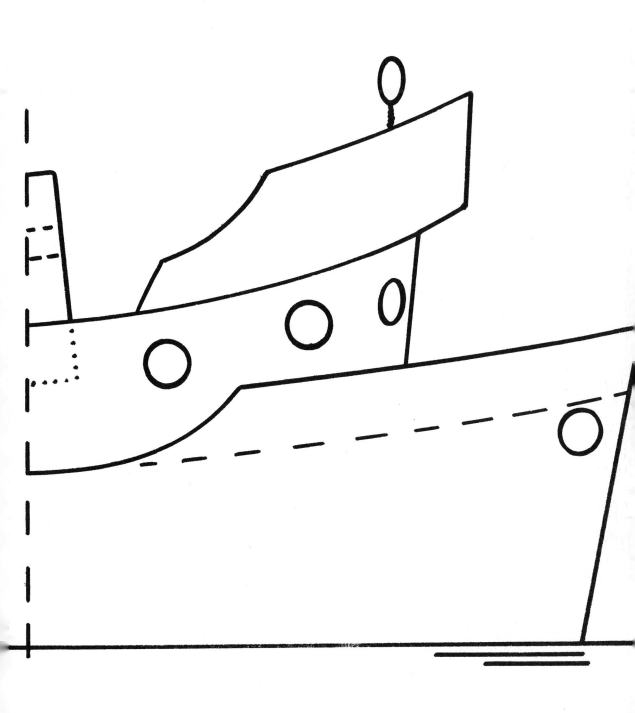

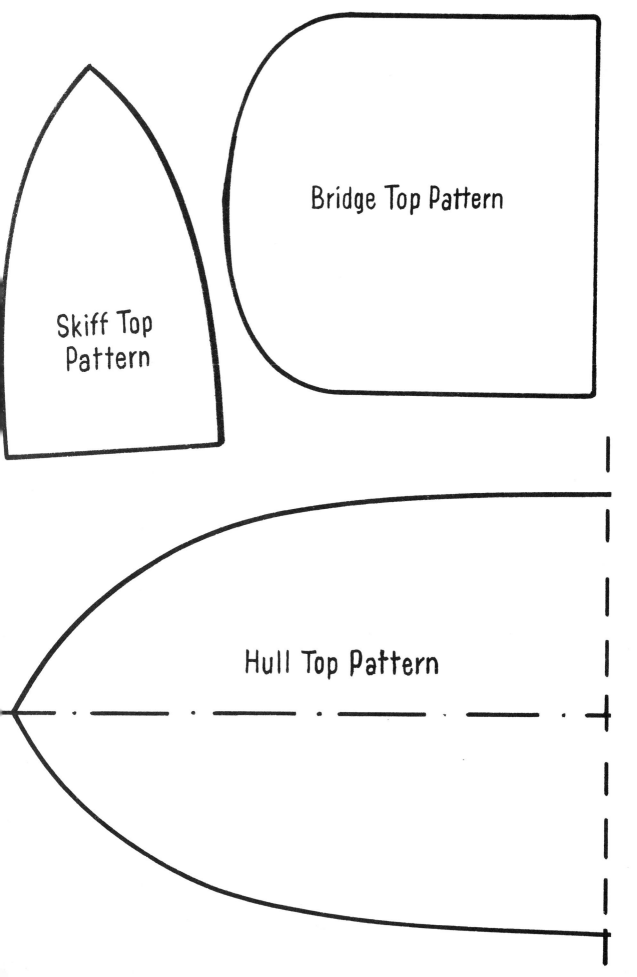

Skiff Top Pattern

Bridge Top Pattern

Hull Top Pattern

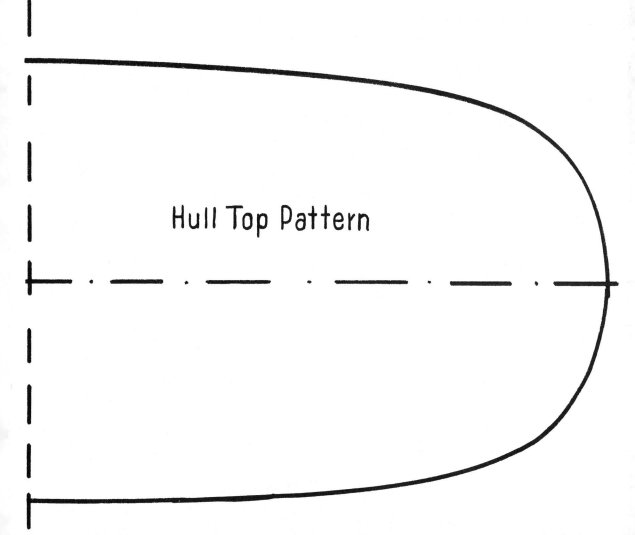

Deckhouse Top Pattern

Hull Top Pattern

Chapter 17

The Barn

Without a good barn, the best-equipped farm—even a toy farm—looks like nothing more than a loose collection of animals and machinery. So what the eager young agronomist needs most to get him started down the straight and narrow is a good barn in which to store his more agricultural playthings.

This offering is scaled to fit most toy-tractor sizes and sports not only doors that open and slide, but also a roof that lifts off so you can get to the lofts, and a hoist for getting things into the lofts in the first place.

Step One: Cutting

The sides and floors are cut from ⅜″ plywood. A ¼″ plywood can be used, making the barn lighter, but gussets would have to be placed at the corners, making it harder to put together.

Mark onto the plywood the dimensions of the two side walls, the two end walls, the lofts, roof braces, and floor, and cut these out with a carpenter's handsaw, a portable electric saw or a table saw. To mark on the outline of the first end wall, draw a squared center line, then plot the positions of the angles down and out from this. Use the first wall as a pattern for drawing the second.

Now mark the dimensions of the four roof pieces on ⅛″- or ¼″-thick masonite, or ¼″-thick plywood. The top vents are cut from 2″×2″ stock with a band, jig, saber or coping saw.

Next rip out four pieces of 1′-long stripping, about ½″ thick and ¾″ wide.

Mark the positions of the end doors, side doors, end window and side

170

windows, as shown. Cut these out with a saber, keyhole, jig or band saw. If
you have a saber or keyhole saw, drill a ⅜″ starter hole in the windows and
then cut them out; or cut a line straight down the wall and into one side of
the window. When cutting out the doors, try to save the cutout piece to be
used as the door. Otherwise (if the saw wanders) cut new ones to fit the
openings.

To give the effect of boards on all the walls, cut ⅛″-deep grooves with a
carpenter's saw, extending vertically up all wall areas, and spaced about
⅝″ apart. This can also be carefully done on a table saw or with a hacksaw.

Step Two: Assembling

The four 1′-long strips of wood are to form slides for the side doors. Place
the floor of the barn in front of you, with one end toward you. Nail one of
the strips to the floor about ½″ in from the right side and flush with the
far end. Now nail the other strip to the floor about ½″ in from the left side

171

and flush with the near end. Bend the nails over, or snip them off, if they stick through the bottom. Use white glue at all joints, of course.

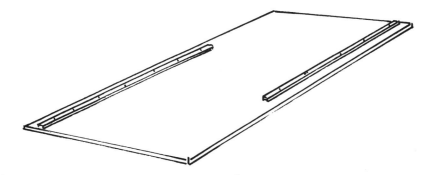

To nail the other strips to the bottoms of the lofts, place a loft on a flat surface in front of you with one end toward you. Nail a strip about ½″ in from the left side, flush with the far end. Then repeat this process for the other loft.

The sides can now be glued and nailed to the barn floor at the lower edge.

Nail through the end walls into the ends of the sides and the floor. Now place a loft, with the slide on the bottom and next to the side wall inside the barn. The lofts should be level and ⅜″ above the top of the side doors. Nail in through the side and end walls to attach the lofts.

Attach the fixed side of the roof by nailing down through the roof pieces and into the tops of the walls. If you're using textured masonite, attach the roof pieces with the textured side up. Nail the removable roof pieces to the angled side of the two roof braces, with the braces mounted 4″ in from either end.

The top vent pieces are mounted on the top edge of the removable roof

172

side. Drill two ⅛″ screw holes about ¾″ down from the top edge of this roof side, and about 5″ in from both ends. Place the bottom V-notch of a roof vent over the top edge of the roof, with one of the wings of the bottom V-notch over one of the holes. Then sink a short wood screw in through this hole, and into the bottom of the vent (using glue, of course). Repeat, to attach the other vent. Now the removable side of the roof can be fitted on the barn by hooking the bottom V-notches of the vents over the top of the fixed roof.

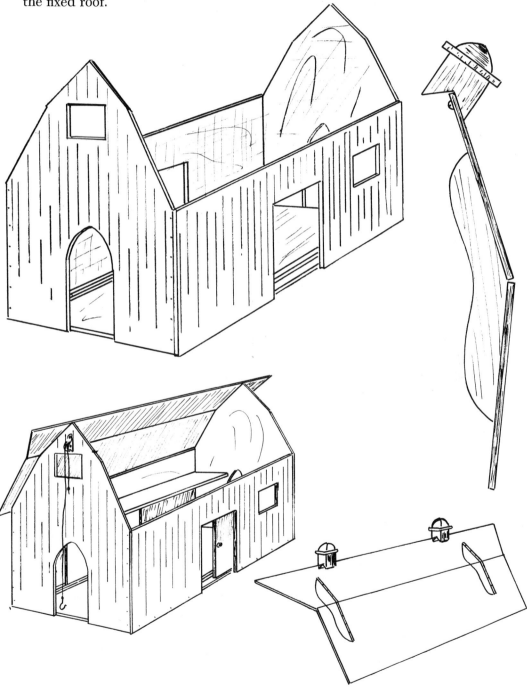

The side doors can be slipped in through the door openings and into sliding position. Place a tack or short nail in the track to keep the door from sliding out when fully closed. The end doors can be attached with small, 3/4"-square brass hinges. Nails or tacks can be used as door handles.

Sand the barn inside and out to remove possible splinters. Then paint the walls, as well as the sides of the vents, what else?—barn red. The roof and tops of the vents are green, and the trim around the doors is white.

A hoist is made from a wire hook, a piece of string, and a pulley from a curtain slide or sliding-door wheel, and can be mounted above the end window for storing away a winter's supply of toys. And don't forget a hex sign to be painted on the end wall to keep out the evil spirits.

LUMBER LIST
for the
BARN

A 4' × 4' piece of 3/8" plywood
A 2' × 2' piece of 1/8" masonite or 1/4" plywood
A 2' length of 1" × 4" stock, any wood
A 6" length of 2" × 2" stock
Six 1" wood screws
Three dozen 1 1/2" nails
Eight 3/4"-square brass hinges
One small pulley with a mounting hole

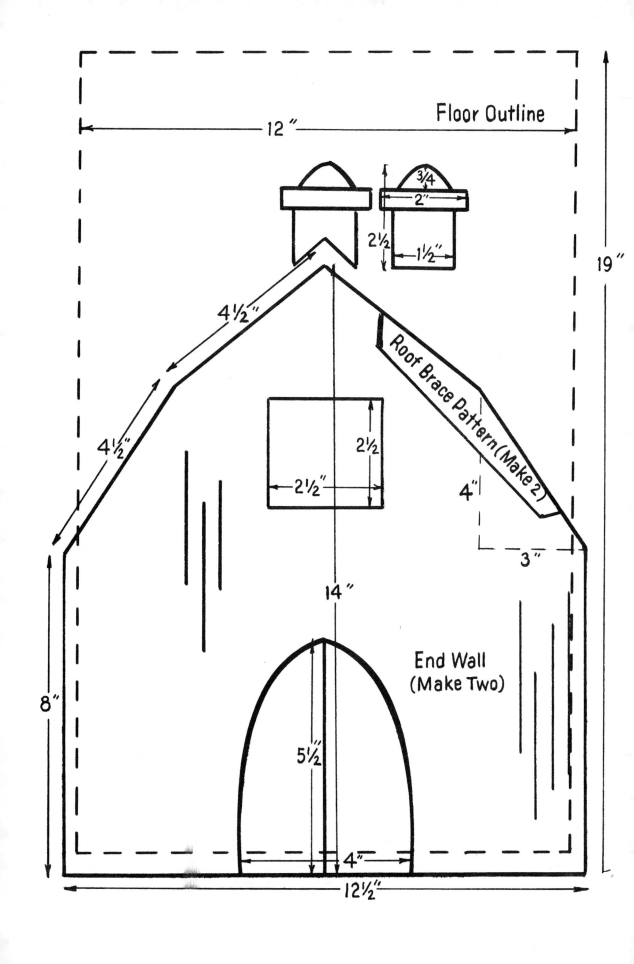

Floor Outline

12 "

19 "

3/4

2"

2½

1½ "

4½ "

4½ "

Roof Brace Pattern (Make 2)

2½

2½ "

4 "

3 "

14 "

End Wall
(Make Two)

8 "

5½ "

4 "

12½ "

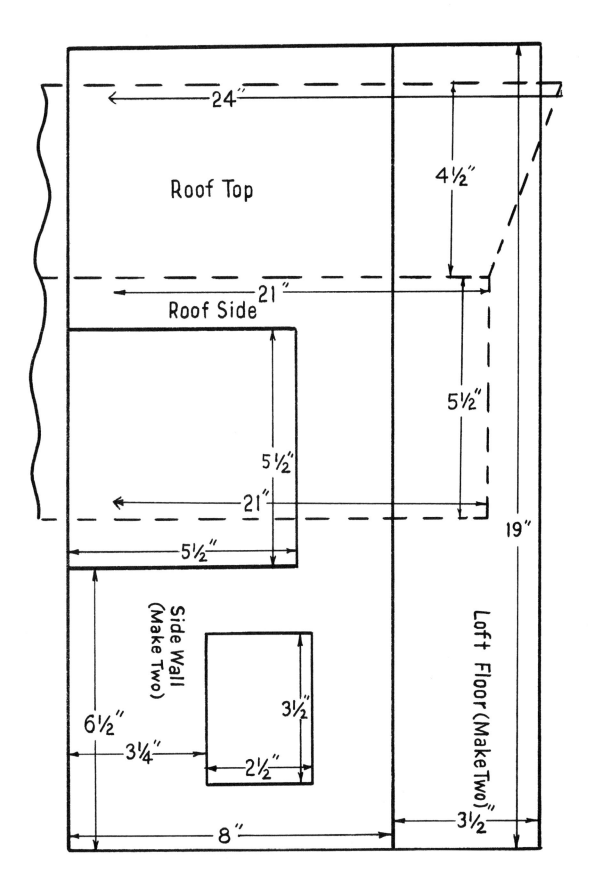

Roof Top

24"

4½"

Roof Side

21"

5½"

5½"

21"

5½"

19"

Side Wall
(Make Two)

Loft Floor (Make Two)

6½"

3¼"

3½"

2½"

3½"

8"

Chapter 18

The Airplane
Teeter-Totter

Old airplanes fascinate kids and so do teeter-totters, so what we've come up with here is a combination teeter-totter/airplane we think will make the most hard-core young victim of boredom prick up his (or her) ears and say, "Gosh! Here's a toy worth spending some time with!" In fact, we had a hard time keeping kids out of it while we were trying to finish the thing.

If you have ever been hit by the urge to join the birds and feel the rush of the wind in your face, the pull of the wings, lifting you up over the fields to swoop through the fleecy clouds of spring, etc., then you can understand the kids' fascination with airplanes—especially the old planes. It was the smaller, more personal open-air jobs that seemed to cry out to be bounced from one wheat field to another and gave birth to a whole generation of barnstormers.

These wandering braves of the air would flit from farm town to farm town, giving rides at so much a pound to any right-thinking locals who were bursting with zeal to become part of the "Air Age." Territories were closely guarded and frequently fought over by these early airmen, and any new section of the country that hadn't already been picked over by barnstormers was money in the pocket of an enterprising aviator.

But of course, years of thumping down into unfamiliar potato fields, and huddling under the wings during all-night thunderstorms, and fighting off herds of hungry cattle, all lusting after a meal of wing fabric, took their

toll. And many a rosy-cheeked lad who set out on a gypsy life of barn-storming returned home with a leathery squint and a repertoire of strange oaths.

This refugee from those distant flying-circus days serves as both a plane that the young barnstormer can climb into and in his imagination soar off o'er the treetops, or a toy that he can use as a teeter-totter. When he has friends and relations in, they can sit on the tips of the wings (which pivot like a teeter-totter) and get a bit of exercise. And the whole machine unbolts and comes apart for easy storage.

If there happen to be three teeter-totterers, the third gets a free ride in the cockpit as the wing riders do the work.

Almost all of the plane is made from a 4′×8′ sheet of ⅜″ plywood. Mark on the dimensions of the straight cuts of the parts. Then sketch in the curves. The parts for the engine and the propeller are cut from a 4′×4′ sheet of ¾″ thick plywood. When drawing on the circles, drill two small holes through a yardstick or any thin stick, positioning the holes as far apart as the radius of the circle is long. Stick a nail through one hole and onto the plywood, then insert the tip of a pencil through the other hole, and draw the circle around the nail held in the center.

Step One: Cutting

Using a portable electric circular saw, or a carpenter's handsaw, cut out the parts for the fuselage and the tail, making the straight cuts and rough-cutting the curves outside the lines. Then make the final curved cuts with a band, saber, jig or coping saw. The dotted circle marked on the second bulkhead should be cut out to permit added foot room.

To allow the sides of the fuselage to bend back to the tail, the insides of both side pieces are scored. Cut vertical grooves about ⅛″ deep and 1½″ apart up the *insides* of both side pieces, using a carpenter's handsaw or a portable circular saw. It's not important that these cuts be neat or parallel,

178

but make sure you have the grooves on the opposite surfaces of both sides, so you don't end up with two left sides. Cut the first vertical groove about 4″ forward of the tail end. Then progress forward, spacing the grooves as described until you reach the back of the seat.

Step Two: Assembling the Fuselage Box

Most of the joints in the fuselage are butt joints, with the edge of one piece running up against the side of another, and screws sunk in through the side and into the edge grain. To make it easier to sink the screws into the center of the edge grain, take the time to draw a line on the side piece, marking the position of the edge of the other piece. Then drill ⅛″-diameter screw holes along this line to guide the screws into the center of the edge. When attaching the edge of a piece, line up and sink the two end screws first, then the other screws along the line will automatically fall into place. Use plenty of white glue at every joint, except where a reason is given not to.

First mark with a straight edge the positions of the bulkheads, dashboard, and seat assembly on the outside of one side. The line for the front bulkhead should be positioned about ¼″ back from the front of the side piece. The back bulkhead should be flush with the front of the wing cuts on its back side. Now place one side piece directly over the other, and drill the screw holes along these lines, spacing them three to four inches apart. Countersink the screw holes on the outside, if you like. Drill the two ¼″ holes at the rear end of the side pieces for the tail skid.

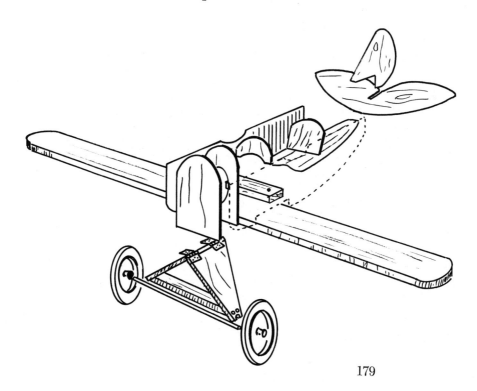

Using 1¼″-long, Number 8, flathead wood screws, attach the side edges of the first and second bulkheads to the *inside* of one side. Next, attach the seat bottom to the seat back, leaving it loose enough to slant back, as shown, and then attach the seat back and the seat bottom (only as far back as the seat back) to the side piece. Now, before these joints get too dry, attach the other side edges of these pieces to the other side piece in the same way. Pull the tail ends of the side pieces together, and bolt them together through the ¼″ holes with 4″-long bolts, threaded to the head. Now screws can be run into the edges of the seat bottom, behind the seat back. Attach the dashboard in place wih two screws on either side.

The curved top of the fuselage, in front and back of the cockpit, is covered with 1″×¼″ slats. Attach the top, center slat to the top of the front bulkhead with glue and 1″ galvanized box nails. Then bend the slat back down to touch the top of the dashboard, and glue and nail there. Cut off the slat about 4″ behind the dashboard. Attach the other front slats the same way, down to both sides. The bottom slat on each side will have to be cut into a wedge shape to fit against the top of the side.

Once the front slats are on, cut off a 13″ length of hardwood 2″×3″ stock and position it between the sides, under the seat, and flush with the top of the wing cutouts; then sink screws (with glue) through the side pieces and into the ends of the 2″×3″. Also cut out the tail skid from the 2″×3″ stock. Then prop the fuselage up on a bench, with the tail hanging out over the edge. Mark and drill the bolt holes through the tail skid, then unbolt the tail and glue the skid. Sandwich the skid between the side pieces, and bolt tightly, using spacer wedges at the front of the skid if need be.

Now the slats covering the top rear of the fuselage can be attached in the same way the front slats were nailed on, cutting off the back ends of the slats flush with the sides of the fuselage.

With a carpenter's handsaw, cut off the front ends of the rear slats flush with the seat back. Cut off the fronts of the front slats flush with the first bulkhead. Mark a curve, as shown, forming the front of the cockpit. Then, with a coping saw, saber saw or very carefully with the portable circular saw, cut off the rear ends of the front slats in the curve, running about 2″ behind the dashboard at the front, and blending back down into the cockpit cuts in the tops of the sides.

Step Three: The Front End

Mark the circles for the cowl and the spinner, as well as the engine, propeller, and landing-gear parts, onto the 4′×4′ piece of ¾″ plywood. Cut these pieces out. Drill three screw holes in through the round cowl piece, and then attach this piece to the front bulkhead, flush with the slats, and round off the edge of the cowl with a shaper. With a ⅜″ bit, drill a hole through the center point of the cowl, and on through the bulkhead. Then drill ⅜″ center holes through the engine, spinner, and propeller. Round off

180

the edge of the spinner to a flat, bowl shape, and then round off the edges of the propeller, also with the shaper.

Step Four: The Landing Gear and Wing

Cut the axle carrier to the length shown, with the 45° end cuts. Then cut a ½"-wide groove down the center of the longer bottom side, about ½" deep.

Butt the tops of the landing-gear sides, with the longer side overlapping the edge of the shorter one, and drill screw holes through the longer piece, and into the edge of the shorter. With glue, screw these pieces together. Now place the angled ends of the axle carrier between the lower insides of the landing-gear side pieces, and drill through both side piecs with a ¼" bit, extending the holes down through the ends of the axle carrier on both sides of the axle groove. With glue and four 2½"-long, ¼"-diameter, round-head bolts, attach the axle carrier to the sides of the landing gear.

Next, place two 3"-square butt hinges or two strap hinges (brass or galvanized) so that the hinge pins lie along the apex of the landing-gear triangle formed by the sides and axle carrier. Both hinges should lie with one half on the same side of the landing gear so that the hinge pins will lie along one axis.

The wing is cut from a 10' length of 2"x12" fir stock. Trim off the semicircular ends, then mark a center line across the midpoint where the board will balance. Then place the board with the center line up, and attach the other halves of the hinges to the bottom of the wing so that the hinge pins lie along this line. Cut off a 26"-long piece of ⁷⁄₁₆"-diameter iron rod, and drill ⅛" cotter-pin holes through it about ⅜" in from both ends. Then place the rod in the axle groove and hold it in place either with nails driven part way in and then bent over the axle, or with short strips of metal or wood over the axle, just to hold it in place when the plane is lifted.

Slip the wheels on the ends of the axle, then prop the wing up so that it sits horizontally. Lift the fuselage up over the wing and then let it down with the wing cutouts fitting over the wing. With the ⅜" bit, drill two holes down through the 2"×3" wing brace, and through the wing itself. Space these holes about 2" in from the sides of the fuselage. Bolt the wing in place with 4"-long, ⅜"-diameter, roundhead bolts. To permit an easy disassembly, don't glue the wing to the fuselage. The wing is then attached to the back bulkhead by drilling three screw holes in through the front of this bulkhead near the bottom, and running the screws through the bulkhead into the front of the wing.

Step Five: The Tail

To attach the tail surfaces (or empennage, as it's known around the airfields), place the horizontal tail surface (the stabilizer) centered over the flat tops of the fuselage sides at the rear, and draw lines on the bottom of

181

the stabilizer marking the positions of the fuselage sides. Drill two screw holes just in from these marks on both sides, and then sink screws, after gluing the tops of the sides and tail skid, down through the stabilizer into the tops of the fuselage sides. Drill two more screw holes, and sink screws down into the top of the tail skid.

Place the rudder in position, and sink two screw holes angled down through the side of the rudder at the bottom, and into the stabilizer on the other side, spacing the screws about 6" apart. Then, from the other side sink a third hole between the other two, down through the side of the rudder near the bottom and just into the stabilizer. With glue and 2" or 2½" screws, attach the rudder to the stabilizer. Square the rudder from the front, then carefully drill a screw hole in through the back edge of the rudder, below the stabilizer, and sink a long, narrow screw in through the edge of the rudder and into the back of the fuselage and tail skid.

Step Six: Shaping

Round off all exposed edges, especially the tail and wing edges, and smooth off all potential splinters with a shaper. Sand the plane thoroughly all over, since enterprising wing walkers end up riding it in every conceivable position.

Step Seven: Painting

Paint the slats, dashboard, and propeller with a dark stain, and then wipe. The stained surfaces can be given a couple of coats of satin-finish varnish to keep the grain looking nice. Paint the fuselage sides, the stabilizer, and the rudder a bright, sky blue with two coats of gloss enamel.

Then the wing, landing gear, wheels, cowl, spinner, seat, and cockpit sides can be painted with a couple of coats of deep gold-yellow gloss enam-

182

el. Spray the engine flat black. To install abstract instrument dials on the dashboard, remove both ends of a soup can and place one end of the can firmly against the dashboard in position. Now spray flat black into the open end of the can, holding the nozzle about an inch away from the end of the can. It takes only two or three short squirts—any more will end up in drips. Hold the can in place for a few seconds after spraying, then remove the can, and *voila!* one dial, if a little abstract. Repeat until you have a full complement of instruments.

Step Eight: Final Assembling

Insert a 4"-long, ⅜"-diameter, roundhead bolt through the hole in the engine, and then into the hole in the front of the cowl. Drill three screw holes in through the engine spaced around it about 3" out from the center. Screw the engine to the front of the cowl, with one cylinder centered at the top. Now remove the bolt, insert it through the spinner, and back into the hole in the engine. Space three screw holes around the center of the spinner, and attach it to the front of the engine.

Remove the bolt once more, and run the ⅜" bit through the hole in the center of the front of the plane a few times to clean it out. With a ½" bit, evenly space eight ¼"-deep holes around the propeller center, 3" out from the center hole. Place dabs of glue in these holes and tap ½" roundhead wood plug buttons tightly into them. Insert the ⅜" bolt through the front of the prop, and then in through the hole in the front of the plane. Place a washer on the other end of the bolt, then run on a nut and a locknut and tighten against each other, leaving the prop free to turn.

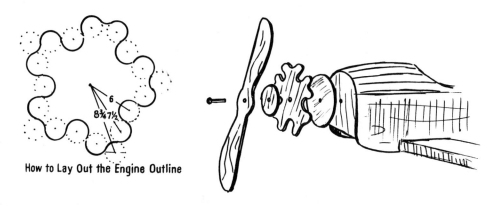

How to Lay Out the Engine Outline

Fasten the wheels in place with washers and cotter pins.

To put the red, white, and blue stripes on the rudder use a roll of red and a roll of white 1½"-wide plastic tape. Place the white tape, running it back from about the middle of the rudder, 1½" up from the stabilizer, around the back of the rudder, and then up to about the middle of the other side horizontally. Place the bottom edge of the red tape 1½" above the top of the white tape and alternate strips of red and white up the sides of the

183

rudder. Then place the short side of a square on the stabilizer, point the long vertical side of the square running up the side of the rudder to the peak. Cut off the ends of the tape along this line, using a razor blade.

Now it's about time to roll her out onto the field where Tailspin Tommy, Skeeter and the rest of the flying circus can yell, "Contact" and "Switch on" and "Say, listen, where'd you learn to fly like that?!" until dinnertime brings their interests back down to earth.

LUMBER LIST
for the
AIRPLANE/
TEETER-TOTTER

One 4′×8′ sheet of ⅜″-thick, exterior, A/C grade plywood
One 4′×4′ sheet of ¾″-thick, exterior, A/C grade plywood
One 5′ length of 2″×3″ hardwood stock
One 10′ length of 2″×12″ fir stock
Four 8′ lengths of 1″×¼″ slat
Two 12″ tricycle or soapbox-derby wheels
One 3′ length of $\frac{7}{16}$″-diameter iron rod
Two 3″ square butt hinges or large strap hinges
Three 4″-long, ⅜″-diameter, roundhead bolts, with four nuts and washers
Four 2½″-long, ¼″-diameter, roundhead bolts with nuts
Two 2½″ flathead screws
One thin 4″-long flathead screw
Eight ½″-diameter, roundhead wood plug buttons
Two $\frac{7}{16}$″ washers and two cotter pins

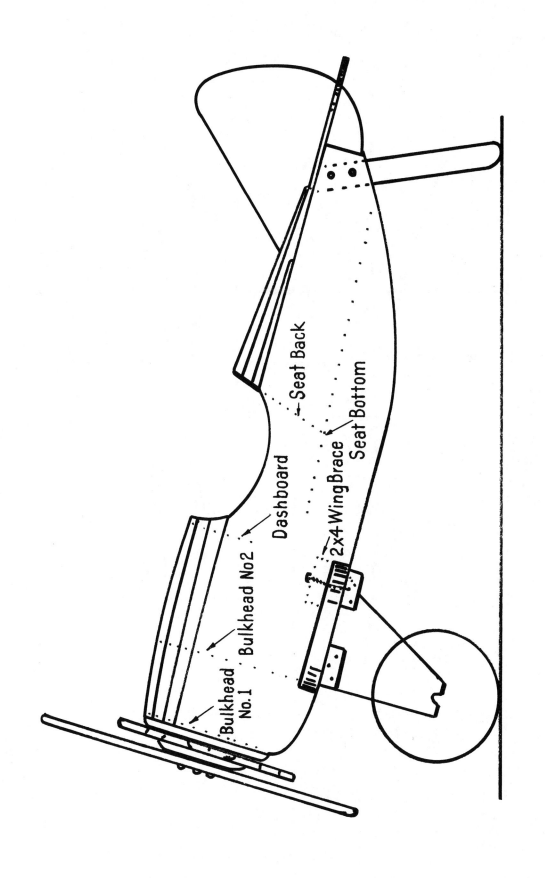

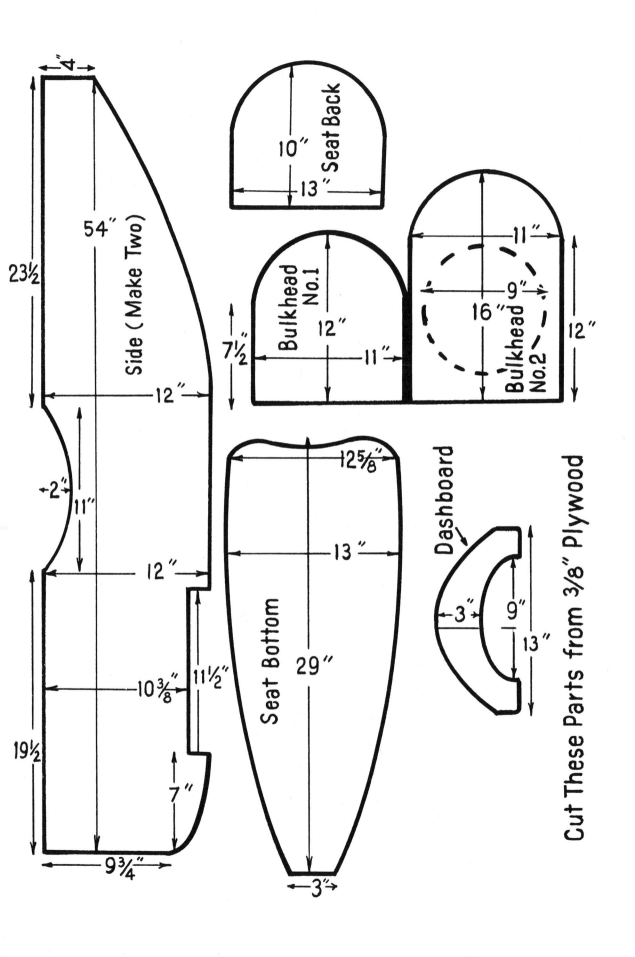

Side (Make Two)

4"

54"

23½

12"

2"

11"

12"

19½

10⅜"

11½"

7"

9¾"

Seat Back

10"

13"

Bulkhead No.1

12"

11"

7½

Bulkhead No.2

11"

9"

16"

12"

Seat Bottom

12⅝"

13"

29"

3"

Dashboard

3"

9"

13"

Cut These Parts from ⅜" Plywood

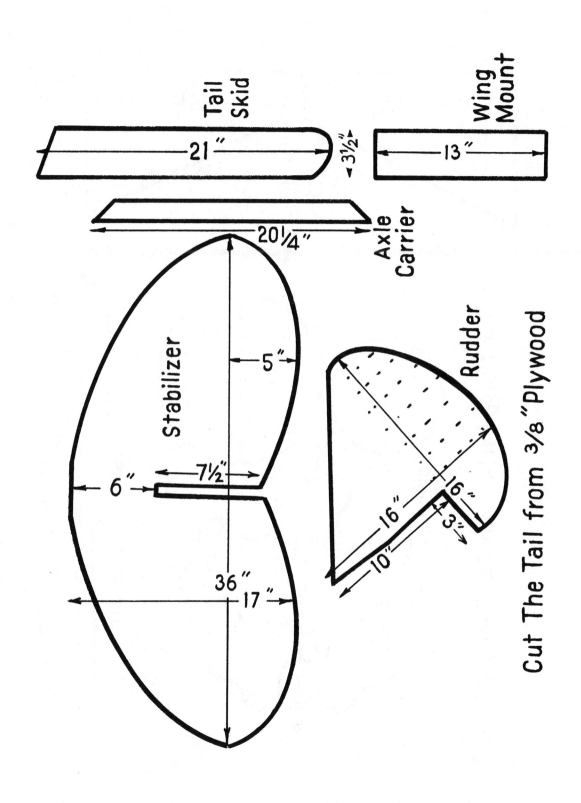

Tail Skid

21″

3½″

Wing Mount

13″

Axle Carrier

20¼″

Stabilizer

5″

7½″

6″

36″

17″

Rudder

16″

16″

16″

3″

10″

Cut The Tail from 3/8 ″Plywood

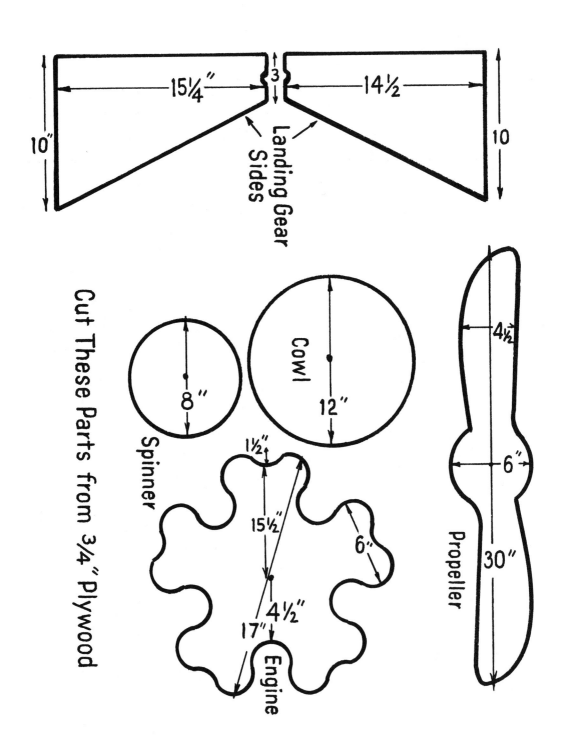

15¼"

3

14½"

10"

Landing Gear
Sides

10

Cut These Parts from 3/4" Plywood

8"

Spinner

Cowl

12"

4½

1½"

15½"

6"

4½"

17"

Engine

6"

Propeller

30"

Chapter 19

The Wheelbarrow

The wheelbarrow is a simple, sturdy, useful tool that no self-respecting young tiller of the soil should be without. This one is taken from an old English illustration and has stood the test of time without a flinch. It can be made from any wood you happen to fancy working with.

Step One: Cutting

Mark the basic dimensions, then sketch the outlines of the parts onto a 6' length of 1"×10" stock. Next mark the outlines for one frame handle and one leg on one of the 4' lengths of 2"×4" stock. Cut these pieces out, using a band, jig, saber or coping saw. Use these pieces as patterns to cut one more frame handle and one more leg from the other length of 2"×4".

Step Two: Drilling

With the ⅜" bit, drill four holes into the outside of the wheelbarrow box sides, equally spaced with the centers about ⅜" deep. Drill the box sides positioned in opposite directions so you don't end up with two left sides to the box. Now drill three more holes in the sides in the same manner, equally spaced about ⅜" in from the front edges of the sides.

Step Three: Assembling the Box

On a flat surface, place the box front piece and one of the side pieces, bottom edges down, then run a line of white glue down the end edge of the end piece; butt the end piece up against the side piece, flush with the end,

189

and sink 1¼″ flathead wood screws in through the holes in the side and into the edge of the end piece. Repeat this to attach the other side to the front. Now run a line of glue around the side and front edges of the box bottom piece, insert the bottom against the sides and front, flush with the bottom edges, and then sink screws in through the holes along the bottom of the sides and into the edges of the bottom piece. Drill three ⅜″ holes near the bottom of the front side of the box, and sink screws in through these holes into the front edge of the bottom piece.

Step Four: Attaching the Frame

Insert the notched part of the frame handle into the notched part of the leg. Now drill a ⅛″ screw hole through the handle where the handle overlaps the legs, and then countersink this with the ⅜″ bit about 1″ deep. Place glue on the joining surfaces and screw the handle to the leg. Repeat this performance on the other leg-handle set, but with the leg on the other side of the handle so you don't end up with two left-hand sets.

Place the top of the handle frame against the bottom of the box bottom so that the handles extend back behind the side a little less than 6″, and so that the front corner of the box hangs out over the side of the frame about 1¼″. Now drill three countersunk holes down into the top of the bottom piece, and after gluing, sink three screws down through the bottom piece

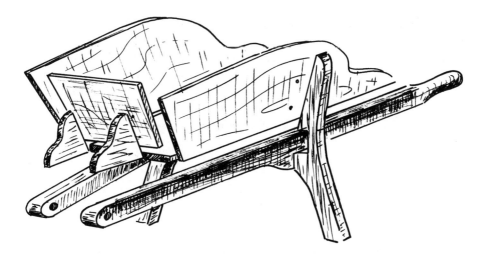

and into the top of the frame, checking the position, and making sure that the inside of the leg piece rests against the outside of the side piece. Drill another $\frac{3}{8}''$-diameter, $\frac{3}{8}''$-deep countersunk hole into the inside of the side piece, and sink a screw through the side and into the leg.

Repeat this to attach the other leg-frame assembly in the same relative position, so that the insides of the frames at the very front are 2″ apart.

Now attach the corner braces between the box front piece and the tops of the frames, drilling countersunk holes into the back side of the front piece of the box, directly over the frames, about $1\frac{1}{4}''$ up from the bottom piece. Sink a screw through each hole and into the braces, with all joining surfaces glued, of course.

Now, with a jig, hack or table saw, cut off about two dozen short stubs of $\frac{3}{8}''$ dowel, no longer than $\frac{3}{8}''$. After placing a dab of glue in every countersunk hole, tap the stubs of dowel down into the holes until flush with the wood.

Step Five: Shaping

With a wood rasp or a shaper, round off all exposed edges, especially around the tops of the wheelbarrow box. The handles, up to the backs of the sides, should be completely rounded, forming comfortable grips. Sand all surfaces to remove potential splinters.

Step Six: Finishing

When the wheelbarrow is shaped, drill a $\frac{3}{8}''$ hole through the side of each frame, 1″ back from the front of the frame piece, so that both holes are aligned, for the axle bolt. Insert the 5″-long, $\frac{3}{8}''$-diameter axle bolt through the hole in one frame, then through the center hole in the wheel, and finally through the hole in the other frame, tightening the nut securely.

Now the wheelbarrow can be stained, varnished, painted or antiqued to your taste. The example pictured was first stained with a dark walnut stain, then wiped, and finally varnished with satin-finish varnish.

191

LUMBER LIST One 6' length of 1″×10″ stock
for the Two 4' pieces of 2″×4″ stock
WHEELBARROW Two dozen 1¼″, Number 8, flathead wood screws
A 1' piece of ⅜″-diameter wood dowel
A 5″-long, ⅜″-diameter hexagonal-head bolt with
nut
One 8″-diameter tricycle wheel

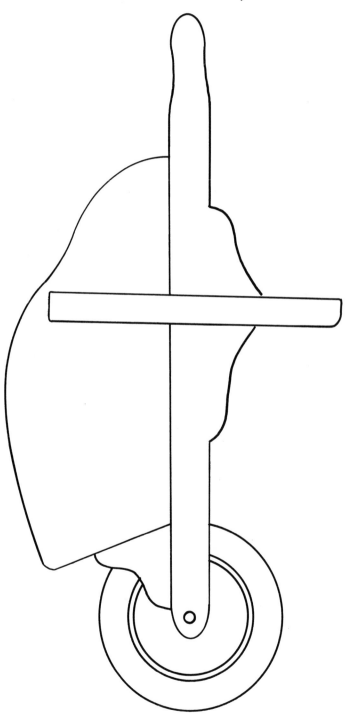

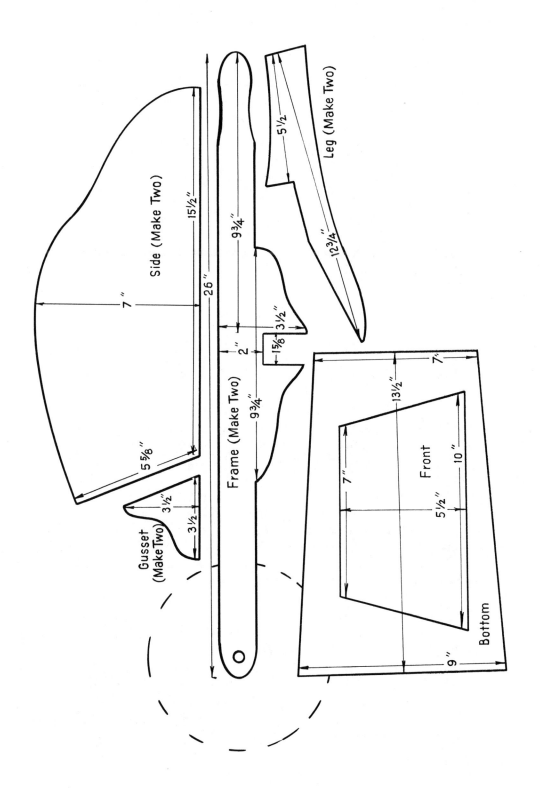

Side (Make Two)

15½"

7"

26"

5⅝"

Gusset (Make Two)

3½"

3½"

Frame (Make Two)

9¾"

9¾"

2"

1⅝"

3½"

Leg (Make Two)

5½"

12¾"

Front

13½"

7"

5½"

10"

7"

9"

Bottom

Chapter 20

The Castle

The castle project is a little ambitious for the scope of this book. It always seems to excite comment, however, so we've included a brief explanation for those hardy souls with lots of free time and tenacity.

The design is a genuine composite, taking a turret here, a crenellation there, to try to capture a good, well-rounded taste of the days of yore. The short towers around the gateway (portcullis, for the purists) are Old English. The front wall and main front towers are later Italian, the rear towers are French, and the gabled house on top is Swiss.

The general layout could be copied in wood, using squared towers throughout, so we're also including a couple of plan views for those who would like to pursue that route.

The example pictured was made out of a material we happened upon which we call "supercrete." It's an extremely hard but heavy casting material which can be mixed in a bucket and which sets rock-hard, without firing, in about one hour.

To make a mold for the castle, a wood and foam mock-up was covered with plaster, and the walls and roof surfaces were smoothed flat. Then the details of the blocks, windows, and roof shingles were carved in. The finished surface of the plaster was then painted lightly with a thin gloss paint. Next the mock-up was divided into three sections that would be cast separately: the main bottom box; the roofed house and side towers; and the tower roof.

194

Each of these sections was given about five to seven coats of latex rubber mold material, which is painted on with a brush.

Next each of the mold sections was backed up with about 2″ of supercrete to form a buck which would hold the rubber mold in shape when the actual casting was made.

To make this magic mixture, mix up a *very* hot (lots of catalyst) batch of polyester (fiber glass) casting resin. Then add enough beach sand so that the mixture is no longer soupy, but still not too stiff to work with.

The supercrete was then packed around the outside of the rubber mold and allowed to go off (harden). (Actually, the buck from the large, bottom-box part of the mold was made with dividers at the corners so that it could be taken apart, and put back together again, to get the piece out without breaking the mold.)

195

Once the supercrete had hardened to its customary hard, heavy mass, the bucks were pulled off the latex molds. Then the molds were peeled off the plaster mock-ups, and the rubber molds cleaned of any bits of plaster that had broken off.

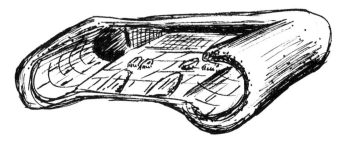

Next the cleaned-out molds were replaced inside the supercrete bucks, and a new batch of supercrete was mixed. This was packed into the tower-top mold about an inch thick, and then packed onto the front wall of the bottom mold and the front wall and front roof side of the house mold, about

½″ thick. When this batch went off, the molds were rotated, and the tower top was pulled from the mold.

Then a new batch was mixed, another tower top cast, and the rest was packed into one side wall of the bottom box, and into the rear roof side of the house mold, and up the sides to meet the first packing.

Then, at long last, a final, smaller batch was mixed, the box mold was rotated, and the final third wall of the castle bottom was packed with supercrete. When this went off, about an hour later, the mold was turned toward the sun to cure for a few hours. Because of the amount of sand, the mixture cures slowly compared to unmixed resin, and is rather spongy if taken out too soon. In fact, it won't really appear to have much strength at all until a few days later when the resign begins to shrink in earnest around the sand, and the substance slowly gets harder and harder, ending somewhere between stoneware and cast iron.

When the sides were deemed reasonably rigid, the bucks were taken off, the molds peeled off, and there for the world to see were all the mistakes we'd made along the line. On about the third try, however, it began to look like what we had in mind with the mock-up. The components were then glued together with more supercrete and plywood floors were inserted and held in place with that mystical stuff. Once the castle was in one piece, the roof surfaces were painted bright orange-red, then the whole castle was antiqued by painting with a thin, dark brown paint and then wiping with a rag, which brought out all the laborious detail and made a nice, rich tone for the roofs.

A chessboard, made from small black and white squares cut from floor tiles, was glued to the upper floor with linoleum paste. And small holes were drilled down into the tops of the tower roofs, and nails inserted to serve as flagstaffs.

It takes a bit of work, it's true, but it may last awhile, if that's any consolation. And even if you have little inclination to spend so much time on one project, the development of supercrete, with all its strange new properties, may inspire you with new ideas on how to use it for entirely new, heretofore unthought-of purposes.

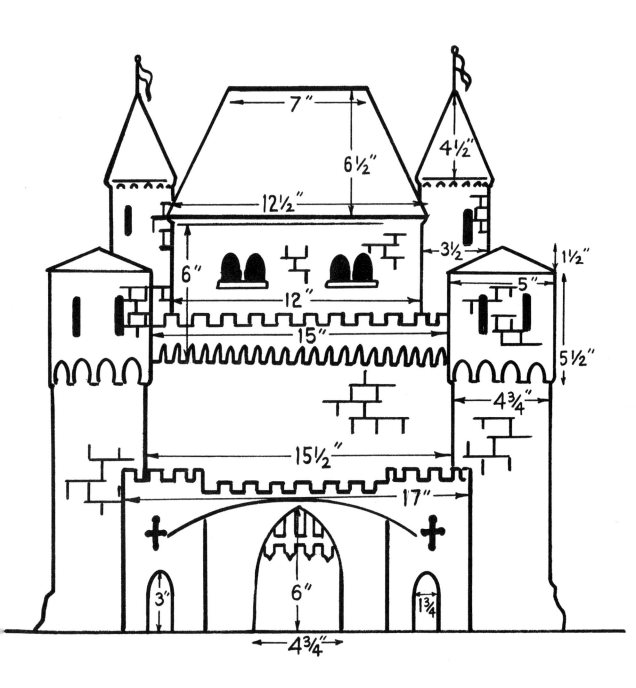

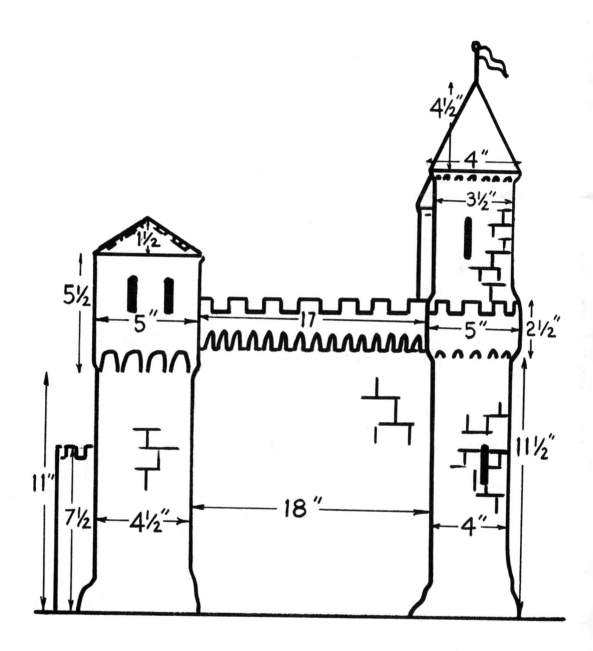

Chapter 21

The Gypsy Wagon

Rumor has it that gypsies are supposed to be crazy about making off with the kids in the neighborhood. Now, whether this is a lunatic plan or not is open to debate. But just to be on the safe side, we've come up with a child-sized version of the gypsy's wagon to help satisfy that urge to travel o'er the distant horizons, to trudge down new roads, and then to pull up at night in a cozy little home away from home. In off seasons, between forays to the far end of the yard and back, this wagon can be used as a gypsy dollhouse or simply as a portable toy bin.

Over the centuries the design of the traditional gypsy wagon slowly improved until by the end of the last century they had become extremely well made and well thought out. While remaining light and strong, they still sported lavish decorations (after all, with no yard work, how else could a gypsy be kept from enjoying a lazy Saturday afternoon?).

To make this combination dollhouse/wagon/toy bin, start by marking the dimensions of the side walls and end walls on a $4' \times 4'$ sheet of $1/4''$ plywood or paneling. Try to mark the dimensions on the better side of the plywood, with the side panels opposed so you don't end up with two left sides.

Step One: The Basic Box

Cut out the side and end walls with a carpenter's saw, portable electric saw or table saw. Mark the position of the window on one side, place the sides aligned back to back, and then drill through the $1\frac{1}{4}''$-diameter holes that form the windows, using a hole-saw attachment for the power drill.

On the back wall cut out the door hole by cutting straight down from the top edge and into one side, then around; or by making ⅜″ starter holes and using a saber or keyhole saw.

To make the framing around the sides, rip a 6′ length of 1″×8″ softwood stock into five strips, just under 1½″ wide. Place this frame stripping on the side pieces themselves in the positions shown, and cut them off to the lengths indicated. Run a line of white glue along the back of each frame piece as it's attached, and nail through the back of the side piece and into the frame strips with ¾″ or 1″ nails. After all frame pieces have been nailed onto the sides, being careful not to end up with two left sides, of course, attach the frame pieces along the top and bottom edges of the end walls. Then rip a 4′ lengh of ¾″×¾″ strip from the remaining frame stripping. Cut the ¾″×¾″ strips to be attached to the side edges of the end walls, and attach these in place.

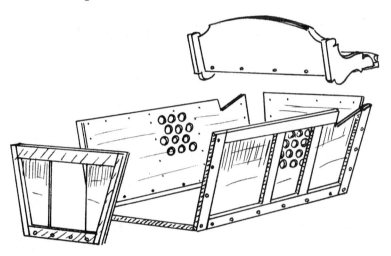

To assemble the sides of the box, 1¼″, flathead wood screws are sunk in through the side walls and into the edges of the end walls. To bring this about, drill ⅜″-diameter countersunk holes down the side walls, spaced about 4″ apart down both ends, with the centers about ⅜″ in from the ends of the walls. The ⅜″ countersunk holes should be drilled about halfway through the frame stripping.

Now, with white glue and screws, attach the back end of one side wall to the edge of the back wall, and then attach the front end to the front wall. Repeat this procedure to attach the other side.

The floor is cut from ¾″- to ½″-thick plywood or hardwood to the dimensions shown (or 1″×12″ stock can be used with a bit of stripping on the edge). Place the box on a flat surface, flop the bottom down in between the sides, drill countersunk holes around the bottoms of the sides, about ⅜″ up from the bottom edge, spaced about 5″ apart, and then attach the floor to the walls with screws and glue.

201

Step Two: The Seat

Cut the seat back, bottom, and sides from 1″×8″ softwood stock. Join the back to the back edge of the bottom with screws and glue after drilling countersunk holes about 4″ apart. Now attach the bottom to the top edge of the front wall and then attach the seat sides to the end edges of the seat back and bottom with glue and screws after drilling countersunk holes. Attach the side walls to the insides of the seat sides by nailing from inside the box, through the wall and into the seat side pieces.

Cut the flower boxes from 2″×2″ stock, and the shutters from a 36″ length of 1″×3″ stock. To make the flower boxes, rip the 2″×2″ so that, when viewed from one end, the side facing outward leans out toward the top. The box should be 1⅝″ or 1½″ wide at the top, and 1″ wide on the bottom. Drill holes in the top for pots or plastic flowers if you like. To make the shutters, mark a center line down one side of the 1″×3″, then drill a 1″ hole through the center line, 2″ from one end. Now drill four more 1″ holes through the center line, with the centers spaced 7½″ apart. Next make square cuts across the 1″×3″ through the center point of each hole to form the four shutters. Attach the flower boxes with glue and nails running through the back of the side walls and into the boxes. Attach the shutters by gluing and nailing them to the frame pieces next to the window.

The time has come to slice off ⅜″-long stubs of ⅜″-diameter wood dowel to use as plugs to fill the countersunk holes. Cut off about three or four dozen of these plugs, then place a dab of glue in each hole and tap a plug in flush with the surface of the wood.

Step Three: The Roof

To make the roof, cut the three arched bulkheads from the 1″×6″ stock, lopping off the ends of the middle one, as shown. Place the bulkheads in line on a flat surface, sitting on their bottom edges. The end bulkheads should be about 2′ apart, with the shortened bulkhead near the center and parallel with the end bulkheads. Two 20″ lengths of the 1½″-wide frame stripping should be placed on edge, between the end bulkheads and against both ends of the center bulkhead. Position the pieces as shown, and after sinking ⅛″-diameter screw holes, fasten the pieces together with screws and glue.

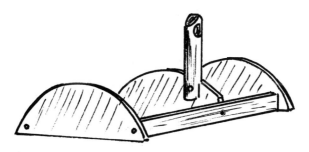

The chimney is made from a 1¼″- or 1½″-diameter wood dowel (or an old shovel or hoe handle). Drill a ⅞″-diameter hole through the dowel, then cut off the angles of the gabled end (for the gabled roof on top) about 1″ above the center of the hole. Next cut off the other end of the dowel 8″ from the gabled end. Slice off a flat surface on one side of the dowel at the bottom end so that this surface is parallel with the top line of the peaked roof. Then rest the flat surface of the dowel against the back of the center bulkhead, drill two screw holes through the bulkhead and glue and screw the chimney vertically to the back of the bulkhead and about 4″ to one side from the center. Cut small roof halves to be glued and nailed to the gable angles at the top of the chimney.

To shingle the roof, cut six 8″×24″ pieces of ⅛″ or thicker masonite or plywood. With a saber, jig, coping or band saw, cut a randomly wiggly line approximately along the center line of each piece, as shown. Then with a band, jig, or table saw or carpenter's handsaw, make the short cuts, spaced about 1½″ to 2″ apart, between the shingles, as shown. The strips of shingles can now be glued and nailed to the top edges of the roof bulkheads, starting from the bottom and overlapping, working up both sides to the top center point. Naturally, a hole will have to be cut for the chimney when you come up to it.

To cover the top joint between the two top rows of shingles, cut twenty 1½″×3″ individual shingles and attach them along the top, overlapping peaked side-by-side pairs, as you work toward the front, as shown in the photos.

Trim the front ends of the shingle strips flush with the front bulkhead.

Mark a curved back line for the roof, starting at the top about 2″ behind the rear bulkhead, curving down both sides and angling slightly toward the front. Make this cut with a saber, coping or band saw.

The roof is attached to the top of the wagon box so that it will hinge up backward for toy storage. Cut two ⅛″-deep, 1½″-long hinge notches in the top edge of the rear wall, and then attach two 2″ butt hinges, first to the top of the wall and then to the bottom of the rear roof bulkhead, with the pins to the outside. If you like, use ornamental butterfly hinges mounted to the back of the wall and the bulkhead instead.

Step Four: The Chassis

The wagon is about ready to be set on its wheels. Mark and cut the rear axle holder, front axle holder, rear braces and front brace on 2″×6″ stock. Mark the positions of the axle holes on the ends of the axle holders, then drill in from both ends with a ½″ bit. Butt the back edges of the rear braces against the front side of the rear axle holder, about 2″ in from both ends, and then sink screw holes through the axle holder and glue and screw the braces in place against the front of the holder. Attach the front brace to the center of the front axle holder in the same way.

Center the rear axle holder in place beneath the floor 3″ in front of the bottom edge of the rear wall, and then drill screw holes; glue and screw the rear holder and braces to the bottom of the wagon box. Drill a ⅜″-diameter hole down through the top of the front axle holder in the center, then drill a hole through the center line of the box bottom position for the pivot hole for the front axle holder 4″ behind the bottom edge of the front wall. Cut off a 12″ length of 1″-wide iron strap, and drill a ⅜″ hole,

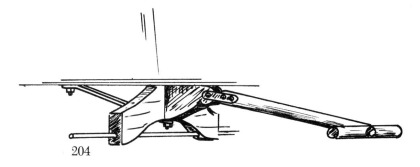

204

¾″ in from one end, and a ¼″ hole, ½″ in from the other end. Run a 7″-long, ⅜″-diameter, roundhead bolt down through the hole in the front of the box, then through a wide, ⅜″ washer, then down through the hole in the center of the front axle holder, through the larger hole in the strap, and finally attach a nut and a locknut. Extend the strap back along the center line of the bottom of the floor, and bend it up to sit flat against the bottom of the floor. With the end of the strap centered, drill a ¼″ hole through the strap hole and through the bottom of the floor. Attach this strap with a 1½″-long, ¼″-diameter, roundhead bolt inserted down from the top.

Cut a 1½″- or 1¼″-diameter tool handle or doweling to about 17″ long. Then cut off a 4″ length of the dowel and drill a ¼″ hole across the center of it. Cut one end of the long piece to a concave, semicircular shape to fit the side of the short piece, then drill a ¼″ hole into the center of it, about 1″ deep. Sink a 3″-long, ¼″-diameter lag screw through the short piece and into the end of the long piece to form a handle crossbar. (As an alternative, a short iron strap can be bent around the end of the crossbar and bolted to the handle shaft on both sides.)

Cut two 6″ lengths of 1″-wide iron strap. Drill a ¼″ hole about ½″ in from both ends of both straps. Then drill a ¼″ hole through each strap, 1½″ from each of the end holes in both straps.

Place the handle down flat on a bench top, and position the two iron straps on both sides of the handle with the single-hole ends of the straps sticking out beyond the handle about 3″. Mark the two 1½″-apart holes on the side of the handle, so that they can be drilled through parallel with the crossbar of the handle. Bolt these straps to the handle with 2″, hexagonal-head bolts. Bend these straps out and then back parallel to sit against both sides of the front axle holder brace. Now drill a ¼″ hole through this center brace to attach the ends of the strap, so that the handle can be pivoted up and fastened with a locknut.

Step Five: Finishing

Attach ¾″ × ¾″ stripping around the edges of the rear door, as shown, with glue and nails, and then fix the door to the back wall with two small, ornamental butterfly hinges.

With a wood rasp or a wood shaper, round off the edges of the seat pieces, and smooth off all edges and joints. Round off the inner corner edges of the frame pieces with the shaper or a drum power rasp. Sand off all potential splinters with medium-grade sandpaper.

Insert two 3′ (standard length) pieces of 7/16″-diameter iron rod through the axle holes. Then slip 12″-diameter tricycle wheels onto the ends of the back axle, and 8″ or 10″ "tryke" wheels onto the front axle. Cut off the axles, leaving about ½″ sticking out both sides beyond the wheel hubs, then drill ⅛″ cotter-pin holes through the ends. Fasten the wheels on with a $\frac{7}{16}''$ washer on both sides and a cotter pin through the end holes of the axles.

Of course, the variety of color schemes suitable for gypsy wagons is endless. But to color yours like the example shown, stain the chassis, box, seat, and handle with a dark walnut stain; then wipe clean and put on a coat or two of satin-finish varnish. Paint the windows, wheels, and chimney a warm yellow. Color the roof brick red and the shutters olive green. If you like, any number of the nicely cast ornamental stick-ons found at lumberyards nowadays can be used for added interest. Oh, yes, and don't forget to paint the hole in the chimney flat black.

With that, your toil is done, and it's ho, for new horizons and the rich, satisfying smell of the dusty open road, etc.—at least to the far end of the homestead.

LUMBER LIST
for the
GYPSY WAGON

Two 6′ lengths of 1″×8″ softwood stock
One 4′×4′ piece of $\frac{1}{4}''$ plywood or paneling
One 1′ length of 2″×2″ softwood stock
One 13″×24″ piece of $\frac{3}{4}''$ to $\frac{1}{2}''$ plywood or hardwood
One 6′ length of 2″×6″ stock
One 2′×4′ piece of $\frac{1}{8}''$ masonite or plywood
A 2′ length of 1″-wide iron strap
A 3′ length of $1\frac{1}{2}''$- or $1\frac{1}{4}''$-diameter dowel (or tool handle)
Two 2″ butt hinges (or ornamental butterfly hinges)
Two 1″ butterfly hinges
Four dozen $1\frac{1}{4}''$, Number 8, flathead wood screws
A 3′ length of $\frac{3}{8}''$ wood dowel
Two 3′ lengths of $\frac{7}{16}''$ iron rod
Two $3\frac{1}{2}''$ wood screws
One 7″-long, $\frac{3}{8}''$-diameter, roundhead bolt with nut and locknut
One $1\frac{1}{2}''$-long, $\frac{1}{4}''$-diameter, roundhead bolt with nut
Three 2″-long, $\frac{1}{4}''$-diameter, hexagonal-head bolts, with four nuts
One 3″-long, $\frac{1}{4}''$-diameter lag screw
Two 12″-diameter tricycle wheels
Two 8″, 9″ or 10″ diameter tricycle wheels
Five $\frac{7}{16}''$ washers
Four cotter pins

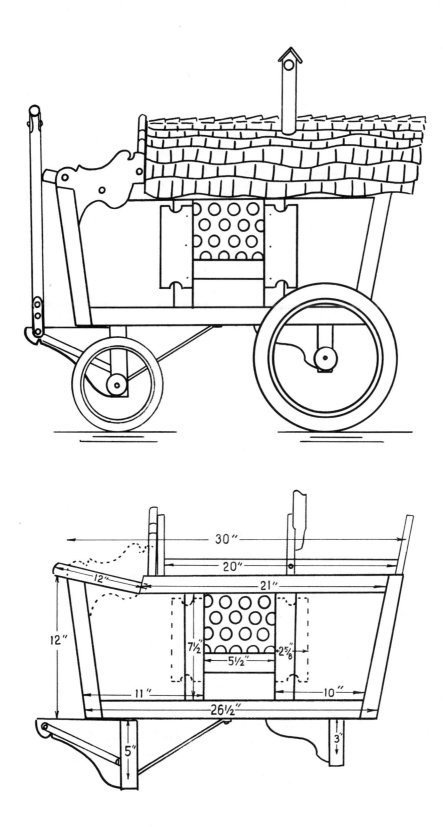

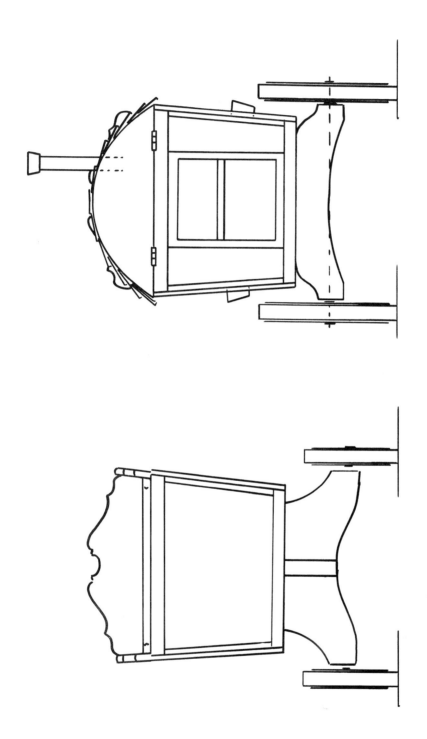

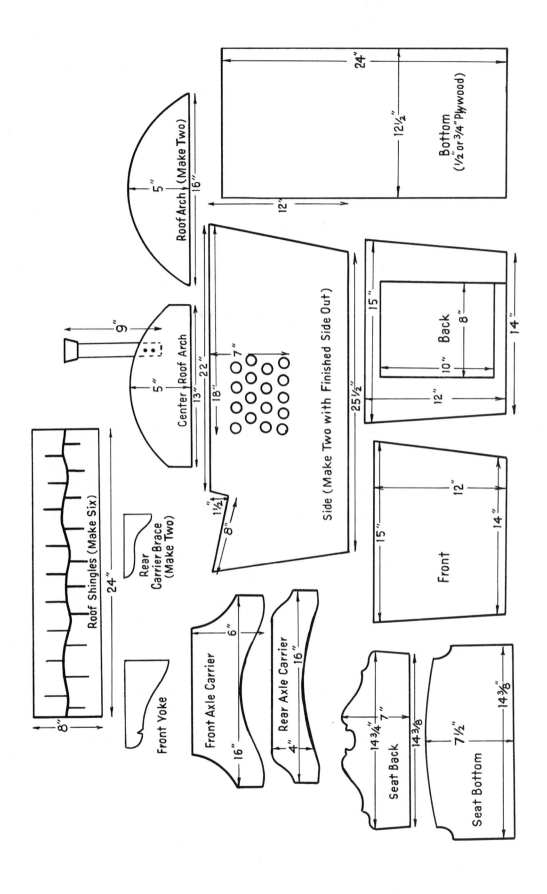

Chapter 22

The Pedal Truck

The pedal truck is a piece of equipment no enterprising young man, or even woman, of action can afford to be without. It serves the purpose of both a stake wagon and a pedal car at the same time, and the basic layout can easily be converted for use as a fire truck, crane truck, dump truck, or whatever kind of truck strikes your client's fancy at the time. As it stands, the stakes can be lifted out for conversion to a flatbed for carrying bulkier loads.

The truck is light, but strong, carrying 200 pounds in the bed without a whimper, and the direct drive makes it a bit slow, but able to pull loads and make grades and whatnot. As an added attraction, both the seat position and the wheelbase are infinitely adjustable to fit both the driver and the job.

The design is taken loosely from the old Mack trucks that seemed to turn up everywhere, through decades and decades of the good old days.

Be warned, however, before warming up the saws and drills, that it's probably not the best project to begin your career with. Both the truck and the moon-crawler in the following chapter are not really intended as projects for the beginners in the crowd. There's nothing magical about either project, and no special, hard-to-master skills are involved in either piece. It's just simply that to make propelled vehicles, even a pedal vehicle, complete with drive train and steering, takes a lot of steps, however easy each step may be.

So, if you're not yet ready to flex the frontal lobes a bit, and take each

step slowly, keeping all the details in place, perhaps it would be better to save these projects for when you've developed your confidence with tools a bit.

This isn't meant to discourage the old masters from tackling these, of course. There's nothing quite like seeing your own creations tooling over the countryside with a full load of youngsters getting a good dose of fresh air, exercise, and excitement—especially if he's carrying loads of dead leaves to the trash in the bargain.

Step One: Cutting

Most of the body parts are cut from a 4′×4′ sheet of exterior, A/C grade plywood. The steering and drive parts of the chassis are largely recruited from the plumbing department of the lumber store. To draw on symmetrical curves, sketch them first on a folded sheet of paper, cut out, then unfold and use the paper as a pattern.

Sketch the dimensions of the grille, dashboard, bed, seat pieces and axle carrier onto the plywood. Make the straight cuts with a carpenter's handsaw or portable circular saw, and rough-cut out the parts to the outside of the curved cuts. Then make the curved cuts with a band, saber, jig or coping saw. The bed is shown on the plans with the top grooves drawn in. Simply cut out the 14″×22″ rectangle, and the grooves will be cut later.

Rip an 8′ length of 1″×8″ straight-grained pine or fir stock so that you end up with one 8′ board 3″ wide, and two 8′ boards 2″ wide. Cut the

3″-wide board to two lengths, 44″ each. Using a table saw, set it to a shallow, ⅛″-deep cut (or use a carpenter's handsaw), and cut parallel grooves down into the top of the bed piece, spaced about 2½″ apart, as shown in the plans.

Now drill ⅛″ screw holes down through the bed along both sides, spaced about ⅜″ in from the sides, and about 5″ apart. Countersink these holes so that the 1¼″, Number 8, flathead wood screws will sit flush with the top when set.

Step Two: First Assembling

Place the two 44″ frame rails on a flat surface, on edge, and run a line of white glue along the top edges a distance of 22″ from one end. Now align the bed flush with the outside and the glued end of one rail, and sink screws down through the bed and into the top edge of the rail. Repeat this to attach the other rail to the other side of the bed, with both rails flush with one end of the bed.

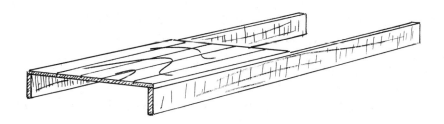

The two back axle carriers look like a football shape attached to a rectangle. Place these axle carriers over one another, and mark a center line, perpendicular to the edge opposite the curved edge, so that the line runs through the position for the axle hole. With the pieces sitting over one another, drill through both pieces, making the $\frac{3}{8}''$ axle hole and three $\frac{1}{8}''$ screw holes spaced up the line above the axle hole.

Now, using plenty of glue, sink screws through the holes in one axle carrier and into the edge grain of the axle-carrier spacer (a rectangular piece with one concave side), so that the long, straight edge of the spacer is flush with the top, straight edge of the carrier. Repeat this to attach the other axle carrier to the other end of the spacer.

Place the bed/frame-rail assembly upside down, and insert the axle-carrier assembly, straight edge down, in between the rails. The outsides of the axle carriers should rest against the insides of the frame rails. With the back ends of the straight edges of the axle carriers positioned 3″ in front of the back edge of the bed, sink two $\frac{1}{4}''$-diameter holes through each frame rail and adjacent axle carrier, and fasten securely with four, $1\frac{1}{2}''$-long, $\frac{1}{4}''$-diameter, roundhead bolts. To allow the wheelbase to be adjusted later on, if you decide to lengthen or shorten the truck, don't glue these joints.

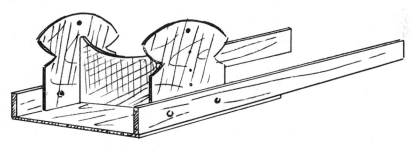

Step Three: The Body

The radiator front sits butted up against the front edges of the frame rails. Drill two screw holes spaced about $\frac{3}{8}''$ in from both side edges of the radiator, and then sink screws in through these holes and into the front end grain of the rails, using glue, of course.

The bottom point of the dashboard is held to the top edges of the frame rails with 90° iron corner braces, with two screw holes in each 2″ arm. These braces are found near the hinges in the hardware department.

Place one of the braces on top of each rail, with the horizontal arm extending forward of the vertical arm, and with the back side of the vertical ram positioned 7⅜″ behind the front of the truck. Sink screws down through the horizontal arm. Then place the bottom tips of the dashboard on top of the rails, with the back of the dashboard up against the front of the vertical arm, and sink short, stubby screws in through the arm and into the dashboard.

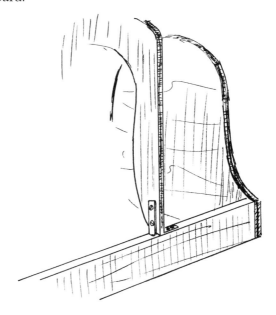

In the hardware department, or sometimes the housewares department, can be found a rack of 2′×4′ pieces of aluminum grillwork and sheeting; use this soft aluminum or iron sheeting for the hood. Cut an 8″×30″ piece to approximately the size needed for the hood. As it is attached, you can trim the piece to shape with the tin snips. Any soft sheet stock will work, but aluminum is best. Bend the sheet to a rough U-shape, and insert it over the outside of the radiator shape, and inside the dashboard shape. Once the sheet is trimmed so that it sits flat against the outside of the radiator, the inside of the dashboard, and on the top edge of the frame rails, drive ¾″, roundhead tacks or other small, roundhead nails down into the edge of the radiator, and up into the edge of the dashboard, spaced about 2″ apart.

Cut out the small, arched steering-column holder, and position it against the back of the dashboard, straddling the center line horizontally, and about 1″ down from the top of the dashboard. Draw a light line around the bases of this holder when it is in place, then drill a screw hole through the back of the dashboard where the holder rests against it. Now countersink the holes from the front of the dashboard and attach the holder to the back with glue and screws sunk through the front and into the bases of the holder.

214

Step Four: The Seat

The bottom side pieces of the seat, which rest against the insides of the frame rails, butt up against the seat back along their back edges. Drill three screw holes through the seat back, about ⅜″ in from both edges, and using glue, sink screws through these holes to hold the bottom side pieces of the seat to the seat back. Then place the seat bottom on top of the bottom side pieces, and against the seat back, and drilling the appropriate holes, run screws (don't forget glue) down through the seat bottom into the tops of the side bottom pieces, and then in through the back of the seat back into the rear edge of the seat bottom. Now drill, glue, and screw the upper sides of the seat to the top of the seat bottom and to the seat back.

The seat bottom sides can now be inserted down in between the frame rails and fastened to the frame with four 2″-long, ¼″-diameter roundhead bolts coming in from the outside. To position the seat as in the sample truck pictured, drill the holes through the center of the frame-rail sides, about 15″ and 21″ back from the front of the truck, and position the seat back up against the front edge of the bed with the top of the seat 12″ above the bed. The seat should also slant back a few degrees.

Step Five: The Stakes

The stakes are made from the 2″-wide strips ripped from the 1″×8″, as are the holding brackets.

215

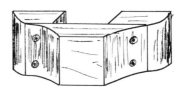

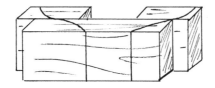

Consult the sketch to get the drift of how to fabricate the four stake brackets. Cut four stakes, 15″ long, and then round off one end of each, and cut a ½″×2″ notch out of the bottom corner edges, so that the stakes will slip down into the brackets. Cut four more stakes 18″ long, and round off both ends of each stake. Then place two short stakes on a flat surface, side by side, 12″ apart; place two longer stakes across these, so that they're centered and square, in the position shown. Glue the joining surfaces, drill screw holes, and sink a screw through the longer stakes and into the shorter at each crossing. Make another set of stakes in the same way. Then hold the sets in place against the sides of the frame, mark the position of the shorter, vertical stakes, and then glue and screw the brackets to the sides of the frame. Insert the sets of stakes to make sure they actually will insert, and make adjustments, if necessary.

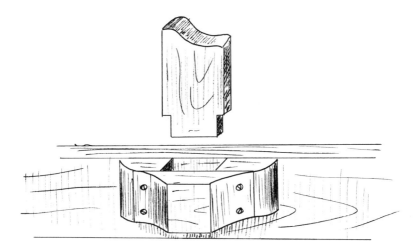

Step Six: The Chassis

To fashion the chassis, it's a good idea to try to drum up a pipe vise, or perhaps a regular vise, and possibly a pipe cutter. Sometimes with the help of a golden tongue, the lads at the lumberyard will take a little time to make a few well-marked cuts, if you hit them during a slack period.

216

Start by drilling a 1″-diameter hole through the front of the radiator, centered about 1¼″ up from the bottom on the center line. Then drill another 1″ hole through the seat back piece, about 1″ above the bottom point, and on the center line. The front-wheel drive-steering unit is made, for the most part, from a 1″ *outside* diameter galvanized pipe (which is known by its inside diameter measurement as ¾″ pipe), running lengthwise down the middle of the truck, and a ¾″ *outside* diameter galvanized pipe (known as ½″ pipe) running up through the bigger pipe, forming the steering-wheel column. Take a close look at the photo to help understand the whole scheme.

To make the 24″, lengthwise piece, cut off a 14″ and an 8″ length of the 1″ outside diameter pipe. Join these two pieces with a right-angle, four-way cross fitting, and set the joints tight with a good-sized pipe wrench. Insert the end of the shorter piece through the hole near the bottom of the radiator; then insert the end of the longer piece into the hole near the bottom of the seat back. With the pipe in place, run a two-hole wall flange onto the front end of the pipe (seen in the photos near the bottom of the radiator), tighten it down, and then run two screws in through the screw holes and into the front of the radiator. The empty holes of the four-way, right -angle cross piece should point straight up and down.

Now cut off and thread both ends of a 16″ piece of galvanized pipe with a ¾″ outside diameter. Run a T-fitting on one end, tightening this fitting on as firmly as possible. In the plumbing section are found short stubs of pipe, threaded from both ends. Run a 1½″-long threaded stub into both openings in the T-fitting. Next run cap plugs onto the ends of the threaded stubs, and then tighten the caps down until they fit up against the ends of the T-fitting. Now, with a ⁷⁄₁₆″ twist bit (or if you have only a ⅜″ bit, enlarge the ⅜″ holes by applying side pressure to the drill), drill a hole in through the center of the end of one of the caps, and then through the end of the other cap, making a bearing for the front axle to turn on.

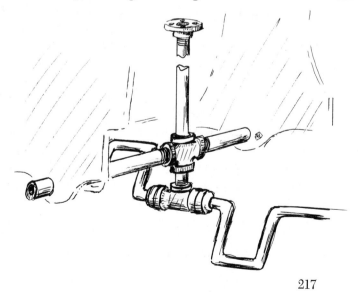

The pedal crank axle in front is made from a 3′ length of $7/16$″-diameter iron rod. The 90° bends are made by holding the rod securely in a pipe vise or bench vise near the mark showing the position of the bend. Then a 3′ or 4′ length of $1/2$″ inside diameter pipe is slipped over the rod down to the bend mark, and the bend is made by applying a little brawn to the free end of the pipe.

Make the first 90° bend $7\frac{1}{2}$″ from one end of the rod. Then make a mark for the second bend, 3″ farther along, on the long arm of the rod. Move the rod in the vise so that it's near the mark for the second bend, then use the pipe to bend the rod back up, parallel to the $7\frac{1}{2}$″ length of the rod. Check the alignment from all angles and correct any side bends as you go along. Now make another mark, 3″ farther on, move the rod in the vise, and make another 90° corner, bending the rod up, parallel to the first 3″ length of the crank. Now repeat this process to make another 90° bend 3″ farther along, bending the rod back to the same axis as the first $7\frac{1}{2}$″ length of the crank.

Now insert the long end of the crank rod through the $7/16$″ holes through the ends of the T-fitting, making sure the rod can turn freely in the holes. Then make the four remaining 90° bends in the rod, spaced 3″ apart, to form the other pedal throw of the crank exactly the same as the first, except that the second throw should be positioned up when the first is down, as shown. When the crank axle spins freely and the $7\frac{1}{2}$″ end lengths of the crank are aligned to your satisfaction, insert the free end of the 16″ steering column up through the empty holes of the four-way cross-fitting in the 1″ pipe mounted along the center of the truck, then up through the steering-column holder at the back of the dashboard. Now run a four-hole wall

218

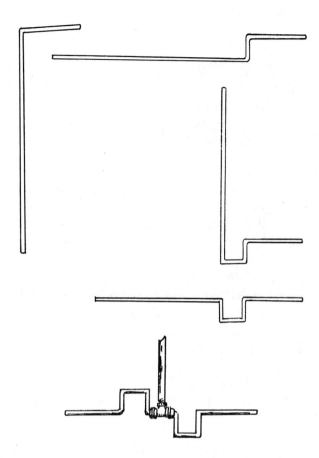

flange down onto the threads at the top of the steering column and tighten this fitting down as best you can. Put a tube over the handle of the pipe wrench, if necessary, to get extra leverage.

Cut the bell-shaped front axle guides from the ⅜″ plywood, if they haven't already been cut out. With glue and screws, attach these to the outside of the frame rails, flush with the top and with their center lines 9″ back from the front of the truck, so that an imaginary line joining the center points of their tops will pass through the center of the steering column.

Cut two 8″ lengths of ½″-wide iron strap. Bend the ends of the straps down, making 1″ ears at both ends, sticking straight down. Drill three ⅛″ screw holes spaced along the center lines of both straps, then countersink these holes so that the flat screwheads will rest just below the surface of the strap on the side of the strap facing the bent ears.

Sink screws up through these straps and into the bottom edges of the axle guides, holding the straps firmly in place with the ears pointed down, as shown.

Mark and cut out the steering wheel, if this has not already been accomplished. To mark a satisfactory circle, drill two ⅛″ holes in a yardstick, or any thin stick, positioning the holes as far apart as the length of the

219

radius of the circle. Insert a nail through one hole and hold it in place against the plywood. Then, with the tip of a pencil through the other hole, draw a circle around the nail center point.

Now draw a line through the center point of the wheel, and then another line through the center point, but at right angles to the first line. Mark each line $2\frac{1}{4}$" in from the edge of the wheel at both ends of each line. Drill four $2\frac{1}{4}$"- or $2\frac{1}{2}$"-diameter holes through the wheel, using these marks as center points. Place the wheel, centered over the top end of the steering column, and mark on the bottom of the wheel the four hole positions of the wall flange. Drill these holes through the wheel with a $\frac{1}{4}$" bit, and then enlarge the holes in the flange to $\frac{1}{4}$" if needed. Run four $1\frac{1}{2}$", $\frac{1}{4}$"-diameter, roundhead bolts down through the wheel and the flange and tighten securely.

Step Seven: Attaching the Wheels

Cut a 24" piece of $\frac{7}{16}$" iron rod to serve as a rear axle, and drill $\frac{1}{8}$", or smaller, cotter-pin holes about $\frac{3}{8}$" in from both ends. Insert the rear axle through the rear axle holes, and oil all moving parts, allowing oil to soak up into the wood bearings.

Cut two 3" lengths of $\frac{3}{4}$" outside diameter pipe, and then two $4\frac{1}{2}$" pieces of $\frac{3}{4}$" outside diameter pipe. Slip the 3" pieces over the ends of the rear axle, and then slip on the rear 12"-diameter tricycle wheels. Soapbox derby disc wheels may be substituted at a sacrifice of the looks. Oil the rear wheels, and fix them on with washers and cotter pins. Then slip the $4\frac{1}{2}$" pipes over the ends of the front axle, and run on the front wheels.

Now it's always a nuisance to have to bring someone else in on the job, but there's only one way we've found to fix drive wheels to axles really permanently, and that's by welding.

If you don't have a welding rig, or a friend who does, there are a number of different shops in nearly every town that will do a little welding for you. Just load up the truck and pack it off to a lawn-mower, bicycle, or dune-buggy shop, or practically any automotive shop, and ask the man to simply tack *one* of the front-wheel hubs to the end of the axle, on the outer side. It won't take more than a couple of minutes of torch time, and shouldn't cost much, if anything, to have done. Fix the other front wheel on with washers and a cotter pin, and oil.

Step Eight: Painting

If the truck is to be modified for other uses, like a fire truck for example, attach the bells and ladders, or whatever, and paint to suit the use. If you like the finish on the example pictured, after sanding away all potential splinters stain the bed, stakes, and dashboard with a dark walnut stain, then wipe clean. Next paint the hood, radiator front, outside surfaces of the seat, frame rails and center of the steering wheel (leaving a 1" band around the edge unpainted) with a medium-dark green gloss enamel. Two coats should do it. Then paint the wheels, the top edges and inside surfaces of the seat, and the two-hole wall flange on the bottom front of the radiator with a warm, orange-yellow (commonly known as "implement yellow") gloss enamel.

Finally, sketch a grille shape onto a piece of paper held against the front of the radiator, fold the paper in the center, cut out the half shape, and then sketch around the pattern centered on the front of the radiator. Paint this shape flat or semi-gloss black, as well as the front axle guides, rear axle carriers (inside and out), and the iron pipes and rod axles.

It was a bit of a long haul, creating this noble little truck, but then, as somebody is nearly always saying, "You sometimes get out of things just what you put into them." And young truckers in the area will no longer suffer the usual hesitance—at least, for a few days—at the prospect of cleaning up leaves, hauling out trash, and/or policing the yard.

LUMBER LIST	One 4′×4′ sheet of ⅜″, exterior, A/C grade plywood
for the	
PEDAL TRUCK	One 8′ length of 1″×8″ straight-grained fir or pine stock
	One 2′×4′ sheet of soft aluminum or iron sheeting
	Two 3′ lengths of ⁷⁄₁₆″-diameter iron rod
	Four 12″-diameter tricycle wheels
	Four dozen 1¼″, Number 8, flathead wood screws
	Two dozen ¾″ roundhead tacks
	A 14″ and an 8″ length of 1″ outside diameter (¾″ inside diameter) galvanized pipe, threaded on all ends
	Galvanized iron pipe, ¾″ outside diameter (½″ inside diameter) of the following lengths: one 16″ and two 1½″ (all threaded on both ends); two 3″ and two 4½″ (all nonthreaded)
	One ½″ T-fitting
	One ¾″ four-way cross-fitting
	Two ½″ caps
	One four-hole, ½″ wall flange
	One two-hole, ¾″ wall flange
	One 16″ length of iron strap, ½″ wide
	Twelve 1½″-long, ¼″-diameter, roundhead bolts and nuts
	Six ⅜″ washers
	Three cotter pins
	Two right-angle corner brackets, 2″ on a side

221

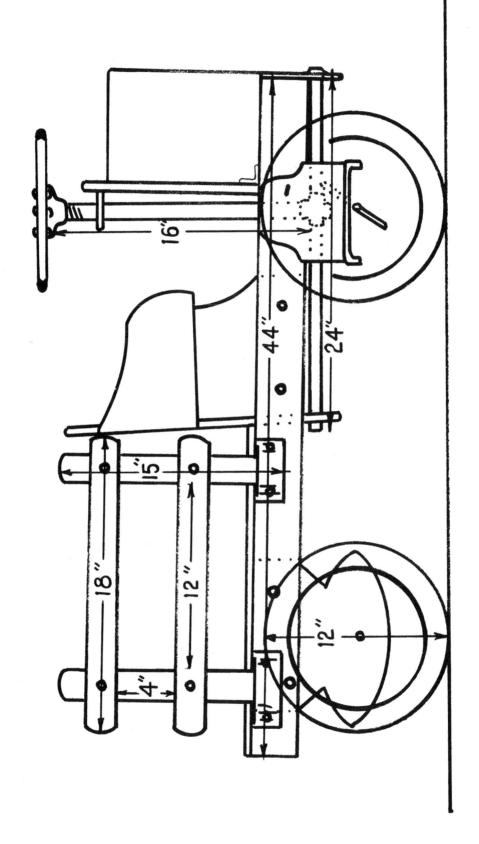

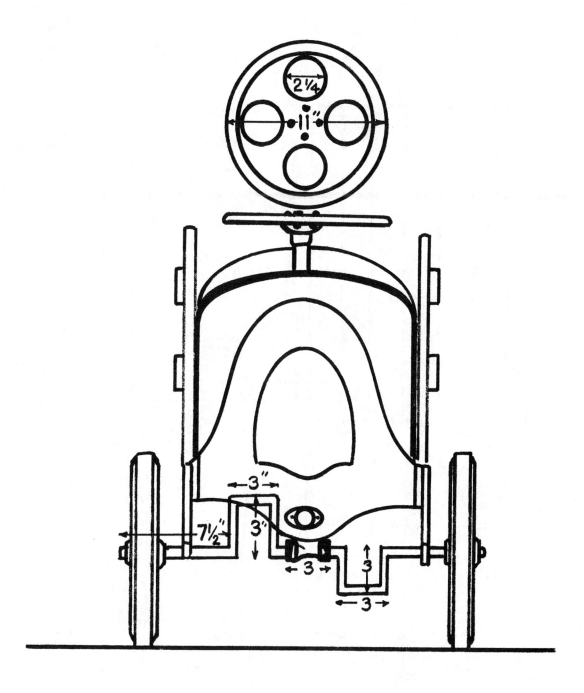

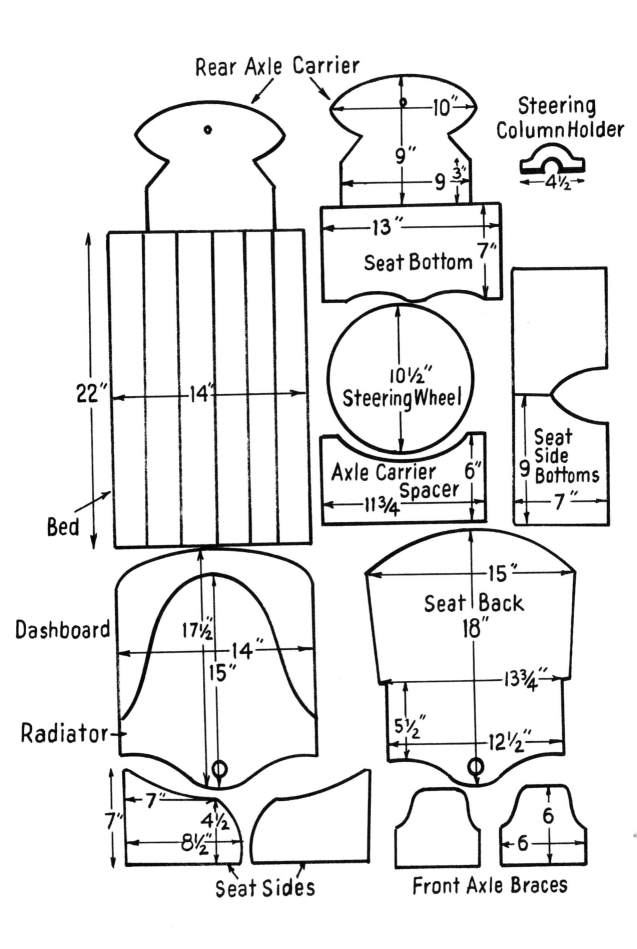

Rear Axle Carrier

Steering Column Holder

10"

9"

9

3"

13"

Seat Bottom

7"

Steering Wheel 10½"

Axle Carrier Spacer

11¾"

6"

Seat Side Bottoms

9

7"

22"

14"

Bed

Dashboard

17½"

14"

15"

Seat Back

18"

15"

13¾"

5½"

12½"

Radiator

7"

7"

4½

8½"

Seat Sides

6

6

Front Axle Braces

Chapter 23

The Moon-Crawler
[Lunamog]

Never ones to walk when we can ride, it seems that the first thing we ferry to the latest Last Frontier is some sort of machine to keep us from suffering the indignity of having to hoof it. And the odds are that the moon is the target for the next big all-terrain vehicle, or dune-buggy truck. So if your own representatives of the younger generation hope someday to spend time touring the moonscape in a moon-mobile or moon-crawler or Lunamog, or whatever the machine will be called by then, here is a small pedal-powered version they can practice with at the beach, or just over the vacant lot, and get a little exercise in the bargain.

The Lunamog (a lunar takeoff from an all-terrain truck called the "Unimog") features front-wheel, or rather front-crawler, drive, with rear-crawler, lever-controlled steering and articulating rear suspension.

As with the pedal truck, while it takes no special genius to make one, there are a lot of steps to the project, simple though they may be. So if you're a newcomer to the world of tools and the ways of kicking things until they work, perhaps it would be a good idea to warm up on some simpler toys before going after this one.

Step One: Cutting

Start out by marking the dimensions and the straight sides of the pieces onto a ⅜″ exterior, A/C grade plywood. Then sketch in the curves. Cut

226

out the sides, the center frame, the seat bottom, seat back, rear deck, back piece, back center frame brace and dashboard. Cut the straight sides first with a portable electric saw or carpenter's handsaw, then cut the curves with a band, saber, jig or coping saw. On a 16″ length of hardwood 1″×3″ stock, draw a line across the center point, using a square. Then make two marks on one edge of the 1″×3″, 7⅛″ out from the center line on both sides. Make two more marks on the other edge of that side, 6⅜″ out to both sides from the center line. Connect the two edge marks on the two ends and cut along these lines to form the brace that will tie the sides of the machine together at the bottom front.

Step Two: Assembling the Body

The body pieces are joined together with butt joints, running the edge of one piece up against the side of another piece. As all the joints are made in pretty much the same fashion, we might as well go over the process thoroughly once, so we won't be boring everyone with repetitions. White glue and 1¼″, Number 8, flathead wood screws are used through-out. To get a good grip into the end grain of plywood, it's important to sink the screws into the center lamination. To do this, draw a straight line on the side piece marking the position of the center of the edge to be butted up against it. With a ⅛″ bit, drill screw holes spaced about 3″ or 4″ apart along this line. Then countersink these holes slightly for a nice finish. Place plenty of white glue along the edge of the joining piece, and sink the two end screws first, making sure they hit the center of the end grain. Then the rest of the screws will usually sink right into the center, if driven in straight.

Now, to assemble the pieces, draw a screw-hole line about ¼″ down from the top of the rear deck edge on the side piece. Then draw another line about ¼″ in from the back edge of the side piece and then mark the lines showing the positions of the seat back and seat bottom, as well.

After placing the side pieces aligned over one another, drill screw holes along these lines, spaced about 3″ apart, and countersink them on opposing sides of these pieces, so you don't end up with two left sides.

Mark a center line down the middle of the rear deck piece, the seat back and the seat bottom, and drill and countersink screw holes along these lines.

Now, using glue throughout, attach the seat back in position against the center-frame edge, and sink screws through the holes and into the edge of the center frame. Next attach the seat bottom in place on top of the center frame, then run screws through the rear of the seat back and into the rear edge of the seat bottom. Then attach the rear deck piece to the top edge of the center frame; sink screws through the front of the seat back and into the edge of the rear deck piece.

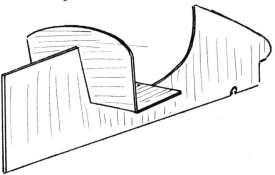

Now attach one side to the rear deck piece, flush at the top and rear. Then attach the side piece to the seat back and seat bottom, and to the edge of the back side.

Try to make certain that the bottom lines of the two side pieces and the center frame will sit touching a flat surface, as you attach the other side piece in the same manner. With the bottoms aligned, run the 1″×3″ front brace between the two sides at the front, bottom corner of the machine, sinking screws through the sides and into the ends of the brace.

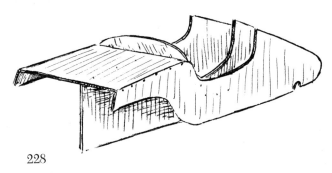

228

Attach the dashboard in position with two screws running in from both side pieces. Attach the center frame brace also, which butts against the back end of the center frame, by running screws through the center line of this brace and into the edge of the center frame, then running screws into the edges of the brace, through the rear deck piece and sides.

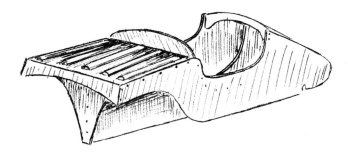

Cut off five 9″ lengths of 1″ half-round molding and glue and nail them in position to the top of the rear deck with short finishing nails.

Step Three: The Drive Axle

The front axle-pedal crank is bent from a 3′ length of $\frac{7}{16}$″ iron rod in much the same way that the front axle of the pedal truck in the previous chapter was bent. However, if you missed out on that one, we'll divulge the process once more.

As can be seen in the front plan view, the axle crank is a series of eight 90° corner bends. These are made by placing the rod in a pipe or bench vise near the mark for the bend, then slipping a $\frac{1}{2}$″ pipe about 3′ or 4′ long over the rod, up to the mark, and then making a good, sharp bend. After each corner is bent, the next is marked 3″ farther along the rod, and the rod is then moved in the vise so that the jaws are once again about $\frac{1}{2}$″ away from the next bending place. See the previous chapter for the illustration.

Looking at it from the front, the axle is bent 90° down, $7\frac{1}{2}$″ from one end. Then 3″ farther along the axle is bent 90° up again, then 3″ farther another 90° up-bend, and so on, as illustrated, until two opposing throws of the crank have been formed. After each and every bend, however, check the axle from the top also to make sure no unseemly side bend is creeping into the work. After all the corners have been bent, place the crank axle on a flat surface to check for a side bend, and correct this if necessary. Then cut the notches in the bottoms of the center frame and the sides for the axle, place the axle in these notches, and spin it to see if the ends of the axle are aligned; bend to correct.

The front crawlers are mounted to the front axle by means of drilled straps which are welded to the axle. As we said in the previous chapter, it's always a nuisance to have to bring an outsider in on the project, but it's a very simple welding job that won't take more than a couple of

229

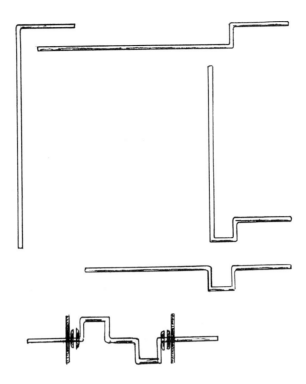

minutes of torch time at the local automotive shop. And it makes a permanent assembly that you'll never have to think of again.

To make the straps, cut four 6″ lengths of 1″-wide iron strap, usually found near the hinges in the hardware department. Drill a $7/16$″ (or $3/8$″ enlarged by using a rotated side pressure on the drill) hole through the center of each strap, then drill $1/4$″ holes 1″ in from both ends of each strap.

The axle is held onto the side pieces with $1/2$″, two-hole wall-flange pipe fittings. Since these will be mounted inboard of the crawler straps, they should be run on the crank-axle before the straps are welded on. To get these on the axle in the right order, slip them over one end of the axle in the following order: The first flange is slipped on rounded side first; the second, flat side first; the third, rounded side first; and the fouth, flat side first. Then each end of the axle is inserted into the large center hole of one of the straps.

With a piece of chalk or a pencil, make a weld mark 4″ in from both ends. Tell the man with the torch (if you don't have your own set) to tack the strap around the center hole to the axle, attaching both straps in place. Once back in your shop, bend the straps to square them at right angles to the axle, and check the alignment of the axle end once more. Now, sandwich the side pieces (around the axle notches at the bottom) between the flat sides of the two-hole wall flanges and drill through the other flange holes with a $1/4$″ bit. Bolt these flanges against the side pieces with $1\frac{1}{2}$″-long, $1/4$″-diameter, roundhead bolts, with the bolts to the inside of the Lunamog. After

230

the axle has been attached to both side pieces, spin it to make sure it's still straight, and then apply a little grease to the bearing surfaces.

Step Four: The Steering

The rear axle is mounted at the bottom rear of the center frame on a universal joint to allow the crawlers to pivot both vertically, for bouncing over rough terrain, and horizontally, for steering.

To set up this universal joint, make the axle carrier from a number of ½″ inside diameter pipe fittings found in the plumbing department.

Place a T-joint in a pipe or bench vise with one end toward you, and the middle arm pointing up. Run a 3″ stub into the near end of this T-fitting, and tighten the joint firmly. Next run the end of another T-fitting onto this stub and tighten firmly, with the middle arm to the right, 90 degrees from the direction of the middle arm of the first T-fitting. Now run another 3″ stub into the near end of the second fitting and tighten. Finally, run a third T-fitting onto the end of the stub and tighten it so that its middle arm points up in the same position as the first T-fitting held in the vise.

Now, with the ⁷⁄₁₆″ twist bit (or ⅜″ bit and then enlarge the hole to ⁷⁄₁₆″), drill a hole through the side of the middle arm of the center T-fitting, perpendicular to the direction of the 3″ stubs. Then drill a ¼″ hole through the middle arm of both end T-fittings, perpendicular to the directions of the stubs and to the direction of the ⁷⁄₁₆″ hole as well (it's best to have the part in front of you before trying to understand what all this means).

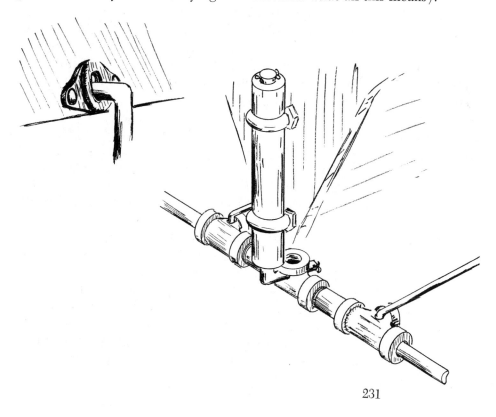

231

Cut a 10″ length of $\frac{7}{16}$″-diameter iron rod, and drill a small cotter-pin hole about $\frac{3}{8}$″ in from both ends. Make a 90° bend, $1\frac{3}{4}$″ from one end. Next, cut off a $5\frac{1}{2}$″ piece of $\frac{1}{2}$″ inside diameter, galvanized pipe and then cut two more pieces, each 2″ long.

The vertical arm of the universal-joint bent rod is mounted to the back of the center-frame end brace with $\frac{5}{16}$″-diameter U-bolts which are about 2″ long from apex to tips, having tips spaced 1″ apart on center. To assemble the vertical arm holder, first run a nut onto both ends of each U-bolt, and run them all the way up to the end of the threading, about $\frac{3}{4}$″ from the apex.

Now, run one of the 2″ pipes onto the long arm of the $\frac{7}{16}$″ universal joint rod, up to the bend. Then run the end of the long arm through one of the U-bolts between the nuts and the inside of the apex. Next, slip on the $5\frac{1}{2}$″ pipe, then another U-bolt, and finally, the other 2″ piece of pipe. Put a cotter pin through the end hole to hold the pipes and bolts on. Now position the tips of the U-bolts up against the back of the rear center frame brace so that the vertical axis of the rod lies along the center line of the rear brace, and the short arm of the rod is positioned about 1″ below the bottom of the center frame. Mark the position of the tips of the U-bolts when the rod is positioned thus, and then drill out these holes with a $\frac{5}{16}$″ drill bit. Insert the tips of the U-bolts through the holes, and then run nuts on from the forward side of the brace and tighten the bolts in place.

After checking to see that the rod can turn freely on its vertical axis, point the short end of the rod toward the front of the machine. Then, with the middle arm of the center T-fitting down, and the middle arms of the end T-fittings pointing to the front, insert the short arm of the universal joint rod through the $\frac{3}{8}$″ hole in the middle arm of the center T-fitting.

Now cut a $\frac{7}{16}$″ iron rod to 24″ long, and drill cotter-pin holes through, about $\frac{3}{8}$″ in from both ends. Insert this rod through the end of one T-fitting and on through the whole assembly, to form the back axle.

The control levers are made from either $\frac{1}{2}$″ inside diameter galvanized pipe or $\frac{3}{4}$″ thin wall tubing. The levers should be 15″ long, with a 90° elbow and then a 3″ handle at the top. Drill a $\frac{1}{4}$″-diameter hole through each lever, 1″ from the bottom end, and parallel to the top handle. Drill another hole through each lever, 5″ from the bottom end, parallel to the handles and the first holes.

Now drill a $\frac{1}{4}$″ hole through the center frame 10″ in front of the bottom of the seat back and $1\frac{1}{2}$″ down from the top of the center frame. Insert a 3″-long, $\frac{1}{4}$″-diameter, hexagonal-head bolt through the hole in the lever 5″ from the end, with the head resting on the side of the lever toward the direction of the top handle. Then insert the bolt through a washer, through the $\frac{1}{4}$″ hole in the center frame, through another washer, and finally through the other lever with its handle pointing away from the first handle. Secure this bolt with a nut and locknut. Cut the end of the bolt off flush with the locknut.

The ¼" holes through the bottoms of the levers and the ¼" holes through the middle arms of the end T-fittings of the rear axle carrier are joined with a ¼" rod. Cut two 20" lengths of the ¼" iron rod, and drill a small cotter-pin hole near both ends of each rod (use a pointed center punch to locate these holes). Bend a 90° corner 1" from one end of the two rods with a vise, then insert these bent ends in through the holes near the bottoms of the levers, and secure with a locknut.

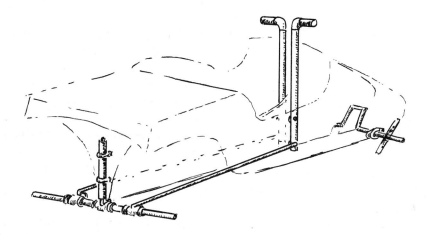

Now place the top handles side by side, positioning the rear axle flat and exactly straight (that is, perpendicular to the center line of the machine) and then mark the place on both rods where they should be bent to be inserted down through the holes in the end T-fittings. Insert these ends, and secure them with cotter pins.

Check to see that the steering really does steer, and the articulating suspension articulates.

Step Five: The Crawlers

If you haven't already guessed, the crawlers are made from ribbed, flexible plastic buckets, roughly 13" in diameter and about 16" deep. They're a popular item in all sorts of houseware supply stores, but if you can't run some down, practically any bucket about the same size will do.

The buckets are backed up, of course, with plywood discs spaced apart inside each bucket. Since the rear crawlers are wider than the front crawlers, the sizes of the back-up discs and the widths of the spacers will be different for the front and the rear.

To mark circles on the ½" or ⅝" plywood, drill two small holes through a yardstick, or any thin stick, as far apart as the distance of the radius of the circle. Insert a nail through one hole to hold a center point on the plywood, and then with the tip of a pencil through the other hole, rotate the stick, drawing a hole around the center nail.

In this way (if you don't happen to have a better way), mark two

233

12″-diameter discs, two 11″ discs, and four 10½″ discs onto the plywood. Drill a ⁷⁄₁₆″ (or ⅜″ enlarged) hole through the center of each disc.

Now place two 12″ discs and two 10½″ discs in one pile for the rear crawlers, and the two 11″ discs and two 10½″ discs in another pile for the front crawlers.

To cut the spacers for the front crawlers, rip a 4′ 1″×3″ to 2½″ wide, and then cut this into four 10″-long pieces. Place these on the front-crawler pile. Then rip a 1″×8″ to 6″ wide, and cut the board into four 10″ lengths. Throw these on the pile for the back crawlers.

Next glue the edge of one of the spacer boards, position it on the 10½″ disc with its ends near the edge of the disc, and nail through the back of the disc and into the glued edge of the spacer. Nail another spacer to this disc surface, parallel to the first, on the other side of the center hole. Place the disc on a flat surface with spacers up, and then place the larger disc over the glued top edges of the spacers. Insert a ⅜″ or ⁷⁄₁₆″ rod, dowel or bolt down through the center hole in the larger disc and into the center hole of the bottom disc. With a square held against the dowel or rod to check the alignment, center the top disc directly over the bottom disc, and then nail through the edges of the spacers. In this way, all four crawler-bucket frames can be made.

Slip the back crawler frames over the rear axle and attach with washers and cotter pins. Slip the front frames over the front axle and mark the position of the ¼″ holes in the welded mounting straps on the discs facing them. Drill these holes through the larger discs, slip the crawler frames back on halfway, slip the unwelded straps over the ends of the axles, and then put the crawler frames all the way on. Sandwich the inboard, larger discs between the welded and unwelded straps, then insert 1″-long, ¼″-diameter roundhead bolts through the holes in the welded straps, run on the nuts, and bolt tightly. It would be a good idea to let some oil soak into the wooden bearing surfaces before attaching the buckets.

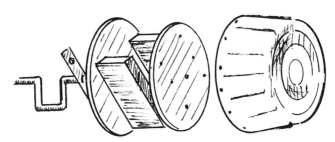

Cut around the side of the buckets about an inch above the depth that will provide the proper diameter to fit over the discs. Slip the bucket over the disc, check to see that it's on squarely by spinning the crawler, and adjust if it's necessary. Then nail ¾″ or 1″ roundhead tacks or other small nails through the side of the bucket and into the edge of the large, inboard disc. Then trim off the bucket rim flush with the side of the disc.

234

Step Six: Finishing

Attach a 2'×2' sheet of soft aluminum or iron (usually found with the heating supplies) across the bottom front with screws running through the metal and into the bottom front edges of the side pieces. Bend the sheeting back, and up to the top of the dashboard and fasten temporarily to the tops of the side pieces next to the dashboard ends. Trim the sheet to about 1" outside the top edges of the sides with tin shears, then begin driving ¾" or 1" roundhead tacks or small nails through the metal and into the top edge of the side pieces, working up and back to the dashboard after having removed the temporary screws at the back. Space the tacks no more than 2" apart. Once the tacks are in on both sides, sink two securing screws back into the holes made by the first positioning screws, and then trim the metal flush with the side pieces and the back of the dashboard. Round off the corners, and smooth the edges with coarse garnet paper.

Sand the whole machine to remove potential splinters, and round off the ends of the five pieces of half-round molding on the rear deck. Wrap the control handles with black tape.

It goes without saying that the Lunamog can be colored any unearthly color you like. White seems to be the vogue for extraterrestrial runabouts nowadays. This one, however, was finished with several coats of orange gloss enamel, with flat black axles, levers, beltline, and the egg-shaped whatzits, added on the hood for a little character. The seat and inside of the cockpit are "implement yellow," our old standby.

With the last stroke of the brush, the countdown draws nigh its close, and woe betide any Martian (or neighbor's cat, for that matter) who thinks he can escape this pedal machine by jumping off the pavement and heading for rough country.

LUMBER LIST for the MOON-CRAWLER	
	One 4'×8' sheet of ⅜" exterior, A/C grade plywood
	One 4'×4' sheet of ½" to ¾" exterior, A/C grade plywood
	One 4' length of 1"×8" hardwood stock
	One 6' length of 1"×3" hardwood stock
	One 4' length of 1" half-round molding
	One 4' length of ½" inside diameter galvanized pipe
	Two 3' lengths of 7⁄16"-diameter iron rod
	One 2'×2' sheet of soft aluminum or thin iron sheeting
	Two 5⁄16" diameter U-bolts, 2" long and 1" between tip centers, with four nuts each
	Four two-hole ½" wall-flange pipe fittings
	One 2' length of 1"-wide iron strap

(Continued overleaf)

Two 2' lengths of $\frac{1}{4}$" iron rod

Four flexible plastic ribbed buckets, around 13" or 14" wide and 16" to 18" deep

Three $\frac{1}{2}$" galvanized T-fittings

Two 3" threaded $\frac{1}{2}$" inside diameter stubs

Two $\frac{1}{2}$" inside diameter 90° elbow fittings

Half a gross of $1\frac{1}{4}$", Number 8, flathead wood screws

Two dozen 1" finishing nails

Four dozen $\frac{3}{4}$" roundhead tacks

Eight $1\frac{1}{2}$"-long, $\frac{1}{4}$"-diameter, roundhead bolts with nuts

One 3" long, $\frac{1}{4}$" diameter, hexagonal-head bolt with two nuts

Assorted washers and cotter pins

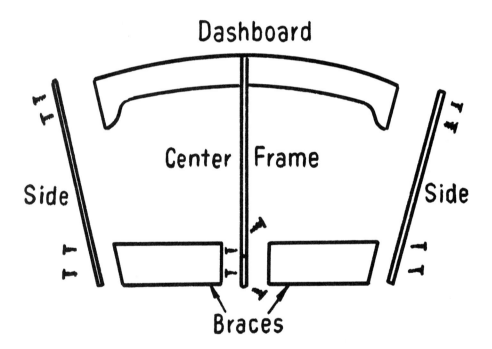

Dashboard

Center Frame

Side   Side

Braces

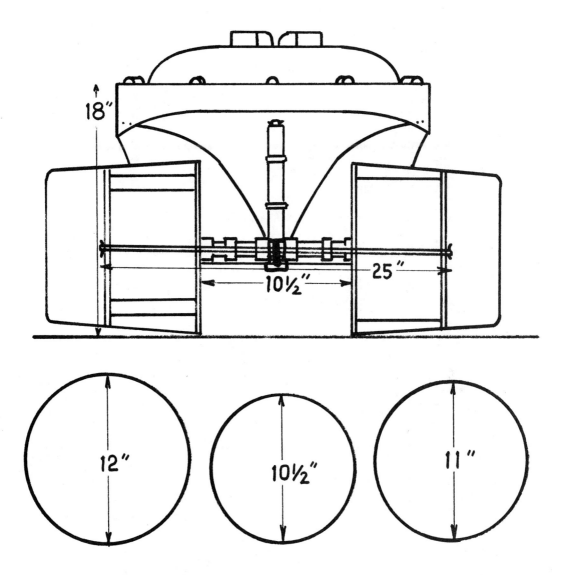

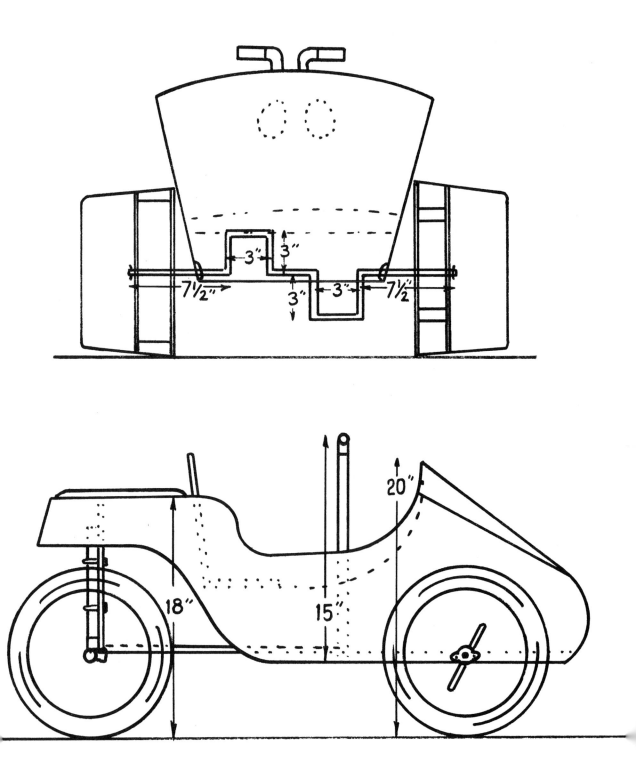

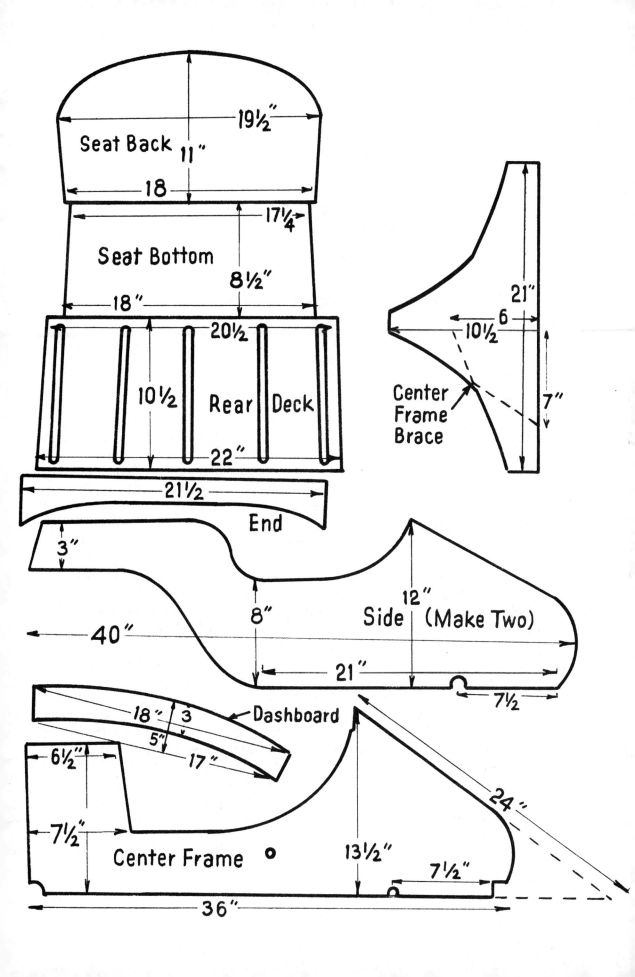

Seat Back 19½"

11"

18

Seat Bottom 17¼"

8½"

18"

20½"

10½" Rear Deck

22"

21½"

End

3"

8"

12"

Side (Make Two)

40"

21"

7½"

21"

6

10½"

Center
Frame
Brace

7"

18" 3

5"

Dashboard

17"

6½"

7½"

Center Frame o

13½"

7½"

24"

36"

Chapter 24

The Pedal Racer

It's always fun to take something that someone else has already done the hard work on, pick up where the original constructor dropped the ball, and make those minor modifications that can sometimes change a lackluster product into a really satisfactory piece of work. The pedal racer is the one toy in the book that is really just a conversion of a factory-produced, store-bought toy. We've tried to keep within the limits of those materials that can readily be found in typical lumberyards and home-supply stores with the rest of the projects. But the great popularity and amazing performance of this little pedal racer conversion seemed to demand that it be included with the rest of the collection. Besides, the commercially made toy on which it's based is seen nearly everywhere and is easy to find even in secondhand shops for a very nominal sum.

The pedal racer is based on an inexpensive little red pedal-powered go-cart called a "hotrod for tots," or some such sporting title. It comes in varying degrees of finery, costing about $15 when new. They've been cranking these little machines out for quite a few years now, to the point where they practically litter the floors of the secondhand and charity stores. In fact, we've even spotted a couple, in repairable condition, set out for the trashman, to give you an idea of their availability. But if you're not addicted to picking through the neighbor's trash, they're still not hard to find.

The design of the racer body in this project is a composite of a number of Edwardian racing machines that used to roar around the old dusty country lanes at appalling speeds, even by today's standards. The hood and grille

shapes are ones that seemed to be favorites with early automotive manufacturers. We gave up counting after we found no fewer than fourteen
different makes with this same radiator-grille shape.

The gas tank behind the cockpit helps to support the seat, which gets
quite a beating in fiercer competition.

But the most important reason for converting this little go-cart (other
than doing something about its looks) is to make it really fun to use.
Admirably engineered in many ways though it is, the production model
still falls short of the perfect pedal car for one simple reason. To keep the
price down, dinky wheels were used as original equipment, making the
gear ratio so low that performance was downright boring to a child old
enough to pedal it at all. Also, the small wheels tended to fall into every
crack in the sidewalk and stay there.

But all these problems were solved in one stroke when a set of
12″-diameter tricycle wheels was fitted on all four corners. The gearing was
suddenly perfect for touring along at a respectable clip, and the wheels no
longer brought the car to a sudden stop when encountering the slightest
obstacle. Since then, the car has never failed to draw a crowd of young
scrutineers wherever it goes, and it has been used so steadily and enthu-
siastically that it's already in need of a new set of tires. In short, we
recommend it highly.

The Once-Over

When you've located a chassis that seems ready for modification, give it
a close look to see that the steering and drive train are well oiled and in
good running order. Try to find a chain-drive version of this go-cart rather

than the pedal-lever model that has also been produced (but which doesn't get around quite as well). The pins connecting the steering tie rod to the steering arms of the axle stubs are probably loosened, and can be fixed by drilling them out with ¼″ bolts and locknuts. The front-axle stubs are also frequently bent back a little, and can be aligned by taking off the wheels and straightening them with a pipe wrench.

If the 12″ wheels are a little too wobbly on the axles, ⅜″ inside diameter copper tubing will just fit inside the axle hole in the wheel, and over the outside of the axle. Cut three 2″ lengths of this tubing for the three, free-wheeling hubs. With a pointed center punch, mark the positions of the cotter-pin holes through the two front and right rear axle stubs, and about ¼″ in from the tips. Drill these out with a ⅛″ or smaller drill bit. Insert the tubes in the wheels, grease the axle stubs, and fix the front wheels on with washers and cotter pins.

To fix on the fourth, drive wheel, we'll have to use a welding torch, for no other really permanent method has been found, around here at least. If you don't have a welding set, or a friend who does, most lawn-mower, bike, dune-buggy, and automotive shops will do a little welding for you. Remove the nylon bearing on the drive-wheel axle stub, and ask the man to simply tack the outside end of the drive-wheel hub to the tip of the axle. It won't take more than a couple of minutes of torch time, and shouldn't cost much. Then when you're back at work, slip the chassis away from the inside of the drive wheel, cut the nylon bearing down one side with a sharp knife, slip the bearing cut over the top of the axle between the chassis and the wheel, and then insert the bearing back into the hole in the chassis, with the cut on the bottom. Now the other rear wheel can be attached with washers and a cotter pin, after greasing.

Once the wheels are on, the chassis should be ready for preliminary testing. The results should be gratifying, for the car will suddenly show a nicely tuned performance, almost up to the bicycle level of efficiency. And for some, this may be as far as you'd care to take the project.

For those others who would like to add a little nostalgic, good-old-days flavor to this worthy machine, start by unbolting and cutting off the tubes attached to the top of the seat and the frame at the back. Also remove the front grille piece and hood sides (if any). Unbolt the center tube running down from the steering column to the front center of the frame. At the point where this center tube begins to bend down toward the front of the frame, cut the tube off. Then, with a wrench or a larger piece of pipe, bend the end of this tube up vertically just in front of the chain case and about 10″ in front of its apex at the steering-column hole.

In most hardware departments, near the hinges, can be found iron strap,

right-angle corner braces, ⅝″ wide and 4″ long, with two screw holes in each arm. With a ¼″ bit, drill out one of the holes near the corner, and then cut off the arm ¼″ beyond this ¼″ hole, making two of these angle braces exactly the same.

Remove the front bolt from each bracket that holds the two front-axle stubs to the frame tube. Then insert this bolt down through the ¼″ hole in one of the corner straps, and back down into the hole from whence it came, and tighten the nut back on, with the vertical arm of the corner strap to the inside of the bolt through the frame tube. Repeat this on the other side of the chassis frame to mount the other corner strap.

Now sketch the dimensions and outline of the radiator shape onto a piece of newspaper, fold the paper, cut out both halves at once, unfold the paper, and use it as a pattern to draw the radiator shape onto the 16″ length of 1″×12″ hardwood stock, or ½″ to ¾″ plywood. Cut this shape out with a band, saber, jig or coping saw and then cut notches near the bottoms of the side edges so that these edges sit snugly against the insides of the vertical arms of the corner straps. Drill a 1″ hole 6″ up from the bottom of the radiator shape, on the center line. Round off the edge of this hole on the front edge of the radiator piece. Now remove the tie rod at the front end of the steering column, insert the radiator shape down between the angle straps, with the end of the steering column sticking through the hole in the radiator. Then replace the tie rod with the steering column end in place in the center bracket. Sink screws in through the holes on the straps to attach the radiator front, then with a ¼″ bit, drill in through the radiator front and through the vertically bent end of the center tube in front of the chain case. Bolt the radiator to this tube with a 2″-long, ½″-diameter, flat-head bolt and nut, after countersinking the bolt hole a little from the front.

The hood is cut from a 3′×3′ piece of thin, soft aluminum or iron sheet, found with the heating supplies. Mark the shape on the sheeting and cut it out with tin shears. Mark crease lines along the positions of the dotted lines, as shown in the plans, and bend the sheeting over the sharp edge of a bench or piece of angle iron. Next give the hood a little preliminary bend over the top, and then insert the bottom, back ends of the sides down into the cockpit under the seat, and over the rear axle. Bend in the sides of the hood at the front, and insert them between the frame tubes and down onto the top of the radiator. Now attach the front of the hood to the top and sides of the radiator by sinking 1″ roundhead screws through the sheeting and into the edge of the radiator, spacing the screws about 3″ apart down the sides. Then attach the rear of the hood sides to the insides of the frame tubes by sinking sheet metal screws or ⅛″ bolts every 5″ along the tubes. Attach the top of the center frame tube to the hood by drilling a ⅛″ hole through both and fastening with a hefty sheet metal screw.

To protect shins from the bare cockpit edge, split a 28″-long, ½″-diameter rubber tube along one side, and slip the cut over the cockpit edge, running the tube around the front of the cockpit, after painting the inside of the tube and along the edge with contact cement.

Cut the gas-tank ends (sides) from the same stock used for the radiator front. Drill two ⅛″ screw holes through the sides of the body under the seat and sink screws through the body sheeting and into the gas-tank end pieces in place. Check that the ends of the tank are lined up, then cut a length of 1″×3″ hardwood stock to fit between the tank ends. Position this 1″×3″ with the top edge about 2″ down from the tops of the end pieces and about ½″ in from the back edges of the tank ends. After gluing, sink screws in through the tank ends and into the end grain of the 1″×3″. Drill two screw holes through the front of the seat back to run one roundhead screw into the front edge of each tank end piece.

Cut out the pattern of the metal sheeting covering the tank, using the dimensions shown in the plans. Attach this, with the concave end up, to the edges of the tank ends just as the hood was attached to the edge of the radiator.

To attach the spare wheel (which is optional, of course, as are the radiator cap, crank, and horn), drill a $\frac{3}{8}$" hole in through the center line of the tank covering, and through the center point of the 1"×3" spacer. Then insert a 4"-long, $\frac{3}{8}$"-diameter bolt through the hub of the spare wheel, through the hole in the sheeting and the 1"×3", and then tighten up a nut and locknut to hold the wheel in place.

To mount a radiator cap, find an old worn-out garden hose and cut a 1' length off the end that doesn't attach to a faucet. Drill a 1" hole down through the hood at the top, just behind the radiator stock, and then insert the cut end of the hose down through the hole. With the base of the hose coupling down on top of the hood, nail through the hose at a couple of places, fastening it to the back of the radiator. Use a garden-hose end cap for a proper radiator cap.

The crank is bent from a 12" length of $\frac{1}{4}$" rod. With a $\frac{1}{4}$" bit, drill out the hole in the center of the frame tube running around the front, then drill on through the radiator front. Make a 90° bend 3" from one end of the rod, and then another 90° bend 4" farther along, but in the opposite direction, forming a crank. Insert the long end of the crank through the center hole in the front, and then with the rod sticking through the back of the radiator about $1\frac{1}{2}$", bend this end over with a hammer, so that the crank can turn but not fall out.

A brass or chrome bicycle bulb horn mounted on the side of the hood adds a lot of interest and is great for clearing the sidewalk during a speed run.

File off any rough edges of the metal with a file or garnet paper. Then the car can be painted any color you like. The color on the example was copied from the beige-yellow of a favorite old Peugeot racer in the Briggs Cunningham Automotive Museum, with a warmer shade for the wheels. "Implement yellow" would make a good Stutz Bearcat color.

Using a folded piece of paper to make a symmetrical pattern, sketch the grille shape on the front of the radiator, after the yellow is dry, and paint this in with flat or semigloss black enamel. Paint the cockpit edging black also, and then paint the number on the hood, the radiator cap, and the crank a dark green. Finally, wrap black plastic tape around the handle of the crank to make a grip.

The steering wheel may look a little out of place now that the rest of the car has been so radically altered. An 8" aluminum pulley can make a nice-looking wheel. Run a piece of slit tubing around the edge of the wheel, and then wrap the edge with black plastic tape. Remove the set screw in the hub of the pulley, fit the pulley-wheel over the steering column, and mark where the set-screw hole sits on the steering column. With a $\frac{1}{4}$" bit, drill a very shallow hole just into the side of the column rod to make a flat seat for the set screw. Instead of replacing the set screw in the pulley hub, however, run in a short hexagonal-head bolt of the same size and thread. Then slip the hub over the column, and with a wrench tighten the bolt very securely against the seating hole in the column.

That's about the whole story of this pedal racer from the days when men were men, etc. Give the crank a turn, lean heavily on the horn and go roaring off to outrage the local gentry.

LUMBER LIST
for the
PEDAL RACER

One 4′ length of 1″×12″ stock or a 2′×4′ piece of ½″-to-¾″-thick exterior A/C grade plywood

Four 12″-diameter tricycle wheels (five with a spare)

One 3′×4′ sheet of soft aluminum or iron sheeting

Three dozen 1″ roundhead wood screws

Two dozen ¾″ sheet metal screws

A 12″ length of ⅜″ inside diameter copper tubing

One foot of ¼″-diameter iron rod

One 2″-long, ¼″-diameter, flathead bolt with nut

Two ½″-wide iron corner braces with 2″ arms

One-foot length of garden hose (male end), with end cap

One 4″-long, ⅜″-diameter, roundhead bolt, with two nuts

One 8″-diameter aluminum pulley

One 3′ length of ½″-diameter rubber tubing

One 3′ length of ¾″-diameter rubber tubing

One bicycle bulb horn

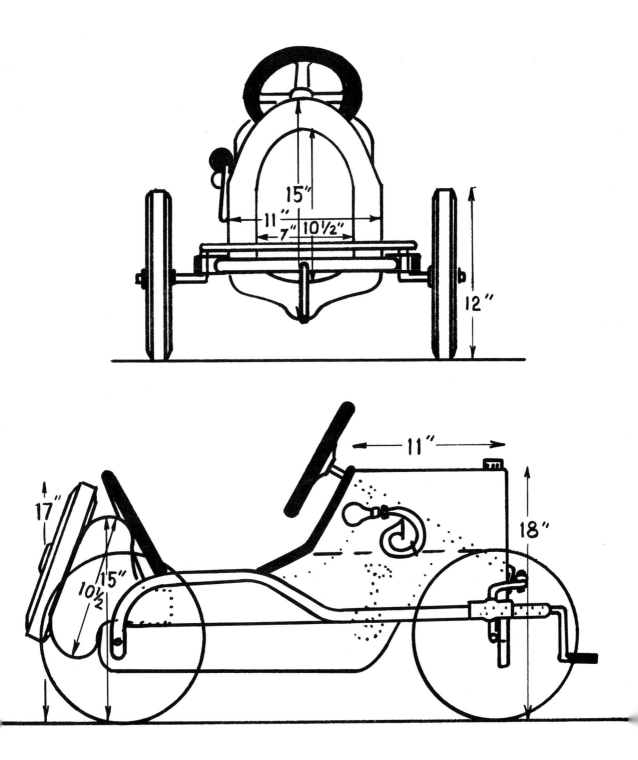